The Making
of a Reader

MARILYN COCHRAN-SMITH

University of Pennsylvania

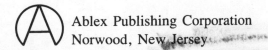

Ablex Publishing Corporation
Norwood, New Jersey

Portions of children's books are reproduced in this monograph by permission of the publishers:

Animals Should Definitely Not Wear Clothing by Judy and Ron Barrett, copyright 1970, Atheneum.
Barbapapa's New House by Annette Tison and Talus Taylor, copyright 1972, Talus Taylor.
Father Christmas by Raymond Briggs, copyright 1973, Coward-McCann.
Fish Is Fish by Leo Lionni, copyright 1970, Random House, Inc.
Florina and the Wild Bird by Selina Chonz, copyright 1953, David McKay, Inc.
Fossils Tell of Long Ago by Aliki, copyright 1972, Harper & Row.
The Good Bird by Peter Wezel, copyright 1964, Harper & Row.
In the Night Kitchen by Maurice Sendak, copyright 1970, Harper & Row.
My Mama Says There Aren't Any Zombies, Ghosts, Vampires, Creatures, Demons, Monsters, Fiends, Goblins, or Things by Judith Viorst, copyright 1973, Atheneum.
The Silliest Pop-up Riddles Ever, Bennet Cerf, Random House, Inc.
Snow White adapted by Jane Werner, copyright 1952, Western Publishing Co.
The Sweet Touch by Lorna Balian, copyright 1976, Abingdon Press.
What Do You Say Dear? by Sesyle Joslin, copyright 1958, Addison-Wesley.
Would You Rather? by John Burningham, copyright 1978, Harper & Row.

Printed in the United States of America.

Library of Congress Cataloging in Publication Data

Cochran-Smith, Marilyn, 1949–
  The making of a reader.

  Bibliography: p.
  Includes indexes.
  1. Language arts (Preschool) I. Title.
LB1140.5.L3C62 1984   372.6   83-25795
ISBN 0-89391-187-9
ISBN 0-89391-219-0 (pbk.)

Ablex Publishing Corporation
355 Chestnut Street
Norwood, New Jersey 07648

Contents

CHAPTER **4**

If You Don't Read, How Do You Know?:
Community Attitudes, Values, and Beliefs 37

CHAPTER **5**

Time and Space: Nursery-School Plant,
Material, and Organization 60

CHAPTER **6**

Are You Sure the Pen is Mightier Than
the Sword?: Reading and Writing off the Rug 72

CHAPTER **7**

Rug-Time, Framework for Storyreading: Sitting,
Listening, and Learning New Things 102

CHAPTER **8**

What Do You Say Dear?: Storyreading
as Interactive Negotiation 125

CHAPTER 9
What is Given is No More Than a Way of Taking: Life-to-Text Interactions   174

CHAPTER 10
Just Like They Did in the Book: Text-to-Life Interactions   236

CHAPTER 11
Conclusions   252

Preface to the Series Language and Learning for Human Service Professions

This series of monographs is intended to make the theories, methods, and findings of current research on language available to professional communities that provide human services. From a theoretical and practical point of view, focus on language as a social process means exploring how language is actually used in everyday life.

Communication between and among adults and children, professionals and clients, teachers and students, as well as the effect of changing technology on communication in all these contexts, has become the object of study in disciplines as varied as anthropology, cognitive psychology, cognitive science, education, linguistics, social psychology, and sociology. The series provides a forum for this research analyzing talk in homes, communities, schools, and other institutional settings. The aim is to shed light on the crucial role of language and communication in human behavior.

The monographs in the series will focus on three main areas:

- Language and Social Relationships
- Language and Helping Professions
- Language and Classroom Settings

We hope that these books will provide rich and useful images and information about how language is used.

CHAPTER 1

Introduction

Parents, teachers, and critics of education are asking hard questions about how children become readers. Researchers in several fields have argued the need for information concerning children's early experiences with print and printed materials. The present need is for studies that are longitudinal, naturalistic, and systematic in terms of observation, interview, and analysis. These studies would be based on a perception of context that includes both the immediate verbal and physical environment and the value system of the adult community. They would document young children's experiences as they learned to use both the oral and written language strategies of home, school and community.

The study described in this monograph was designed with the unanswered questions of parents, teachers, and researchers in mind. It offers to parents and teachers an expanded image of the ways adults in one setting "make readers," that is, of the ways these adults socialize their children into particular patterns of literacy by helping them develop the literary and social knowledge needed to use and understand print. Specifically, this monograph focuses on adults and children observed over a period of 18 months at Maple Nursery School,[1] a private, cooperative preschool in a residential section of Philadelphia. The mono-

---

[1]To provide anonymity for participants, the names of nursery school adults and children and the school itself have been changed.

1

graph highlights both what these children seemed to know about print and some of the ways they seemed to be coming to know it. Particularly, it provides insights into how the adults in this setting acted on their assumptions about how children learn to make sense of written texts.

The result of this study is the description of one model for the making of readers in one environment. Whether or not the model occurs in other settings is still to be shown. My intention is to share this model, but not to prescribe it for other groups or hold it up as a yardstick against which other models ought to be evaluated. As the body of research in the area of early literacy continues to grow, educators, parents, and researchers will be able to describe and compare models for the making of readers in various social groups. Right now, however, our concern is with the making of readers in one particular group, and not with global statements about the making of readers everywhere.

The ten chapters that follow build two arguments: First, it is shown that the adults in the community studied were making readers of children—long before they were able to recognize texts in first grade primers, or write neat sentences on composition paper. The children of Maple Nursery School were learning ways to use and understand the written word prior to their learning the more or less mechanical skills of encoding and decoding print. Second, the adults in the community were not involved in a deliberate effort to teach their children to read and write, or even to get them ready to learn these skills. On the contrary, the making of readers in this community was the result of a process of gradual socialization, rather than direct teaching.

In this setting, socialization into literacy occurred partly because children were constantly exposed to and involved in literacy events[2] as part of their routine social interaction with adults, and eventually with

---

[2] The concept, "literacy event," was used in this study as a conceptual tool. Heath (1978, 1982a) has described a literacy event as "one in which written materials are integral to the nature of the participants' interactions and their interpretive processes" (1978, p. 35); and Anderson, Teale and Estrada (1980) have viewed it as "any action sequence, involving one or more persons in which the production and/or comprehension of print plays a role" (p. 59). Like the speech event (Hymes, 1974) from which it is derived, the literacy event is structured according to certain interactional norms. These norms often center on relationships between oral and written language strategies and how these are used by participants in order to understand, discuss, apply, respond to, play with, evaluate, build upon, or refer to various kinds of printed materials. The notion, "literacy event," serves as a particularly helpful conceptual tool for looking at children's early print experiences.

one another. Print was interwoven into social interaction not in order to create convenient opportunities for teaching literacy skills, but because print was an effective way for the adults and children in this coummunity to fulfill a variety of social, transactional, and informational needs in everyday life.

The second chapter of this monograph describes how and where this study of young children's early experiences with texts fits into current bodies of research on storyreading. The four aspects of storyreading research I have examined are: children's comprehension or story processing; the role of literature in children's lives; children's conceptions of stories and literature; and ways children are introduced to literacy experiences at home.

Chapter 3 describes an approach to the study of storyreading events within a social-interaction framework. Chapter 4 describes the literacy-related beliefs, values and attitudes of the nursery-school community. My theoretical stance is that this literacy orientation forms the outer layer of context for nursery-school storyreading, and locates the school's literacy events in terms of their meaning for the community itself. Nursery-school organization of time and space is discussed in Chapter 5.

In Chapter 6, "off-the-rug" literacy events (almost exclusively events featuring contextualized print) are analyzed. "Rug-time," a framework for groups storyreading, is highlighted in Chapter 7. The way it serves as a physical and psychological signal to the children to use decontextualized print strategies is discussed. Chapters 8, 9 and 10 examine the process of group storyreading itself: Chapter 8 presents a view of storyreading as interactive negotiation; Chapter 9 highlights strategies for using world knowledge to make sense of texts; and Chapter 10 focuses on strategies for using texts in the world. The monograph concludes with a brief discussion of educational implications in Chapter 11.

Constructs Framing the Study

There are two sets of constructs that help to provide both a conceptual and organizational framework for reading and interpreting the findings of this study: (a) the notion of print as contextualized and decontextualized; (b) the notion of multiple layers of context. Before turning to a discussion of the study findings, it will be useful to consider these two sets of constructs in some detail.

The Making of a Reader is an analysis of adult-child interactions around print, both contextualized and decontextualized. One way to read this book is to contrast the children's experiences with these two kinds of print. Chapter 6 highlights the children's experiences with and exposure to contextualized or environmental print. Chapters 7, 8, 9, and 10 examine group storyreading, the children's major experience with decontextualized print.

Contextualized print (e.g., street signs, labels, notes to the milk-man) derives some of its meaning from the context in which it occurs; this context includes both the environment in which the print occurs and its use or function. Part of the meaning of a stop sign, for example, is the print environment: white letters on a red, metal, hexagonal sign attached to a five-foot pole and stuck in the ground. The stop sign's meaning is also derived from the way the print is used—to give directions to oncoming traffic—and from the situation in which the print occurs on a corner facing the right-hand lane of traffic as one street intersects another. With environmental or contextualized print like the stop sign, lexical information—"stop" is a verb meaning to halt or cease—provides only one cue to interpretation. Equally significant as interpretive cues are contextual relationships between print and its environment, its situation, and its use.

As Chapter 6 describes in detail, Maple Nursery School children had many experiences with environmental print, which they were encouraged to interpret in relation to the context in which it occurred. On the first day of school, for example, the children were shown label cards for various nursery school items and locations and were encouraged to interpret these labels in relation to their environments. For instance, the label, "SNACK," was read to the children, and one child was directed to tape it onto a cupboard in the kitchen. The nursery school teacher pointed out: "Now we'll know where snacks go . . . we'll read this sign!" As the teacher's comment reveals, the children were invited to interpret the label in relation to its placement on a particular cupboard in the kitchen and in terms of its purpose as a way to locate nursery school items and places. The adults and, to a certain extent, the children of Maple Nursery School used contextualized print in many situations for a number of different purposes and goals. Each of these uses involved specific strategies for relating print to the contexts that surrounded it. Thus, for the nursery-school children, part of learning to use contextualized print was learning how to derive meaning from the lexical and syntactic features of print in relation to and in terms of the environment, situation, and the purpose it served.

Decontextualized print is quite different from the contextualized print of signs, notes and labels. Essentially, decontextualized print is written language that has meaning independent of the situational and environmental context in which the print occurs. The way we interpret a novel, for example, does not depend on the chair or the room where we choose to sit, or on the color of the paper upon which the book is printed. Of course, the quality of the bookmaking and the comfort of the seating arrangement may influence our enjoyment of the novel. But the way the printed novel is understood does not depend on its appearance on parchment or newsprint, or on whether we read it by candlelight or flourescent bulb.

The meaning of decontextualized print in novels or children's books is derived from the lexical and syntactic features of the printed texts themselves and from the conventions of literature. Making sense of decontextualized print, therefore, involves more than decoding printed symbols; it also involves understanding the demands and nature of the conventions of different literary genres and other texts. From our readings of individual texts within a given genre (e.g., mystery novels, romance novels, alphabet books), we extract a frame or sense of story and an understanding of the literary conventions within the genre. This frame helps to guide our reading of a new text. Hence, information about different genres figures significantly in our interpretation of a new text.

The development of a frame for a genre is facilitated by the existence of general characteristics or conventions within the genre. European-based fairy tales, for example, feature stock characters, formulaic openings and endings, and significant occurrences in groups of three. When we read in a fairy tale about a "wicked stepmother," we are familiar with this figure, and need little more description of character development or motivation. In this way, the conventions of the fairy-tale genre function significantly as cues for interpretation. Unlike cues for the interpretation of contextualized print, however, generic cues are not located in the environment where the text occurs; nor are they related to a specific purpose for which the print is to be used. Rather, these cues are derived from the shared assumptions of the authors and readers of texts, and are, in this sense, decontextualized from the print environment.

The nursery-school children's major experience with decontextualized print was group storyreading. They were encouraged to interpret the decontextualized print of storybooks, using strategies that were quite different from those needed to control contextualized print.

During "rug-time," the physical and psychological framework that surrounded group storyreading, the children were encouraged to interpret storybooks by attending only to the books themselves. Indeed, the children were actively discouraged from attending to the context in which the print and the reading occurred.

Adult-child interaction around storybooks essentially *created a context* for reading and interpreting the decontextualized print of storybooks. That is, in the verbal interaction around books, the storyreader instructed her listeners in how to make sense of texts by helping them to use—or using for them—various kinds of world and literary knowledge. She also guided the children in ways to use book knowledge in their lives.

In this way, the storyreader transformed the usually internalized, automatic, and one-sided reading process of adult readers in this community into an outwardly explicit, deliberate, and joint sense-building process for the children. In learning how to interpret decontextualized print, the children learned when and how to take information from their pools of world knowledge in order to make sense of texts, as well as ways to apply information from texts to real life situations. In this particular literate community, group storyreading served as one key to the children's transition to the strategies needed to interpret decontextualized written language.

The second construct that provides a way of thinking about and looking at the findings of this study is the notion of *multiple layers of context*. The children's major experiences with books occurred at the school during group storyreadings when the teacher read aloud to the whole group of children. Group storyreading was the only reading or writing activity in which the children were required to participate. It was also the most frequent and regular of such activities. As such, storyreading provided valuable insights into the literacy and literary orientation of the nursery school community. By the same token, the larger orientation was part of the context within which storyreading occurred. Storyreading was embedded within several *concentric layers of context,* each of which was, necessarily, part of a study of storyreading.

At Maple Nursery School, storyreading was surrounded and supported by: (a) a physical and behavioral framework, called "rug-time," that served to structure the bookreading experience for the children by providing an interpretive and interactional orientation; (b) a wide variety of "off-the-rug" activities within which literacy events were embedded and to which many different uses of reading and writing were integral; (c) a general nursery-school environment where time and space were consistently organized and correlated to types of activities, uses of materials and interactional norms; and (d) an adult belief system, in which literacy was both a primary method of access to knowledge and a major source of solitary and social pleasure.

Another way to think about these multiple layers of context is to visualize them as concentric circles around a center. Group storyreading forms the core. The rug-time frame wherein the children were expected to sit quietly on a rug and listen to the teacher reading was the most physically immediate and the most conspicuous ring around group storyreading. This frame signalled to the children a particular set of interactional and interpretive norms for storyreading. However, reading-related activities did not occur only *on* the rug, but were also continuously embedded in other kinds of activities. For example, the children's first day of school was replete with references to reading and writing, invitations to use reading and writing for various purposes, and displays of printed materials. The main purpose of the day, however, was not to offer instruction in reading and writing, but to offer assurance to nursery-school newcomers.

Off-the-rug nursery events, into which reading and writing were interwoven, offer many insights into both the community's literacy orientation and into storyreading itself. Hence, the network of literacy events surrounding storyreading formed the second ring of context around storyreading. The third concentric ring around storyreading was the general nursery school environment. At this level, a highly consistent organization of time, space and materials supported storyreading, and helped to establish the interactional and interpretive norms of rug-time. Finally, the first three rings around storyreading were surrounded and supported by a fourth ring composed of the literacy-related beliefs, attitudes and values of the adult community. As the concentric-circle image suggests, all of the circular layers of context were contained in, or were containers for, one another. Each raised questions about, offered interpretations for, and provided insights into each of the others.

Earlier, I suggested that one way of using this book was to compare Chapter 6 on contextualized print with Chapters 7, 8, 9, and 10 on decontextualized print. This kind of reading highlights the contrast between the nursery school children's experiences with contextualized and decontextualized reading. Another way of using this book is to read Chapters 4, 5, 6, and 7 as descriptions of each of the layers of context surrounding and supporting storyreading. This framework for reading the book begins at the outer ring of context, and works inward toward storyreading itself, which is examined in Chapters 8, 9, and 10.

CHAPTER 2

Dimensions of Storyreading: What We Know and Need to Know

One way to begin an exploration of the making of a reader is by looking at what we already know about children's experiences with storyreading. Previous research has outlined four characteristics of children's early experiences with storyreading: Children's efforts at making sense of stories are constructive; storyreading can play an important role in children's lives; children's concepts of "story" and "literature" support their storyreading experiences; and early mother-child storyreadings are like dialogues. Based on a growing body of longitudinal research that has focused on children's early experiences with storyreading and other print in natural[1] settings, we can add a fifth feature of storyreading that essentially reframes the other four: patterns of storyreading are cross-nationally and cross-culturally diverse.

From the previous and current research on children's storyreading, we can thus sketch out a picture of children's early storyreading experiences along five dimensions.[2] As the fifth dimension reveals, this does not mean that these five dimensions are universally characteristic of

---

[1]The word, "natural," is used throughout this monograph to describe storyreading situations that are part of the ongoing, already-occurring activities of various cultural, home, or community groups as opposed to storyreading situations that are constructed, prompted, or initiated by researchers.

[2]For a more detailed discussion of research related to children's storyreading experiences, see Cochran-Smith (1983).

early storyreadings. In fact, it is a premise of this monograph that storyreading patterns are culture-specific and cross-culturally varied. These five dimensions, however, provide us with an initial way of looking at storyreading events, and help us to construct a comparative framework for understanding these events.

In social groups where these dimensions of storyreading do exist, they need to be analyzed as part of our effort to look at storyreading and the making of readers. In social groups where storyreadings do not occur, or where storyreadings are not characterized by the dimensions discussed here, the existing differences give us some insights into how to understand the literary resources and knowledge developed by these social groups.

Making Sense of Stories is a Constructive Process

One dimension of storyreading comes from research on children's comprehension of stories. This research has shown that children's efforts to make sense of stories are constructive, rather than a function of memory alone. That is, children's comprehension of prose does not seem to be the result of simply remembering a story; but instead the result of an integration of memory and the internal mental operations performed by the hearer of a story. Generally, it has been psychologists who have explored comprehension aspects of children's storyreading experiences. The specific questions addressed in these studies are part of larger and more general psychological investigations of human cognition—knowing and/or processing information.

Those who have focused on children's cognition have been especially interested in the developmental aspects of prose comprehension and memory; stories have frequently served as vehicles for eliciting comprehension and memory samples. Researchers in this group have usually concentrated on one or two aspects of comprehension. These include: recalling, recognizing and/or reconstructing specific narrative sequences; reorganizing story material by inferring or creating information in addition to that explicitly stated; and constructing stories based on implied narratives (as in sequences of related pictures).

Although neither their procedural nor conceptual frameworks are uniform, the studies in this group have been based primarily on experimental designs. A typical investigation would proceed something like this: children of various ages are randomly assigned to groups, and stories specifically constructed for research purposes are read aloud to individual children (the story read aloud to individuals in one group may be different from the story read to children in another group, depending on the purpose of the experiment). Individual children are then asked to answer questions about the story they heard, or to perform other tasks in relation to the story, such as recalling or recognizing the sequence of the story. The results of storyreading studies like these are discussed in terms of significant correlations between independent variables (e.g., age of children, length of story, temporal or spatial order of story information) and dependent variables (e.g., accuracy of story recall, type and number of correct inferences made).

Story comprehension research makes many contributions toward understanding children's early experiences with storyreading. Most important is the general evidence that (at least in similar experimental situations) making sense of stories is, indeed, a constructive process, rather than only a function of memory (Paris, 1975). Although there is much that comprehension research does not tell us about storyreading, the idea of making sense of stories as a constructive process lends an important perspective that can be a starting point for many kinds of storyreading research. When we look at adult-child interactions during storyreadings, for example, we are alerted to look at the ways readers and listeners draw inferences from what they read. This research also prompts us to consider whether learning how to make inferences in stories is part of a process of socialization into literacy.

Closely related to work on inferring in storyreading is work on the structure of narratives, or story grammar research (Bartlett, 1932; Propp, 1958). A story grammar postulates the structure of an ideal narrative, which describes the expectations people have about stories (e.g., Mandler & Johnson, 1977; Rumelhart, 1975; Stein & Glenn, 1975; Thorndyke, 1977). Story grammars share the basic assumption that comprehension is constructive, and that both comprehension and retrieval of story information are based on a combination of the specifics of given stories and internal story schemata, which determine people's expectations about stories. These expectations relate to the kinds of information included in stories, the specific placement in stories of certain information, the order in which particular information occurs, and the relationships between various kinds of story information.

Formulations of story grammars which specify these expectations and analyze various stories according to such grammars allow comprehension researchers to make predictions about readers' and listeners' recall and/or reorganization of stories. For example, first grade, fourth grade, and college students were found to be sensitive to the internal structures of stories, and to use these structures to comprehend and recall stories (Mandler & Johnson, 1977). In addition, internal story grammars were found to help children process the stories they heard (Stein & Glenn, 1975, 1977; see also Glenn, 1978 and Day, Stein, Trabasso, & Shirey, 1979 for reports of related research). Story grammar research needs further exploration, because story grammar researchers posit internal schemata, which we use to process texts, but they do not give us much insight into how these schemata develop. Longitudinal, naturalistic observations of storyreadings can provide insights of this kind.

Comprehension research tells us much about storyreading, but it leaves many significant questions about storyreading and its role in everyday life unanswered. These questions about storyreading cannot be answered by the comprehension research undertaken to date, because experimental storyreading situations are so unlike natural storyreading situations. Of major importance are differences in the stories used and the contexts created. The stories used in comprehension experiments are rarely real children's stories; rather, they are stories based on specific story grammars and/or constructed specifically for experimental purposes.

Furthermore, in most of the comprehension studies, actual picture books are not used as the stimulus to which young children are invited to respond. Instead, prepared story scripts are read aloud to children by experimenters, either in person or on audiotape. This procedure precludes investigation of several important issues in young children's interactions with storybooks: What is the role of picture ''reading'' in prose comprehension? How do pictures and texts work together to convey narratives? What is the nature of the task of getting information from pictures? How does this task compare with the task of getting information from print? It seems problematic to separate text and pictures, rather than to treat them as integral parts of the beginning reading/comprehending process.

In addition to differences in the stories used, experimental storyreading situations differ markedly from the situations of natural storyreadings. In the former, social interaction between experimenter and child is intentionally minimized, and the adult storyreader plays only the role of administering the text. In some of the reports that we have of natural storyreading situations, on the other hand, adult storyreaders seem to be playing quite active roles (see, for example, Butler, 1979; White, 1954). This suggests that experimental research may be omitting a factor that is important in understanding how children hear and make sense of stories. Another problem along these same lines is that experimental storyreading events are not analyzed and described within the context of their situations. Rather, they are treated as if they had occurred in isolation.

Further, as the researchers themselves point out, in both story grammar and prose comprehension research, only one of a large number of questions about the storyreading experience is being asked. In Paris's study of prose recall (1975), as in almost all of the studies, "fabrications and extraneous elaborations were not counted" (p. 238). As I will point out later, it is possible that such extraneous information is uniquely able to provide insight into storyreading situations. As Gardner (1978) reminds us, comprehension itself is only part of the storyreading experience:

> Certainly some understanding of stories is vital, and measures of comprehension are a reasonable place to begin any investigation of narrational competence. Yet . . . there is more to the story experience than simple comprehension. . . . I would go so far as to suggest that sheer comprehension . . . is not what the story experience is primarily about. (p. 252)

Gardner's remarks emphasize the fact that there is much about storyreading and comprehension that we cannot understand without considering the larger context within which it occurs.

This is not to suggest that investigators of children's prose comprehension have asked unimportant questions. On the contrary, inquiries into comprehension are fundamental and have alerted us to some important dimensions of storyreading. I would argue, however, that prose comprehension investigators have overlooked some of their opportunities for insights into storyreading, because they have not considered the social and contextual factors of storyreading situations.

Storyreading Can Play an Important Role in Children's Lives

A second dimension of storyreading comes from parent diaries. This work shows that storyreading can play a significant role in the lives of young children. Parent diaries suggest that children's early experiences with stories and books can enrich their experiences outside of books. These experiences can play a part in language and concept development, influence later attitudes toward reading, and stimulate and broaden young children's imaginative development. Those who have given us this information about storyreading are often parents with academic training in either library work or teaching. Unlike researchers in clinical settings, who read experimentally-constructed stories to children they did not know, these parents read actual storybooks to their own children in natural home settings over periods of several years. The parent diaries are personal memoirs, rather than systematic studies. As such, they offer us a very different kind of information about storyreading. Rather than disinterested data analysis, these diaries offer chronologically arranged series of parent-child-storybook incidents, which seem to testify to the powerful influence that books may have on children's lives.

The first full-length account of a child's storyreading experiences, published more than 25 years ago, is frequently cited in works related to children's early imaginative, language, and literary development. White's (1954) diary of storyreading covered a three-year period beginning when her daughter, Carol, was 2 years of age. This description of book and book-related experiences pioneered the parent diary. Writing from the perspectives of both parent and librarian, White vividly described storyreading experiences with her daughter and the patterns of literary response that she saw developing. With warm, personal descriptions of many of Carol's storyreading and play experiences, White portrayed the mutual enrichment of Carol's life experiences and book experiences. Her chronological diary entries also outline a progression of Carol's gradual coming to terms with the nature of written literature. Implicit in White's journal is a description of herself as an adult reader, who played an important role in the relationship between child and books, and significantly affected her child's emerging attitudes toward stories and books.

The idea that an adult reader can play a significant role in a child's early storyreading experiences is a critical dimension for those of us who seek to examine the storyreading process. It alerts us to the fact that we may need to look at more than just a child's responses or questions about the stories he or she hears. Rather, as I will argue in Chapter 3, we may also need to look carefully at what adults do during storyreadings.

During the 1970s, a number of excerpts from parent accounts were published in small journals in Australia and England. As White had done, several parents focused on the early experiences of their own children at home (Graetz, 1971; Lowe, 1975; Saunders, 1976). These accounts generally described early book preferences, reactions to books, and development of book-handling abilities of individual children. In addition to these excerpts from written accounts, parents' observations and recollections of their own children's book experiences were used in several brief papers as testimony to the importance of early reading in shaping reading attitudes and interests (Graetz, 1977; Olding, 1971; McKinley, 1977).

No full-length account of a child's storyreading experiences was published after White's until Butler's account appeared in 1979. Butler's study was based on a three-year period in the life of her granddaughter Cushla, a child born with severe physical and perceptual handicaps, and initially assumed to be mentally retarded. Butler concluded that Cushla's extensive experiences with storybooks, which were first introduced to her when she was only four months old, became a large part of her "therapy," and had a profound positive impact on her development. Particularly, they provided her with opportunities for language, imaginative and visual development, and affirmed the security of home and family.

Crago and Crago drew on data from a four-year longitudinal record of their daughter's book and story-related experiences to discuss several aspects of the child's literary development and response (Crago and Crago, 1976; Crago, M., 1975, 1978, 1979, 1980). These included: a chronological description of the child's primarily preverbal experiences with books, her reactions to pictorial conventions in storybooks, and her responses to repeated readings of single texts over a long period.

Parent diaries of children's early experiences with books describe the storyreading practices that were already occurring in individual families. In contrast to the storyreading information provided by comprehension research, the information that the diaries offer comes from a base of: readings of actual children's books, rather than experimentally-constructed stories; domestic storyreading settings, rather than laboratory-like situations; and participant-observations of adult-child interactions over relatively long periods of time, rather than isolated subject responses during brief single encounters where experimenter participation was minimized.

Furthermore, the parent authors of the diaries were in a unique position to observe the behavior of their own children over long periods of time and in a wide variety of situations, and could thus suggest relationships between important events in the children's lives and their book experiences. Due to time and physical constraints, opportunities for such breadth and depth of study are never completely accessible to outside researchers.

Because of their intimate, long-term participation in their children's lives, parent diarists are able to offer us a great deal of information about children's storyreading experiences. I have already pointed out that White's (1954) diary encourages us to look closely at the role of the adult as a storyreader. From several of the diarists, we also begin to get insight into differences in the ways that families use books in their everyday lives. Some of the diaries provide a sense of the social organization of routinized storyreading scenes and of how adults and children draw from books to make sense of non-literary experiences. These ideas alert us to some of the dimensions that may be important in studies of storyreading: adult's and children's roles in storyreading episodes; reasons for coming to books; kinds of information taken from books; references to books during non-reading situations; and the social organization of storyreading episodes.

One thing that parent reports usually do not tell us is how information was collected or used to draw conclusions about young children and books in general. Usually we are told only that "diaries were kept." We do not know, however, whether records were immediate or retrospective, whether children's responses were written down verbatim, or were summarized by the adult, whether entries were made daily, weekly or on some other regular basis, or whether audio or visual recording devices were ever used during storyreading sessions.

Awareness of the shortcomings of other accounts led Crago and Crago to carefully specify to their readers the procedures they used (primarily audio-tape recordings of sessions supplemented with some note-taking). They described their daughter's literary response patterns via meticulous quantification of her comments in relation to the texts used. Their reporting is, by far, the most precise of the parent accounts in this respect. In their effort to avoid biasing the data, however, they intentionally refrained, as much as possible, from introducing new information, or pointing out unnoticed items to the child during storyreadings. The child's story questions were directed back at her, rather than answered or built upon in further conversation.

They also generally excluded from their analysis any of the youngster's responses that were prompted by their own questions or comments, including only those comments that stemmed from her "unaided grasp" (1976, p. 138) of stories. This procedure minimized the role of the adult in storyreadings, and may be a deficit, rather than an asset, to this research. Such a procedure ignores the fact that they, as parent readers, were verbally interacting with the child during storyreadings. As I will argue later, the verbal give-and-take of adults and children is paramount to the storyreadings that occur in some social groups. By manipulating the story situation to minimize reader-listener interaction, and by excluding their own verbal role in storyreadings, Crago and Crago have ignored the dialogic nature of their storyreadings.

Despite the rich information that some of the storyreading diaries give us, we need to know much more about what storyreadings have to do with the contexts in which they occur. That is, we need to know about inter-relationships between settings and storyreadings. The immediate physical and verbal environments surrounding individual story-reading sessions are described in varying detail by the parent diarists. None of the accounts, however, presents a broad consideration of context, including both the immediate physical and verbal environments and the book and story-related beliefs, assumptions, and experiences of participants. The underlying cultural and social notions of literacy—what it means to "be literate" in various cultural or community groups—are not accounted for. Many of the parent accounts, in effect, seem to imply that children universally develop more or less similar concepts of "story" and ways of understanding and responding to stories by progressing through certain stages toward a given endpoint—specifically, "the literate adult."

Cross-cultural research in several disciplines suggests that this is not the case, and that concepts of, and attitudes toward, literacy are matters that need to be investigated. It would seem important, therefore, for those attempting to observe storyreading in natural situations to include in their descriptions a broad account of context, or what Ochs (1979) has called the ". . . cultural filtering that transforms . . . physical behavior into conventional acts and events" (p. 2).

The parent diaries do well what they set out to do; that is, they offer warm, personal recollections of the book experiences of particular children. When we try to read these accounts at a level that goes beyond memoir, however, we need to keep in mind several of the qualifications that I have outlined above.

Concepts of "Story" Support Storyreadings

A third dimension of storyreading involves the network of children's developing concepts of "story" and "literature" that seem to underlie and support storyreading events. Psychologists and educators who have explored this supportive storyreading network are interested in broader questions concerning children's aesthetic development, specifically their literary development. Researchers addressing these questions are interested in examining not how children process stories, but what children know about stories, and how this knowledge underlies their experiences with stories. As we look at children's early storyreading experiences, literary-development research signals to us that we need to examine the role played by emerging concepts of story.

Applebee (1978), for example, looked at both the young child's emerging ability to assume toward his or her own stories a "spectator role" (i.e., distance between author and story in language, structure and theme) and his or her developing "sense of story" (i.e., implicit knowledge of narrative conventions). He found that these emerging narrative concepts supported and influenced children's abilities to make sense of new stories.

Other researchers have looked at the relationship between aesthetics and human development, including children's conceptions of literature as one of the arts. Howard Gardner and Brian Sutton-Smith have been at the forefront of this kind of research. Gardner and his colleagues (see, for example, Gardner, 1973; Gardner and Gardner, 1971; Gardner and Winner, 1978; Gardner, Winner and Kircher, 1965) found that children's aesthetics are, indeed, developmental and correlated to other developmental schemes, notably Piaget's. As part of an ongoing endeavor to establish a developmental psychology of the arts, Sutton-Smith and his colleagues (see, for example, Sutton-Smith, 1975; Abrams and Sutton-Smith, 1977; Botvin and Sutton-Smith, 1977) explored children's conceptions of literature by analyzing some of the structural aspects of stories that were told by children themselves. Sutton-Smith and his colleagues argued that children progress through a series of storytelling stages wherein plots become more structurally complex, and protagonists handle conflict in different ways. Other researchers have also addressed questions concerning children's concepts of literature by analyzing children's original stories (Stein and Glenn, 1977b; Stein, 1979; Leondar, 1977).

What children know about stories underlies and supports the ways in which they make sense of, or are helped to make sense of, stories during storyreading situations. Studies of children's sense of story and storytelling, therefore, can offer insight into the skills and relationships involved in storyreading. As I will discuss in Chapter 9, for example, an important part of what some adult storyreaders do is help children use their knowledge of narrative structure and literary convention as frameworks within which parts of texts can be understood.

Although the developmental studies suggest to us some important dimensions of storyreading, it is important to remember that they are based on a priori conceptions of the word, "story." In studies of this kind, "story" is consistently used to mean an original, imaginative event or series of events involving a protagonist faced with some obstacle or problem. Other responses given by children (e.g., recountings of personal experiences, retellings of traditional tales, or television materials) are not regarded as stories; children who tell these are asked to try again, and tell other stories. The notion of story relegates many responses to the level of "extraneous" material, and precipitates the loss of what may be important data concerning precisely the question addressed: what do young children think stories are? The developmental studies also seem to assume that children develop universally applicable concepts of story and methods of processing and recalling story information. As suggested by much of the research discussed in the following sections, this assumption is open to serious question.

Mother-Child Storyreadings Are Like Dialogues

In several case studies of mother-child pairs, bookreadings were found to be conversationally interactive experiences, wherein a routinized exchange between mother and child occurred. These studies propose an important dimension of storyreading, and alert us to the need to pay close attention to the language structure of storyreadings. Research by Ninio and Bruner (1978) provides one of the first systematic and detailed descriptions of adult-child interaction around books. As such, it raises many questions, and provides a framework for comparative analysis. A particularly important part of such a framework is the idea that adult-child dialogue supports or scaffolds the labeling of items in picture books. Other researchers have been able to use this notion of a scaffolding dialogue in their analyses of children's storybook experiences (Miller, Nemoianu and DeJong, in press; Snow and Goldfield, 1980, 1982).

Ninio and Bruner's 10-month observational study of one mother and child focused on the linguistic and cognitive development of the child; their purpose was to explore the major mechanisms through which the child achieved lexical labels. Although their focus was not on literacy or literary development per se, Ninio and Bruner's work nevertheless clearly contributes to an understanding of the verbal give-and-take that may surround storyreading sessions. Based on video-recorded samples of play, including "book reading cycles," they found that mother-child interactions around books occurred within a "structured interactional sequence that had the texture of a dialogue" (p. 6). The mother's utterances within the bookreading dialogues all centered around the labeling act, while the infant's part included pointing, smiling, laughing, and vocalizing. They argue that a central element in the achievement of labeling was the child's mastery of the turn-taking rules that underlay the bookreading dialogues and "scaffolded" the labeling that occurred.

Ninio and Bruner's work has been influential in storyreading research. It is important to remember, however, that they studied only one child who was male, English, and white. Despite this limitation, their discussion seems to imply that young children generally achieve the concept of lexical labels through similar scaffolding dialogues around picture books. As I have pointed out earlier, we cannot assume that children universally have similar language and literacy experiences.

Like Ninio and Bruner, Snow and Goldfield (1980, 1982) focused on the book-reading interactions of one mother and a male child during the time when he was between 22 and 33 months of age. They suggest that bookreadings functioned as particularly potent contexts for language learning by providing uniquely predictable and defined situations when the child was able to acquire information and later use it in similar contexts. Snow and Goldfield's work reinforces the framework suggested by Ninio and Bruner: that bookreading can be a conversationally interactive experience wherein a routinized exchange between reader and listener occurs. They also draw our attention to the strong potential of the bookreading situation itself for language learning.

Patterns of Storyreading Are Cross-Culturally Diverse

A number of anthropologists and educators have begun to explore the contexts and situations that introduce children to literacy in various social groups. These researchers are working to identify and analyze the key literacy events that particular social groups require of and provide for their children. This sort of research allows for and invites comparative analysis across communities and cultures. It extends our base of knowledge concerning children's early literary experiences, and emphasizes both that ways of coming to texts are socially organized, and that there is much diversity among patterns of using reading and writing. Descriptions of children's early development in various communities underline the fact that socialization for particular configurations of language and literacy strategies is integral to children's very early social experience.

The theoretical stance of those who have given us cross-cultural storyreading information is rooted in anthropology, in a view that "the meaning" of any kind of human behavior is embedded within the context in which it occurs. For this theoretical position, the concept of context is crucial; it includes not only the immediate physical and verbal environment within which an event or act of some kind takes place, but also and in at least equal measure, the significance of that event for those who participate in it. Thus, understanding the values, attitudes, norms, beliefs, and assumptions shared by participants concerning the meaning or importance of an event is crucial for understanding the event itself.

How children are socialized into particular learning and linguistic strategies and conceptions of literacy has been addressed in several comparative studies of children's early literacy patterns. Scollon and Scollon (1981), for example, compared the linguistic socialization and literacy orientation of their own young daughter with those of several Chipewyan children in Fort Chipewyan, Alberta (Canada). They suggested that in several significant ways, their daughter was "literate" by the time she was two years old; that is, by that age she had adopted their own "typification of literacy," which was "to a large extent an orientation to the discourse patterns of white, English-speaking, educated, middle-class Americans and Canadians" (p. 97). This orientation included the child's view of herself as both reader and writer, and her expectation that reading and writing were routine parts of her everyday life. It was an orientation quite different from that of the Chipewyan children, for whom literacy was a one-sided process in which they could be readers, but not writers, and for whom literacy was primarily the province of the church or the school. Scollon and Scollon argued that training for this literate orientation began almost from birth via the linguistic patterns they used to socialize their daughter, and via the print-orientation of her environment.

Other comparative studies of children's early literacy patterns have raised the question of possible differences in literacy opportunities at home and at school. Heath's eight-year study (1982b, 1983), for example, explored uses of language and literacy in two communities in the Piedmont area of the Carolinas, and, in a separate study, among 15 middle-class mother-child dyads in the same area. Unlike the children from the middle-class, school-oriented homes, children from the two other communities had difficulty in school. Heath suggests that this was due, in part, to the fact that, upon entering school, children from these two communities had language strategies that were not supportive of, or consistent with, those needed for success at school learning tasks.

In one community, Heath (1982b) found that families generally did not read to their children, ask them to label objects in books, intentionally teach their children reading and writing behaviors, or give their children decontextualized literacy tasks to complete. On the other hand, families in the other community, like school-oriented families, did read to their children and ask them for labels and "what" explanations, related to storybooks. Unlike school-oriented families, however, these families did not help their children use book meanings to make sense of their environment. In Heath's words, they did not "carry on or sustain in continually overlapping and interdependent fashions the linking of ways of taking meaning from books to ways of relating that knowledge to other aspects of the environment. They [did] not encourage decontextualization."

Other researchers have also begun to look at the early literacy experiences of children in various cultural and community groups. (See, for example, Anderson, Teale and Estrada, 1980; Miller, Nemoianu and DeJong, in press; Taylor, 1983.) This kind of research raises important issues for those who undertake to study storyreading or other early print experiences that help initiate children into patterns of literacy.

First, this research reveals that particular orientations to literacy cannot be approached as universal, but instead need to be investigated as culture-specific. Second, it emphasizes that the initiation of children into particular literacy orientations ought to be studied in terms of its larger situational and cultural contexts, especially in relation to the literacy of parents and other adult mentors in the community. These studies suggest the need for many explorations of both the literacy patterns of particular cultural or community groups and the ways that children are initiated into these patterns. As I will argue in later chapters, in communities where young children are regularly exposed to storybooks, descriptions of storyreading events are particularly illuminating of how children are initiated into literacy.

Summary

Previous and current research on storyreading allows us to construct a framework for looking at children's early experiences with bookreading. This framework can not give us a global view of storyreading everywhere, but it can provide us with an initial way of looking at storyreading events within particular social groups. It can help us to understand the literacy resources and literacy experiences of young children within these social groups, and it can give us insight into the similarities and differences among the literacy orientations of various groups.

Such a framework for looking at storyreading events is based on the premise, supported by much of the research cited in this chapter, that there are cross-cultural and cross-national differences among the ways that young children are introduced to literature and to literacy in home and preschool contexts. Therefore, it is particularly important that a broad conception of context underlie storyreading research. Within the contexts of particular social groups, previous research alerts us to look at several aspects of the storyreading and other book-related experiences that young children may have. Several important aspects of this framework are summarized below:

1. We need to investigate storyreading via a conception of context that includes the immediate verbal and physical surroundings of storyreading, as well as the literacy values, assumptions, and beliefs of the communities within which storyreading occurs.

2. We need to look for cultural patterns in the storyreadings and other book-related activities, in which various groups of children participate.

3. We need to investigate storyreadings in relation to the patterns of language acquisition and development common to the culture or social group within which the storyreading occurs.

4. Within storyreadings, we need to investigate the construction of story meanings, with special attention to the ways that children make, or are helped to make, inferences about stories.

5. We need to explore the roles in storyreadings of the various people who participate. We especially need to examine adult roles in the storyreading process, the nature and extent of adult and child participation during storyreading, and the extent of adult-child verbal interaction during storyreadings.

6. We need to investigate the ways that particular social groups (whether community, family, preschool, church or other groups) use books in their everyday lives. We need to analyze the kinds of information these groups take away from books, and the purposes for which these groups come to books.

7. We need to analyze the social organization of storyreading events, and the ways that storyreading events are structured in particular social groups.

8. We need to explore children's knowledge *about* stories and

literature, and how they use, or are helped to use, this knowledge to frame individual storyreading events.

9. We need to investigate the language structure of storyreading events, with particular attention to the possibility of a dialogic pattern between adult and child, or children.

10. We need to consider the function of the oral language that is related to storyreadings, and pay special attention to the possibility of adult-child verbal interaction as a kind of scaffolding for children's understanding of various aspects of stories.

The chapter that follows describes a specific method for addressing many of these issues within a study of storyreading and early literacy in one social group.

CHAPTER 3

The Making of a Reader: An Approach to Studying Storyreading

The case study reported in this monograph was designed with awareness of both what we know are some of the dimensions of different kinds of storyreadings and what we still need to know about storyreading in everyday life. The purpose of the case study was to provide detailed description and analysis of group storyreading—a key aspect of early socialization for literacy in one particular community—and, equally important, the network of literacy events that surrounded and supported storyreading.

The ethnographic perspective underlying this study combined several different methods for gathering information: audio-recordings of individual storyreadings, informal and formal interviews with parents and teacher, and longitudinal observations of a broad range of nursery school activities. An ethnographic perspective, however, is not simply a collection of techniques, but a way of looking at and interpreting human behavior, from which a number of methods can be derived and developed. Although the specific techniques for data collection and analysis employed in this study are techniques commonly used in ethnographic research, the overall methodology that combined these techniques was constructed during an exploratory phase of study, and adapted to the unique features of the research situation. As specific events emerged as key events in the early reading and writing experiences of the children attending the nursery school, and as the relationships between particular events became apparent, research techniques were devised and modified to accomodate them.

An exploratory phase of study had three goals: (a) to develop a sense of what went on in storyreadings, in other literacy events, and in the nursery school in general, (b) to create a participant observer's role and develop rapport with the children and adults of the nursery-school community, and (c) gradually to develop a set of fieldwork techniques and a research methodology that would accommodate emerging characteristics of literacy and literary socialization in this particular setting.

Research Design

The details below provide specific information about the nursery-school community described in this monograph. They also describe the way in which a general social-interaction framework led to a specific set of conceptual tools for gathering and analyzing information.

Research site

Maple Nursery School is a private cooperative nursery school, located on a residential street in an old neighborhood on the outer edge of Philadelphia. The parents of the nursery-school children studied identified themselves as school-oriented, middle class families with strong commitments to education. Although the cooperative nursery school is housed in a church building, the school itself has no religious affiliation. The families of the nursery school children live within three to five miles of the school in two adjacent communities. The school is located in one of the communities a few blocks from the boundary of the other. Parents and teacher attend two organizational meetings per year, and a parent executive committee officially runs the cooperative nursery. A paid teacher directs the activities of the school which operates according to the academic or school calendar, from September until June. Parents pay monthly nursery-school tuition for their children and, in addition, "co-op" approximately two days each month by assisting the teacher and children. During the major part of this study, 15 children, ranging in age from three years to five years, four months were enrolled in Maple Nursery School.

Access and researcher role

I gained access to the nursery school community through a colleague who was acquainted with the teacher. Although I eventually became an active participant in many aspects of nursery-school life, I remained an observer of storyreading sessions and literacy events. Observer status in these parts of nursery-school life was important, since I was investigating a socialization process, and was interested in how adults organized literacy events and storyreadings for children.

There is no clear way to assess the impact that I, as a nursery-school participant-observer had upon the actions and interactions of adults and children at the school. Being on the scene over the relatively long period of 18 months, however, helped to insure that the behavior patterns I observed were consistently occurring patterns, and not merely artifacts of the research situation. Furthermore, during this 18-month period, I had the opportunity to observe the nursery-school teacher in a variety of circumstances, including situations when she was observed by potential and current adult members of the nursery school community. Despite the variety of situations, including the presence of observers, the teacher behaved consistently, especially in her organization and direction of bookreadings.

Field Data

The field data for this study was collected both during the exploratory phase consisting of 90 hours of observation two to three days a week from January through April, 1980, and during the study proper, the 1980–1981 academic year from September, 1980 until June, 1981. During September, as school was just beginning, observations were made four to five days a week. This proved to be a particular important time to develop a sense of how patterns of behavior, especially those related to storyreading and reading and writing in general, were introduced and subsequently developed. From October, 1980 until June, 1981, six hours of weekly observations were conducted. During the study proper approximately 200 hours of observation were conducted. In addition, each set of nursery school parents was interviewed during the study. Information was collected at the nursery school in the following ways:

Verbal interactions during storyreadings

Each storyreading event that occurred during observations at the school was recorded in the four ways described below.

Audio-tape recordings of storyreadings. Verbal interactions related to each storyreading event, including discussion that preceded and followed it and the actual reading of the text were recorded.

Hand-written notes. For each storyreading event, detailed hand-written notes to accompany the tape recording were made. These notes, matched to the page numbers of the book being shared, were written on blank notation/transcription sheets, and included the following information, derived primarily from the Hymes (1974) schema of components of speech events and the Ochs (1979) format for transcription of conversations between children and adults:

1. Setting, including time of day and events and activities preceding and following the storyreading, seating arrangement (in diagram form), postures of participants, physical location, psychological framework within which the storyreading occurred, and the general tone or spirit of the event.

2. Identity of participants, including the names of the children and adults present for all or part of the storyreading.

3. Gross nonverbal behavior of participants, including the reader's major gestures, facial animation, and body movements, and the listeners' comings and goings from the reading area, attending behaviors, activities other than attending to the story, and major body movements.

Text. For each storyreading, textual information was recorded—bibliographic data, genre, children's prior familiarity with the book, the apparent degree of difficulty of the story, a description of the pictures that accompanied each page of the text, and the text itself.

Conversations about storyreadings. Conversations with the storyreader about the reading of particular texts were noted, whenever these occurred. These notes were made as soon after the actual conversations as possible, and were not verbatim.

Together the audio-tape recordings, hand-written notes, the text itself, and notes on conversations were used to create an annotated transcript for each storyreading event. The purpose of the annotated transcript was to describe the storyreading event in terms of the verbal interactions of participants.

Environment surrounding and supporting storyreading

Although nursery-school bookreading occurred primarily within one physical and psychological framework, it cannot be understood in isolation. Bookreadings were surrounded and supported by specific activities, attitudes, values and beliefs that helped to model both appropriate reading behavior and response and notions of the functions and uses of reading materials. It was, therefore, important to gather information concerning nursery-school activities in general and literacy events in particular. In order to locate the study culturally and socially, the larger environment into which the nursery-school children were being initiated was also considered as an important part of the context for their school reading and writing experiences. Information about their families' attitudes, values and beliefs about reading and writing, and especially storyreading, was also collected.

General nursery-school environment. Hand-written notes concerning nursery-school procedures, physical set-up, materials, and activities were taken during each observation. These notes were general in their orientation. Special attention was given to the ways in which routines were established, how time and space were organized for and by the children, and how different activities or events were related to one another.

Reading and writing in the nursery school. Hand-written notes were taken on general reading and writing behaviors in the nursery school and on all the literacy events that occurred. These notes included information on:

1. Who wrote and read written materials.
2. How participants interacted with one another in relation to printed materials.
3. For what purposes printed materials were read and/or written.
4. Ways children were involved in literacy events.
5. Circumstances in which references were made to printed materials, or printed materials were displayed.
6. Situations in which children were directly or indirectly instructed in reading and writing.
7. The social situations into which literacy events were embedded.

Following each nursery-school observation, information about the nursery school environment and literacy activities was integrated into anecdotal narratives that described the reading and writing that occurred each day in relation to nursery-school life in general.

Informal conversation and formal interviews. Notes were made during or immediately after each of the following:

1. Informal conversations with parents.

2. Conversations with the nursery-school teacher, including discussion of the purposes and goals of storyreading, general educational philosophy, major goals of the nursery school, rules that needed to be established, the role of the teacher and parents at the nursery school, and specific nursery-school events.

3. Tape-recorded interviews, ranging from 45 minutes to two hours, conducted between January and April, 1981 in the individual homes of each set of nursery school parents. (In five cases, only the mother was interviewed; in one case, only the father was interviewed.) Interviews were open-ended, but centered around the topics in the questions below.

Do you (or does someone in your home) read (or tell) stories to your children?

Why, in general, do you read to your children? Why do you think it's worthwhile to do so?

Do storyreadings occur in particular settings at your house? at particular times?

Do you read for various purposes?

What books are usually shared? Are there particular favorites that are often reread? Who makes selections of books to be read?

What is the source of the books used?

Do you visit libraries or bookstores with your child?

Were you read to as a child?

Does your child ever quote from, talk about, or relate story content to his own experiences? Do you ever do these things for your child?

Do you have book or literacy-related items in your home?

Does your child ever pretend to be reading or writing?

Does your child show an interest in learning to read and write?

Do you ever instruct your child in reading or writing?

Do you want your child to learn about reading and writing at the
   nursery school?
Do you think storyreading is important at the nursery school?
What were your general expectations for the nursery school? Why
   did you choose this particular school?

Anecdotal narratives on reading and writing behavior patterns in the
nursery school, informal conversations with the teacher and parents
during the nursery-school day, and interviews with parents were used
together to create a description of the environment that supported storyreadings at the nursery school.

Annotated transcripts

Transcriptions of the verbal interactions around storyreadings provided the major data base for this study. The reading of an individual
book by the teacher to the nursery-school group generally lasted between five and twenty minutes. One hundred annotated transcriptions of
storyreadings were prepared, each requiring three to four hours of preparation. Transcriptions were based on audio-taped recordings of the
readings, hand-written contextual notes made during storyreadings, storybooks texts, and hand-written notes on conversations with the
storyreader.
   The Ochs (1979) transcription system, coupled with derivations of
the Hymes (1974) schema for examining speech events, provided a
basis for annotated transcripts of storyreadings. Storyreadings, however, proved to be different from speech events in that the texts and
pictures of the books were central to the interactional and interpretive
norms that structured the events. Therefore, the annotated transcripts
accommodated not only the verbal give-and-take of reader and listeners,
but also the textual and pictorial aspects of the books, and relationships
between verbal interactions and textual information.

Transcription Procedures

The procedures used to create the annotated storyreading transcripts
are listed and illustrated below. Following the list is a piece of one
transcript, annotated according to each of the transcription procedures
(Figures 3.1–3.6); relevant aspects of the transcript are marked with
arrows. As the description indicates, the transcripts are to be read in a
generally left-to-right, top-to-bottom manner.

1. The following general conventions apply to the annotated transcriptions of storyreadings:

    a. Three asterisks within or at the end of a storyreading segment indicate that parts of a storyreading event have been omitted.

    b. On most transcripts a far-left "Focal Points" column includes arrows that point to reader or listener behaviors that illustrate particular ideas described in the text.

2. The behaviors of the storyreader appear on the *left* side of the page, verbal behaviors in the second column and nonverbal behaviors in the third column. All unmarked behavior in the reader column is the behavior of Amy, the nursery school teacher. Reader talk that is not from a storybook text is in capital letters. Reader talk that *is* from a storybook text is in lower case letters, enclosed in quotation markes (Figure 3.1).

Figure 3.1 Reader Behavior

	Reader		
Focal Points	Verbal	Nonverbal	
→ →	HE'S GOING STRAIGHT DOWN, DOWN, DOWN, BUT WHERE'S HE FALLING INTO?	points to four pictures of Mickey falling nods	

3. The behaviors of the story listeners appear on the right side of the page, verbal behaviors in the fourth column and nonverbal behaviors in the fifth column. Story listeners are identified by name or, in the case of group speaking, by "all children" or "several children" (Figure 3.2).

4. Information about the situational contexts (e.g., reader refers to a field trip that the class recently took) and discourse contexts (e.g., reader reads in hushed, anxious tone) is *enclosed in parentheses,* in lower case letters (Figure 3.3).

5. Reader and listener behaviors, verbal or nonverbal, that occur simultaneously or overlap with one another appear *parallel to one another.* Listener behaviors that occur simultaneously or

Figure 3.2 Listener Behavior

Focal Points	Reader		Listeners	
	Verbal	*Nonverbal*	*Verbal*	*Nonverbal*
	HE'S GOING STRAIGHT DOWN, DOWN, DOWN, BUT WHERE'S HE FALLING INTO?	points to four pictures of Mickey falling nods * * *		
→			Alice: Mickey cake! (excited)	pointing to RP
→			Brad: Mickey cake!	

Figure 3.3 Situational or Discourse Context

Focal Points	Reader		Listeners	
	Verbal	*Nonverbal*	*Verbal*	*Nonverbal*
		points to four pictures of Mickey falling nods		
→			?: A ho-- Brad: Into the night kitchen (softly)	

overlap with one another are marked with a *single elongated bracket*. Otherwise the transcript is temporally arranged and should be read in a continuous left-to-right, top-to-bottom manner. (See Figure 3.4).

6. Utterances follow the usual conventions of *capitalization and punctuation*. Indiscernible utterances are represented by long underlinings (e.g., _____, _____). Unidentified child speakers are indicated by *question marks* (as above). Storyreader pauses that allow for or invite listener participation are indicated by *three horizontal points (. . .)*. (See Figure 3.5.)

Figure 3.4 Overlapping Behaviors

	Reader		Listeners	
Focal Points	Verbal	Nonverbal	Verbal	Nonverbal
→		points to four pictures of Mickey falling	⌈ ?: A ho-- Brad: Into the night kitchen ⌊ (softly)	

Figure 3.5 Storyreader Pauses

	Reader		Listeners	
Focal Points	Verbal	Nonverbal	Verbal	Nonverbal
→	"Where the bakers who bake till the dawn so we can have cake in the morn . . . (they) mixed Mickey in batter, chanting . . ."	points to four pictures of Mickey falling nods * * *	⌈ ?: A ho-- Brad: Into the night kitchen ⌊ (softly)	

7. Book information appears in the second column on the left side of the page.

    a. A description of each picture (*LP = left picture; RP = right picture; PIC = double-page picture*) appears in the transcript immediately after the storyreader has *turned the page (TP)*. Picture information is enclosed in *brackets* []. Except for proper nouns, information within the brackets is in lower case print. (See Figure 3.6, focal point "a".)

b. The words of picture book texts are enclosed in quotation marks. When the storyreader reads the words exactly as they appear in the text, the text is part of the reader's verbal behavior and simply appears within quotation marks in the verbal column (column 3). Within the quotation marks, minor reader modifications are enclosed in parentheses, and original texts are marked "t." For example, "Mickey (popped out) (t:poked through) and he said . . ." indicates that the text read, "Mickey poked through and he said . . ." but the storyreader said, "Mickey popped out and he

Figure 3.6 Book Information
In the Night Kitchen (Sendak)

Focal Points	Reader		Listeners	
	Verbal	*Nonverbal*	*Verbal*	*Nonverbal*
		points to four pictures of Mickey falling		
			?: A ho--	
			Brad: Into the night kitchen	
a→		nods, TP	(softly)	
a→	[LP: M falls into mixing bowl]			
a→	[RP: 3 bakers come toward him]			
b→	"Into the light of the night kitchen." (with finality)	TP	(total silence)	
a→	[LP: bakers mix with M's head sticking out of batter]			

Figure 3.7 Sample Annotated Transcript
In the Night Kitchen (Sendak)

Focal Points	Reader Verbal	Reader Nonverbal	Listeners Verbal	Listeners Nonverbal	Interpretation of Annotation
	HE'S GOING STRAIGHT DOWN, DOWN, DOWN, BUT WHERE'S HE FALLING INTO? (2)	points to four pictures of Mickey fall-ing (2)			2 verbal reader behavior, non-text
		nods (2) TP (7a)	?: A ho- (3)(6) Brad: Into the night kitchen (3) (5) (softly) (4)		2 nonverbal reader behavior 3 verbal listener behavior 6 unidentified listener 3 verbal listener behavior 4 discourse information 5 simultaneous or over-lapping behavior
	[LP: M falls into mixing bowls] (7a)				7a turns page (TP) 7a book information left picture (LP)
	[RP: 3 bakers come toward him] (7a)				7a book information right picture (RP)
	"Into the light of the night kitchen." (7b) (with finality) (4)	TP (7a)	(total silence) (4)		7b verbal reader behavior, reading text 4 situational context 4 discourse context 7a turns page (TP)
	[LP: bakers mix with M's head sticking out of batter] (7a)				7a book information left picture (LP)
	"Where the bakers who bake till the dawn so we can have cake in the morn . . . (they) mixed M in batter, chanting . . ." (6)(7b)				6 storyreader pause to allow participation 7b verbal reader behavior, reading text 4 discourse information
	(emphasizes 'chanting' with pause for what's to come) (4) [RP: bakers stirring, M's head sticks out of batter] (7a)		Alice: Mickey cake! (excited) (4) Brad: Mickey cake! (3)	pointing to RP (3)	7a book information right picture (RP) 4 discourse information 3 listener verbal and nonverbal behavior 3 listener verbal behavior 1a indicates portion of transcript omitted
		* * *	(1a)		

said . . .'' When the storyreader omits parts of texts altogether or alters parts of texts significantly, the text appears within quotation marks *and* is enclosed within parentheses. This indicates that this part of the text was not part of the reader's verbal behavior. (See Figure 3.6, focal point ''b''.)

c. The book title and last name of the author for each storybook appear at the beginning of each storyreading segment. Complete bibliographic information for these books is included in an appendix at the end of this book. (See Figure 3.6.)

Figure 3.7 presents a sample annotated transcript. It includes all of the notations described and illustrated in Numbers 1 through 7 of the preceding list. Each part of the transcript is followed by a circled number which refers back to the transcript notation list and indicates how the transcript is to be interpreted.

CHAPTER 4

If You Don't Read, How Do You Know?: Community Attitudes, Values, and Beliefs

To talk about nursery school storyreading in a meaningful way, it is necessary to understand its meaning for participants. That is, we want to consider storyreading and the many literacy events that surround it from the perspective of the nursery school community. One way to get at this perspective is to peel away the layers of context into which storyreading is embedded.

These layers include: (a) the literacy attitudes, values and, practices of the adult community; (b) the general nursery-school atmosphere and environment; (c) the network of literacy events that surround and support storyreading; and (d) the immediate physical and verbal environment in which storyreading occurs. The three chapters that follow this one describe and analyze three of the layers of this context—the nursery-school environment, nursery school literacy events, and the rug-time framework for storyreading. In this chapter, *the belief system* of the adult community, as reported in individual interviews with nursery-school families, is described.

Let us begin by looking closely at the children's first day of school. As you read the narrative describing this first day, consider it as the children's introduction to both Maple Nursery School and to school as an institution. We will see the predominance of printed materials and print-related activities that introduce the nursery-school structure and organization. Also we will be introduced to the system of adult literacy beliefs and values that underlie these first-day activities (Narrative Segment 1).

Narrative segment 1: the first day of school[1]

It was September 9th, a Wednesday and the first day for many of the public and private schools in the Philadelphia area. A little boy named Dan was being escorted by his mother up the stone steps of Maple Nursery School. Dan, age three years, two months, had never before been to school; as a matter of fact, he had never before played with more than two children at a time.

Shortly after nine o'clock, most of the children had arrived at the nursery school. Dan's teacher called all the children over to a corner of the room and invited them to sit on a rug facing a wooden puppet stage/playhouse. With herself as both narrator and principal actor, the teacher and Mark, four years, two months, who was beginning his second year of nursery school, created a puppet play for the children and several mothers who remained at the school through most of the morning.

The play was about nursery school—what it was like to go to school, the kinds of activities children participate in at school, the fact that many children feel insecure about leaving their mothers when they first come to school, and the locations and uses of various items at the school. The teacher's puppet expressed uncertainty about coming to nursery school at all: "I don't even know whether I like it here," he said, and speculated about whether or not there would be anything to eat at nursery school.

At this point, the puppet reached for a can of fish food and wondered aloud whether he could eat that. Unprompted, Mark's puppet responded, "No, it's fish food. You can tell by the picture on the can." Then the teacher's puppet reached for a box of crackers, and when the two puppets decided that crackers *were* for eating, the teacher's puppet showed the audience a printed label bearing the word, "SNACK." Her puppet slowly pointed to each letter of the word, and deliberately pronounced, "Snack. Sn-a-ck. This says snack." The puppet told Mark to hang the label on the snack cupboard in the kitchen and assured the audience, "Now we'll know where snacks go—we'll read this sign!"

Next, the teacher's puppet confessed to the audience, "I don't know where the bathroom is either, but I did find this sign." The puppet held out another label card with "BATHROOM" printed on it, repeated the left-to-right, reading/ sounding-out routine, and asked a child to put the label on the

---

[1]All Narrative Segments are based on the researcher's field notes, collected over an 18-month observational period.

bathroom door "so all the kids will know where it is." The reading/sounding-out procedure was repeated for several other label cards.

As the puppet show continued, the teacher's puppet showed the audience a book about guinea pigs and asked, "Do you think I can hear it if I ask my teacher?" Several children shouted "yes." The puppet agreed with them, but told them they would not hear the story right then; instead, he would put the book on the bookshelf behind the rug and they would all hear the book later at rug-time. "This isn't rug-time; now we're just having a little show." At rug-time, the puppet told the audience, they could all use the book to learn about the guinea pig that they had in their own nursery school.

The teacher's puppet then produced a booklet of blank newsprint pages stapled together and titled, "SCHOOL"; the puppet told the children that at nursery school, they would all get a chance to make that sort of booklet about things they liked, or things they thought, or things they did.

The puppet show then became audience-participatory as the teacher's puppet asked each child in the audience to tell the others his or her name. Although some of the children did not respond, most did. The puppet informed them that right after the show, they would make nametags, so all the children would know one another's names. The children were also invited to think of names for their new nursery school guinea pig; all the names would be written down on a big list, from which the children could select.

As the puppet show ended, the teacher shepherded the children to two long tables where materials for name tags were placed. With the help of three adults, the children cut out and pasted cardboard nametags with their names and magazine pictures of animals. Some of the children printed or spelled aloud their own names. Most of the children wore their tags for the rest of the morning, although those who did not wish to were invited to hang them on the wall nearby.

The teacher then sounded a few chords on the piano, and asked the children to come and once again sit on the rug, this time facing toward a low bench backed by a bookcase. She sat on the bench and showed the children several of the books from the case, telling them about some of the stories they would listen to at nursery school in the next few days. The teacher read aloud the promised guinea-pig book, a fictionalized but quite realistic story about a child who took her guinea pig to live in her elementary-school classroom. As the teacher read, she related the information in the book to the real guinea pig in the nursery school classroom; and later, when the children were caring for or playing with the live guinea pig, the teacher referred back to the information in the book.

At the conclusion of the story, the teacher wheeled a movable blackboard onto the rug area, and invited each child to suggest a name for the nursery school pet, which the teacher printed in large letters on the board. After all the suggestions were listed, she asked various children which names they liked best. As they responded, she pointed to the appropriate names and emphasized word parts or individual words.

Near the end of these rug activities, many of the children seemed to lose interest and become restless. The teacher took all of children into the playground outside the nursery school where they played with swings, sandbox, and riding toys. After 20 to 25 minutes of play, the teacher brought the guinea pig outside, and invited the children to sit and form a circle "just like the children in the book did," so the guinea pig could be out of its cage but could not run away.

When the children were called back indoors, they were served a snack, and they sang a rhyming-word song. For the final activity of the nursery school day, the children were again called to sit on the rug. There they listened to another story—a whimsical account of four children who tired of living in a house and experimented with various alternative homes in a cave, a tree, and a stream.

A few mothers arrived early to pick up their children, but waited quietly for the reading to conclude before greeting their children. When the reading was finished, the teacher announced that it was going-home time. She helped the children collect their belongings, and talked to them informally until their mothers arrived to take them home. Dan's first day of school was over!

The nursery school day described above is significant not because it was typical of the nursery-school days I observed during an 18-month period. In fact, the day above was atypical: it had more whole-group simultaneous activities, more teacher direction and domination, less child participation, and less diversity of activities and materials than the typical day. This first day is particularly significant to an understanding of the nursery-school community, however, because it was, for most of the children, the very first day of school of their lives. (Those children who were veterans of Maple Nursery School had been introduced to school with a similar set of activities the previous year.) Many of the activities and routines that were introduced on the first day of school came to be central to the structure and organization of nursery-school life. Similarly, the values and attitudes underlying first-day activities were the values consistently espoused and modeled by adult members of the nursery-school community. The detailed description of the first day introduces several important aspects of both nursery-school storyreading and the environment that supported and surrounded it.

Goals and Expectations of the Nursery-School Community

One of the most striking features of the first day of school described above is the pervasion of print and printed materials. Within a period of less than 3 hours, the nursery-school children, all non-readers in any formal sense, were invited to locate items via printed labels, identify one another according to printed nametags, use a book to acquire information about the new nursery-school pet, consider classmates' suggestions by referring to a printed list, express their own feelings and thoughts by creating printed booklets, and listen to a storybook for entertainment and relaxation.

For those of us whose schooldays were heavy-laden with the basics of literacy, the pervasion of print described above may seem predictable rather than striking. After all, we wonder, what is the purpose of school but to teach children to read and write? The significant point here is that learning to read and write was *not* the purpose of this nursery school. On the contrary, the adult community of Maple Nursery School railed against educational programs that emphasized reading and writing skills, or pushed academic readiness programs for nursery-school and kindergarten children. In fact, many of the parents chose this private, cooperative nursery school expressly to avoid academic emphasis and structure.

What the Maple Nursery School parents were looking for (and, according to their own reports, what they were finding) was an initial school experience with an atmosphere where their children would feel welcome and comfortable, where they would meet and learn to play with many different kinds of children, where they would develop relationships with warm and sensitive adults, where they would be treated as individuals with valid feelings and needs, and where they would have opportunities to participate in many different kinds of activities. The remarks below were typical of parents' answers to questions concerning their expectations for nursery school:

> That [readiness activities] was one thing I was glad that I *didn't* see [when observing the nursery school prior to enrolling her child]. I didn't want Mark seated with a pencil and you know, 'Let's make A's today!' I didn't want that. Nursery school, I think, should be the type of atmosphere that we see here. It's a truly socialization period—playing and learning to get along with others.

The nursery-school teacher's goals were consistent with those of the parents. The teacher stressed the importance of helping the children grow and develop socially and personally. She wanted them to feel comfortable about themselves and about coming to a place called "school." Hence, much of the first day of school centered on assuring the children that nursery school would be a comfortable and non-threatening place for them. Formal academic study and readiness activities were not to be part of the nursery-school program. Rather, the teacher believed that young children learned about reading without instruction, when and if they were ready. The teacher's actions, her explicit commentary on the activities of the first day of school, and parents' comments on their children's introduction to nursery school all testified to the general goal of the nursery-school community: to create for the children a happy and interesting environment, wherein they would learn to cope with the needs and feelings of themselves and others. Neither the parents nor the teacher viewed the purpose of the first day or later nursery-school days as teaching the children about reading and writing.

This is not to suggest that nursery-school adults were not interested in having their children develop as readers and writers; on the contrary, as their interviews attest, they were committed to education and were very much interested in their children's academic futures. However, the reading and writing that were intertwined with nursery-school activities (and, in a less regular manner, with home activities) were simply routine parts of the everyday interaction between adults and children in this community. There was generally no conscious effort to teach reading and writing, and no overt acknowledgement that children were being taught a particular orientation to literacy.

Nursery-school adults did not see as incongruous a first school day in which nearly every activity was print-related and a nursery-school philosophy that de-emphasized reading and writing instruction. They saw no incongruity precisely because the context of the first day was *not* instruction in the uses of print; rather, the first day was designed to assure and establish the children's emotional and physical security in a new place away from parental comfort and care. This feature of the first day was characteristic of nursery-school life in general. Literacy events (those events during which reading and/or writing were produced or used by participants) were consistently embedded within situations or activities whose purposes were not formal or traditional reading and writing instruction. Reading and writing were routinely parts of everyday nursery-school events, but they were the background rather than the focus of planned and organized nursery-school lessons.

Further testimony to the routine rather than imposed or conscious integration of print in nursery-school life was the reaction of the parents of one boy who, by the age of about four years and nine months, was decoding simple picture book texts and a wide variety of environmental print quite accurately. His father was genuinely puzzled about how the child could have learned to read. No one had taught the boy at home, the father knew, and the teacher assured him that she had not taught reading at school. The father concluded that his son had somehow "just naturally learned to read." The little boy's daily exposure to many uses of reading and writing and his daily participation in group bookreadings were not mentioned by the father as possible factors in his son's "natural" learning process.

The father's puzzlement reminds us that it is difficult to acknowledge and examine the learning behind behavior and beliefs that our own communities regard as "natural." However, it is possible and important to do so. Communities with particular patterns of literacy are often used as baselines with which others (with other literacy patterns) are compared. Such comparisons may then be used as the basis of school-wide curricular decisions or compensatory educational programs. Because comparisons of this kind are sometimes made, it is important that we know more about the specific features of many literacy environments. We can begin by looking carefully at individual communities.

Community[2] Literacy-related Attitudes, Values, and Practices

Although Maple Nursery School was located near the boundary between the two communities where the nursery-school children lived, it was not a "neighborhood school," or one that served only families within close physical proximity. Only a few of the children lived within walking distance of the school, and consequently, most of the parents drove their children the two to five miles distance to the school in a number of car pools. Nearly all of the parents chose Maple Nursery School carefully and deliberately because of the philosophy and approach of the teacher. Parents' selections were based on observations at the school, interviews with the teacher, and conversations with other parents whose children had previously attended the school. Parents also

---

[2]The term, "Maple Nursery School community," is used throughout this monograph to refer to the family environments of the children who were observed. The term, therefore, refers to the families' reading and writing practices, their attitudes toward school and learning, and their values regarding literacy and education.

researched and/or observed at other nursery schools located within the general vicinity in order to make comparative decisions.

Demographic characteristics

Although there were many differences among the nursery-school families, there was also a great deal that they had in common. Most of the Maple Nursery School children were from two-parent families and had one or two siblings. Their cultural/ethnic backgrounds included white Eastern and Western European, Jewish, Indian, Filipino, Egyptian, English, and Black American. Two of the children were bilingual (Bengali/English and Filipino/English), and one spoke only Arabic; the others were English-speaking. Cultural and language diversity were valued at the school. Children and parents were invited to share their traditions and to discuss differences among their backgrounds. One mother commented during her interview that she chose Maple Nursery School partly because it was "like a little United Nations."

Despite differences in language, cultural, and ethnic backgrounds, the nursery-school families had striking similarities in their educational and professional backgrounds. Fathers had undergraduate or advanced college degrees and held professional positions in medicine, education, law, architecture, engineering, and library science; most mothers were college educated and had held professional positions in teaching or counseling-related fields, but were working primarily as homemakers while their children were young. Families had close and frequent contacts with several members of their extended families, especially with grandparents. Nursery-School families lived on long-established, residential streets in rented one or two-family houses or townhouses; most had small patches of yard space, and many had front porches. Most of the homes had living room, dining room (or dining area), and kitchen on the first floor, and two or three bedrooms on the second floor. Homes were neatly and attractively, but not lavishly, furnished. Children either had their own bedrooms or shared bedrooms with one same-sex sibling; all of the children had their own possessions—many toys, games, books, items of clothing, and wheeled vehicles.

Nursery-school parents were interviewed in their own homes for periods ranging from 45 minutes to 2 hours. Interviews centered primarily on the book-related aspects of the home environment and the attitudes, values, and beliefs of the parents concerning their children's present and future experiences with books and other print materials. The specific features of these 15 different environments and the parents' attitudes toward reading were remarkably similar, both in general terms and, at times, in precise detail. For example, all the Maple Nursery School families read to their children; and parents often cited the same book titles or authors to illustrate what they meant by "silly" or "worthwhile" books for children, or to pinpoint "my child's favorite" book.

In the following profile, common features of home environments and parental attitudes are described. It should not be inferred from this profile that every feature described was characteristic of any single family, or that, unless specified, any single feature was characteristic of every family. Unless stated otherwise, however, each feature discussed was characteristic of a sizable majority of the families.

Reading practices

Maple Nursery School children had many experiences in their homes with printed materials. Bookreading was by far the most common and frequent of these experiences.

Bookreading. Without exception, nursery-school families regularly read stories to their children. Many parents could barely remember times when their children had not been read to, and some recalled reading aloud to infants as young as three to six months. For the three-to-five-year-old nursery-school children, at-home storyreading was initiated by both children and adults, and occurred at several different times of the day. Bedtime was the most frequent and consistent setting for reading.

Bedtime reading. This was favored and considered particularly appropriate, because it allowed close physical contact and encouraged a calm and peaceful kind of interaction between parents and children. Although bedtime reading was common to all the families interviewed, for about half of them it was a steadfast bedtime ritual, the omission of which was extremely rare. The following comments by one mother provide a sense of this ritual:

> I would say I am extremely interested in reading. I always have been. I love it myself . . . .

> One of the things we most enjoy doing is reading books, and we do it every day. Our time in particular for reading is before going to bed at night. And both of my two little girls, each of them, normally selects a book to read.

And, um, [for] several reasons, it's a nice time: it's a nice time to sort of quiet down before bed; I love to read and they seem to enjoy listening, and also we can be very physically close at that time. It's just a very nice way to be at the end of the day . . . . They both expect it [storyreading] at night, and we've had some scenes if we, if I say for some reason, "I'm late. I have to go out the door. I can't read." [Then] the babysitters always have to. It's just a given that they read before they go to bed.

For the two little girls referred to here, bedtime reading was as much a part of the going-to-bed routine as was teeth-brushing or wearing pajamas. However, it has been pointed out that cross-culturally and cross-nationally the bedtime story cannot be considered a "given" (Heath, 1982b; Schieffelin and Cochran-Smith, in press; Scollon and Scollon, 1981). Heath, for example, studied language and literacy in two Piedmont, Carolina communities during an eight-year period. She found that in one of the communities, parents did not read to their children or teach them reading and writing behaviors. Rather, young children were involved in a rich, almost wholly verbal environment. Similarly, in Fort Chipewyan, Alberta (Canada), it was not a part of adult-child behavior to read books aloud in order to amuse or entertain young children (Scollon and Scollon, 1981).

To understand the Maple Nursery School community, however, is to understand that the bedtime story *was* a "given". In this community, bedtime reading was consistently requested and expected by both children and parents. It marked the close of the day, and provided opportunities for pleasant, intimate parent-child contact. Storyreading was also one of the few activities that could delay bedtime, since parents hesitated to stop reading when their children seemed genuinely attentive and interested. Bedtime reading was such a taken-for-granted part of raising children that some Maple Nursery School parents could not understand or imagine situations in which children were not read to: "I always felt if you don't (sic) read to your child at night, you were doing something terrible."

Daytime reading. The children of nursery-school families were read to at many times other than bedtime. Parents frequently suggested storyreading to provide a one-to-one framework for interaction with their children. Both children and parents initiated storyreading as "something to do" during the day, often when one parent and the child were alone together. Parents read stories to their children, provided books for the children to look at independently, or played cassette tape recordings of texts while children looked at the appropriate book pages during long auto trips to relieve boredom and monotony. Parent-child bookreading also served to quiet children after particularly rough or stimulating periods of active play.

Independent reading. In every Maple Nursery School family, parents reported that children regularly chose to look at books independently in much the same way that they chose to play with particular toys or work with various kinds of materials throughout the day. Sometimes these book activities were social with children sharing books with younger siblings and parents, or with several family members reading together. Most often, however, children spent these times alone in their own rooms looking at books or listening to recordings of texts while following along with the words and pictures in the accompanying books. Many parents reported that children spent portions of nearly every day in solitude, peacefully looking at and "reading" books.

It is especially significant that bookreading provided a prominent framework within which one-to-one adult-child interaction occurred. In many Maple Nursery School families, bookreading times and meal times were the major organized contexts for adult-child interactions that were heavily verbal rather than physical. It is also significant that bookreading was a favored, solitary activity for both children and adults. Underlying both social and solitary bookreading is the message that reading is a worthwhile and approved way to spend time that brings many rewards to the reader.

Print and print-related culture

Maple Nursery School families had wide varieties of reading materials available to children in their homes. Collections included hard and paperback children's books, children's magazines, comic books, and comic sections from newspapers. Books were the form of reading material most frequently found in these homes.

Books. Individual families owned from 40 to more than 100 children's books that had been purchased from bookstores, thrift shops, school-sponsored paperback book clubs, and other mail order sources. Some children also owned books that had been handed down through several generations, and many of the children had in their collections books that had belonged to older siblings or to their parents when they were children. Books were treated as valued possessions by nursery-school parents, and children frequently received hardbook or paperback books as gifts from parents, relatives, and friends. Many of the children had their own bookcases, which were often the most prominent pieces of furniture in children's rooms.

Nursery-school parents regularly took their children to public libraries and encouraged them to select and borrow books. These books were then read to the children upon request as part of regular daytime and nighttime reading. A few nursery school children attended public library story hours or film programs as well. Children also visited bookstores regularly with their parents and were allowed to select books for purchase.

Maple Nursery School homes also had many adult reading materials, including recipe books, reference volumes, magazine and newspaper subscriptions, college textbooks, professional collections, popular fiction and classic literature. Like the children's materials, some books were owned and some borrowed from the public library.

All the parents were familiar with specific children's book titles, authors, and illustrators. Based on selections made at libraries, bookstores, and at home, parents reported that their children had both enduring and changing favorite books. These were requested and borrowed from the library repeatedly. When parents selected books for children, two major criteria were used: the child's current tastes and interests, and literary quality. Although children's current interests were fairly easy for parents to elaborate (e.g., animals, super-heroes, scary books, shell identification guides), almost all parents had difficulty clarifying what they meant by "good literature" for their children.

Of course, defining literary merit is quite complex; it is not a straight-forward question for anyone. Nevertheless, after much qualification and discussion, parents generally defined some criteria according to which they judged children's books. Among the criteria mentioned were: quality illustrations and book design, Caldecott Award winners and runners-up,[3] works by particular authors/and illustrators, imaginative and grammatical use of language, books that not only entertained but also taught the children something, books with appropriate social commentary, books that avoided stereotypes based on sex or race, classics of children's literature, and books that were not silly, vacuous, gimmicky, nonsensical, frightening or based on Disney versions of traditional tales. Parents stressed, however, that they did not impose their literary choices on their children. Rather, because their children chose many of their own books, they were exposed to a balanced selection of literature and had opportunities to read both the good and the bad.

---

[3]The recipient of the "Caldecott Award" is selected annually by a committee of the American Library Association as the most distinguished contribution to American picture-books for children.

Book-related materials. Nursery school children were constantly exposed to book-related or book-based items. They had book/record sets and book/tape sets, composed of paper or hardback children's books accompanied by audio-recordings of adult storyreaders with musical and sound effects. Children also played boxed games based on storybook characters and adventures; went to musical and dramatic productions of storybook tales; watched television or movie productions of storybook tales (and read the original storybooks before and after viewing these shows); and listened to recorded stories. Reprints of children's book illustrations or storybook characters were featured on the youngsters' clothing, wallpapers, furnishings, and room decorations, such as pictures and posters.

Other print and print-related materials. Nursery-school age children were surrounded by a wide variety of writing utensils and materials such as pencils, pens, markers, crayons, chalk, papers, pads, notebooks, chalkboards, and folders. These were available to the children just as toys were available; they were encouraged to play and experiment with them and often saw adults using these things. The children also played with magnetic alphabet letters and letter and number matching/identification games and puzzles. Numerous items of clothing were decorated with printed slogans and phrases. Usually quite early, Maple Nursery School children were taught to sing the "alphabet song" and were shown how to print and recognize their names.

Nursery-school parents emphasized, however, that they did not push their children to learn the alphabet or to practice printing techniques; these interests emerged "naturally," the parents believed. The four-to-five year old children were generally more interested in print than the younger group of three-to-four year olds. The remarks below were typical of parents describing the print interests of the older group:

> Oh my gosh! It's amazing! His father again, with his legal pads and his folders—Mark loves anything like that. His dad'll bring him home a pen, and he thinks that's really neat. He's got three million pens . . . .

> (Later in the interview the mother was asked whether she had made a conscious effort to teach her child about print.)

> It was so easy with him. I mean, he's been doing this for over a year now. With his interests, believe me, I didn't push at all. He, he really is—his favorite tools are pad and pencil around this house. Truly, if you go down to my, uh, downstairs, we have a big table and on it are all kinds of writing things. And he'll sit there . . . he'll be watching the "Brady's" [television show] or something, and he'll lose interest in it and just get a paper and start writing.

Even the youngest nursery-school children recognized and printed some alphabet letters, usually beginning with the letters in their names. According to their parents, all of the children had expressed interest in printed signs, labels, and advertisements by frequently asking adults what the print said. Nearly all of the older children had experimented with and practiced printing skills: they wrote strings of letters and numbers with and without adult models; they asked adults to print certain words and phrases and then copied the words from the models; and they requested and received the spellings of words as they composed their own sentences, notes and letters. Frequently, the children attempted to read back printed messages. Parents reported that these attempts were accurate in terms of the intent of the message and frequently accurate or nearly accurate on a verbatim basis.

Uses of books

When asked, parents concluded that they used specific books with their children for many purposes. These purposes fell into four general categories: (a) entertainment, (b) problem-solving, (c) source of knowledge, and (d) relaxation.

Entertainment. All nursery-school parents stressed the entertainment value of books, both in their own lives and in the lives of their children. They chose books for their children with characters or plots they assumed the child would find appealing; and invited the children to choose their own books based on personal tastes and interests. By suggesting reading as "something to do," by modeling reading as a leisure-time activity in their own lives, and by advocating reading activities as alternatives to watching television parents encouraged children to view reading as an enjoyable and worthwhile way of spending time. Although questions referring to television-watching habits were not asked during interviews, many nursery school parents stressed a preference for reading over television. They brought up this topic themselves and stated that they monitored and limited their children's television watching. In several homes, book-related dramatic play, involving all members of the family, often occurred during the evening hours when many children watch television.

In every Maple Nursery School family, children themselves chose storyreading or book-related activities for their own entertainment. They brought books to parents or other adults to be read to them; independently chose to look at books alone or with siblings; listened to and looked at book/record sets in their own rooms; and drew pictures of book or story-related characters or events. Several parents reported that their children requested and listened attentively to as many as 12 books in one sitting and spent hours each day listening to recorded stories and looking at books on their own.

This is not to suggest that these children never engaged in non-book-related play, or never selected other kinds of entertainment. On the contrary, physically active play and games were extremely popular among nursery-school children, and there were countless occasions when children preferred active play to storyreading. However both nursery-school parents and their children viewed bookreading as a desirable, enjoyable, and entertaining way of spending leisure time alone or with other members of the family.

Problem solving. Although they definitely did not view it as the primary purpose for bookreading, nearly all nursery-school parents periodically used books in order to help their children deal with problems and confront difficult issues. Parents stressed that they did not use this approach in a heavy-handed, didactic, or moralistic fashion. They did not conclude each bookreading with specific admonishments or moral pronouncements to their children (e.g., "*You* need to obey your Mommy and Daddy just like the good little ducklings in the story"). Rather, parents believed that storyreading could be used to initiate conversations around particular topics, and to encourage their children to consider and talk about their feelings in relation to these topics. Nursery school children listened to stories about fictional children with problems or in anxiety-producing situations that come up in real life, such as the birth of a sibling; initial visits to doctors' or dentists' offices; leaving parents to go to school for the first time; dealing with angry feelings; coping with the death or illness of grandparents or pets; staying at home with babysitters while parents went away; quarreling and reconciling with friends; facing and overcoming nighttime fears or fantasies; and understanding and accepting parental discipline.

Parents reported that during these storyreadings children were usually attentive and involved, although often very quiet. Discussions of problems usually occurred after the readings—either immediately afterward, or sometimes days and even weeks later—rather than during the readings, as was true of many other storyreadings. Discussions of issues that were particularly troubling to individual children unfolded over periods of several weeks. During this time children framed questions and remarks about their own lives or situations in relation to the problems of the fictional characters or events in the stories. Parents encouraged their children to see these relationships and used them to explore various aspects of the problems.

Parents expressed uncertainty about whether the books actually helped children solve specific problems, but believed they opened communications with their children about certain matters. These comments were typical:

> I've taken some books with that [problem-solving] in mind. Um, at the beginning of the school year—and this continues—little Elizabeth feels she doesn't have a best buddy. So I've tried to seek out some books that talk about friendship. And when Sally was coming along, I tried to read books to Elizabeth about having a new sister and how the older child didn't always feel that happy about the new arrival. And, uh, I don't know, it's hard, I don't know how much went in. Again, this past summer my mother died. We read some books on death. One in particular that somebody lent me had to do with a turtle that died. And, uh, they've talked very matter of factly about death. . . . My sister-in-law lent a book on sort of early stages of talking about sex. And that opened up a lot of discussion . . . that was one that provoked a lot of questions.

Some parents reported that occasionally their children themselves seemed to use books to work out or deal with troublesome issues. During a period of nightmares, for example, one child repeatedly asked her parents to read "scary stories" to her during the day. Another child, troubled by many angry feelings, requested many readings of "the mad book," and eventually read the book aloud to others at the nursery school on an almost verbatim basis.

Maple Nursery School parents did not believe that all their children's difficulties instantaneously disappeared when they selected the "right" book. On the contrary, many confessed that they had no real idea how the books might ultimately affect the attitudes or actions of their children. They did believe, however, that both fiction and nonfiction books played useful and appropriate roles in their overall strategies for helping children work out social and psychological dilemmas.

Source of knowledge. Nursery-school families introduced their children to books as sources of knowledge or information. Books that were used in this way tended to be nonfiction rather than fiction, and included science, natural history and biography. Often, children had developed interests in particular topics, based on their own experiences; these interests preceded and prompted selection of books on related topics. For example, shell-collecting during summer vacation, acquisition of a pet, and fascination with household gadgets prompted adults to acquire and share books on these subjects. During and after the book-readings, parents encouraged the application of book knowledge to previous and ongoing experiences—e.g., identification and labeling of individual shells based on pictures and descriptions in a book on sea-shells; establishment of a procedure for feeding and caring for a pet canary, according to the recommendations in a book on pets; discussion of how batteries produced power for small appliances, based on facts presented in a book on how things work.

Books also provided sources of information prior to the children's actual experiences; in this way, book information served to introduce children to new experiences or areas of knowledge. These book intro-ductions were both planned and spontaneous. For example, parents selected and read to their children a book on the U.S. space program the day before they planned to view television coverage of NASA's space shuttle flight. In another family after listening to a book on elementary scientific principles, a child spontaneously developed interest in and began to try out simple science experiments at home.

As these examples indicate, in Maple Nursery School homes, a child's interests might prompt bookreadings, and bookreadings could help develop a child's interests. Book information served as one way in which children's experiences were grounded by providing them with both verification and extension of knowledge already gained from direct experience, as well as introducing them to areas not previously experi-enced. Nursery-school parents also used books to introduce their chil-dren to areas of knowledge where first-hand experiences were not possi-ble. Several of the children, for example, were particularly interested in dinosaurs and other prehistoric animals. Although some eventually vis-ited natural history museums, their major experiences with dinosaurs were through books.

Relaxation. Families also encouraged the use of storyreadings for relaxation. Although many of the books selected for the children's relaxation were also used for entertainment, relaxation was primarily aimed at calming the children, so this use was closely correlated with particular circumstances. As discussed earlier, storyreadings at bedtime were perceived by parents as particularly good transitions from the active, physically stimulating activities of daily play to the physically passive activity of nightly sleep.

Readings were also used to quiet children during the day after loud or rough play, when parents felt that their children were becoming too excited, or following temper tantrums. At these times, the physical closeness that storyreading allowed, a soft and steady adult reading voice, and the children's relative inactivity helped to create a calm and restful atmosphere, and achieve the desired relaxation. Some parents commented that the children themselves had acquired this relaxation orientation to reading, and would request storyreadings at times of great agitation and stress, or at times when they were particularly tired.

Parental beliefs about books and reading

When asked to describe their reasons for choosing reading for so many varied purposes, nursery-school parents were at first puzzled by the question. Typical remarks were: ''I would think that the reasons are obvious;'' and ''I don't think we could think of anything else that would fit in more naturally with everything that we do.'' As these and many other comments indicate, reading to their children and encouraging them to participate in book-related activities were for these families routine parts of parenting young children. Parents provided reading experiences for their children as routinely as they provided for their physical well-being.

It is important to remember that reading and literacy are *not* taken for granted in all families. In several working-class South Baltimore families, for example, reading and writing were regarded as the province of the school rather than the home; in these families, literacy was hoped for, but it was not assumed (Miller, Nemoianu, and DeJong, in press). Maple Nursery School families, on the other hand, regarded bookreading and eventual literacy as ''givens'' of childrearing. When pressed to explain why they found reading so important, they came up with two kinds of reasons: they believed that early reading to young children helped them to become competent readers themselves; and they considered reading to be a rewarding activity throughout an individual's lifetime.

Becoming readers. Maple Nursery School parents believed that children's early exposure to books, print-related materials, and reading activities would help them become readers when they entered school and were formally instructed in reading skills. They wanted their children to be readers who had both the ability and the desire to read. Many parents attributed their children's language, vocabulary, and concept developments to early experiences with stories and books. Others believed that storyreading experiences contributed to their children's comprehension abilities and listening skills. One mother, a former teacher, considered early reading experiences to be crucial for school success: "Being read to is so essential . . . it's just a part of growing up. And if kids miss out on it, they really miss a lot, and I don't think it can really be made up. You just can't catch up." None of the parents claimed to understand or have proof of a connection between being read to and learning how to read, but they hoped and believed that listening to stories, having books in their homes, and seeing the adults around them read would somehow contribute to their children's early success at school reading.

In addition to the contributions of early reading experiences to children's learning how to read, nursery school parents believed that such experiences were of central importance in learning the habit of reading and the desire to read. When children learned early that reading was pleasurable and rewarding, they would, parents hoped, be readers for the rest of their lives. "If it becomes a habit early enough on, it will be something carried through life," one parent remarked.

Nursery-school parents attested to the vital impact of reading in their own lives, and most of them considered themselves regular if not avid readers. They wanted very much to pass on to their children what they felt to be the gift of reading. Not all parents were as committed to reading as the parent whose remarks are quoted below, but most of the parents had very positive views about reading.

> Books have been almost the most important thing in my life . . . not *the* most important thing, but the most consistent thing . . . . They're there for entertainment, for knowledge, for comfort, for getting relaxed . . . I read all the time. I read everything from good stuff to junk. If there's a subject, if I become interested in something, if something's happening, the first thing that I do is to go and read about it, and that's a big part of my life, and it's been a rewarding part. And I would like for my children to have the ability to do that if they want to too.

Benefits of reading. Parents believed that reading had offered, and could offer, many benefits to their children for both the present and the future. Parents could offer the rewards of reading to their preschool children by reading to them; later, however, those rewards would not be available to those who were not able to read independently, or who had not acquired a habit and the motivation to read. For those who could read, however, rewards were many including pleasure, mental stimulation, and learning.

All of the parents described reading as a generally pleasurable and entertaining activity for their preschoolers and for the children's future lives. Reading was believed to be a relaxing and enjoyable way of spending leisure time that could offer comfort and escape from the pressures and problems of the outside world. Nursery-school adults reported that story reading served as a focal point for social interaction between adult readers and their child listeners; similarly, they found that ideas contained in books stimulated social interaction between adult readers.

Nursery-school parents also emphasized the role of reading in stimulating their children mentally. Especially in comparison with television, which parents frequently commented was limiting and noninvolving, storyreadings were believed to expand children's imaginative and intellectual interests and to enrich their powers of creativity. One parent linked literary experiences with aesthetic experiences in music and art, and suggested that "reading is extremely important as one part of a whole mode of creativity." Several parents suggested that they wanted their children to understand that books were the results of the creative efforts of several people working in cooperation. In this way, storyreading and follow-up activities creating their own stories and books not only expanded the children's imaginations, but also gave them insight into the creative processes of bookmaking and writing.

Parents described many of the benefits of reading in terms of their children's learning from books; "learning" was used in a variety of different ways, but reading was consistently considered to be its key. Better understanding of the human condition and increased insights into the emotions and needs of other peoples, parents felt, came from wide reading experiences.

> There's so much humanity in books that I feel that you can just enrich their personalities—if there is such a thing as being able to teach through what you're saying—you can enrich their personalities . . . .These little children's books are full of wonderful things . . . .They're so relevant to life.

Parents also spoke of the contributions books could make to children's socialization, that is, to their learning acceptable and unacceptable kinds of social behavior, ways of solving problems, expressing emotions, and living with others. Parents believed that children's books (and later adult literature) passed down to children the traditions of their literary and cultural heritage. The storyreading practices of one nursery school family who came from India clearly pointed up this belief. Although their son had been born in America, both parents were Bengali. They attempted to instill in their son some of their cultural heritage by reading Bengali folk tales to him in both Bengali and in

English translation. Of course this instance was unusual. More often, the families did not choose specific stories and tales in order to broaden their children's exposure to their literary heritage. Rather, parents believed that a knowledge of one's literary heritage is an inherent long-term benefit of wide reading experiences.

Finally, as mentioned before, nursery school parents believed that books in general offered a source of valid information about, as one parent put it, "just about everything." Book information served to legitimate experience and to verify other sources of information. This belief in the power of print was clear in several comments:

> My friends tease me how if I'd found it in writing, found some bit of information in writing, that it becomes real for me. Whereas if someone just tells me something, then I immediately disbelieve it.

Nursery-school parents generally felt that printed sources of knowledge were important to their children's learning in all areas—social, cognitive, psychological, and philosophical. They seemed to believe, as did one parent who concluded her interview, "If you don't read, how do you know?"

Summary

The preceding pages have described the book and book-related values, attitudes, beliefs, and practices of nursery-school families, as reported in oral interviews by nursery-school parents. The home activities of the children and the values of their parents formed a major part of the context that surrounded storyreading and other reading activities at the school. These reports give us important insight into the meaning that reading and writing events had for this community where literacy was taken for granted. The literacy orientation described by parents and the literacy orientation observed at the school were closely allied and supportive of one another. Although book-related practices at the nursery school were more consistent and structured than home practices, literacy experiences at home prepared the children for and supported them in nursery-school activities. Before they entered Maple Nursery School—through both adult models and direct experiences—preschoolers had been exposed to (and had in many cases acquired) these basic conceptions about literature and literacy:

1. Bookreading and other book-related activities are common and appropriate for people of all ages, from infancy to old age.

2. Bookreading is an important activity that often takes precedence and favor over other activities.

3. Bookreading provides intimate, social interaction between children and adults, often on a one-to-one basis.

4. Bookreading can be initiated and terminated by either children or adults.

5. Bookreading is entertaining, pleasurable, and relaxing for both children and adults.

6. Bookreading is an appropriate and pleasurable solitary activity for either children or adults.

7. Book characters, events, and situations are often relevant to real-life situations, and can sometimes be helpful in dealing with real-life problems.

8. Discussion of ideas and events in books, whether immediately or long after bookreadings, are appropriate and encouraged for both children and adults.

9. For both children and adults, reading provides a primary way of finding out about almost anything.

10. Both children and adults can function as readers and listeners.

11. Both children and adults can interrupt, ask questions, and make comments during bookreadings.

12. Plots and stories from books are often translated into other media, including television, movies, records, dance, drama.

13. Books are created by and for people.

14. Both children and adults are appropriate producers and consumers of books and other print messages.

15. Preschoolers may be interested in all aspects of reading and writing.

16. Books are valued possessions and appropriate as gifts, keepsakes, and heirlooms for both children and adults.

17. Individual taste in books varies, and both children and adults are encouraged to make their own selections of reading materials.

18. Knowledge based on personal primary experience or on hearsay can be verified and/or disputed according to information in printed materials.

One salient feature of this literary orientation is the prominence of books and printed materials in the lives of both young children and adults. As has been pointed out, books were very important in the adult community. They were conspicuous in living rooms, dens, and bedrooms. Adults counted books among their treasured possessions, and often lent books to and borrowed them from good friends. Adults instilled these same values in their children. Preschoolers had their own bookshelves filled with books; they brought books from home to show proudly to nursery-school companions; and they regularly borrowed books from the library. Books and other print-related materials were permanent, prominent features of home environments. These concepts about literature and literacy are similar to the literacy patterns of the two-year-old daughter of anthropologists Scollon and Scollon (1981) and of 15 mother-child dyads in mainstream homes in North Carolina (Heath, 1982b).

Another significant feature of the Maple Nursery School literacy orientation is the variety and number of contexts in which books and other printed materials were used. There was no single specific kind of literacy in the Maple Nursery School community, that is, reading was not done only for religious purposes or chiefly to get the local news. Although books were consistently used at bedtime to quiet children and create a calm atmosphere, many kinds of print were used with children in many different situations and for a variety of purposes.

A third important characteristic of the community's orientation to literacy is the view of bookreading as an appropriate social, interactive activity, as well as a solitary, individual activity. As a social activity, bookreading tended to encourage intimacy among fellow readers or between readers and listeners. It structured interactive experiences between adults and children and served as a framework for relating to one another by providing a focus of attention, specific roles for readers and listeners, and a familiar situation that had a clearly marked beginning and ending. Social interaction around books was pleasurable for both children and adults. As an individual activity, bookreading was a favored way for both children and adults to spend leisure time alone. Adults claimed that bookreading provided intellectual and imaginative stimulation, as well as spiritual and emotional comfort and they hoped that books would do this for their children.

Perhaps the most striking characteristic of the Maple Nursery School literacy orientation was the authority accorded to books and other printed materials to verify and extend primary experiences and to legitimate oral information. With the authority vested in them, printed matter provided the Maple Nursery School community with a primary way of knowing that was supported and extended by dozens of nursery-school experiences.

CHAPTER 5

Time and Space: Nursery-School Plant, Materials, and Organization

Narrative Segment 2
"Super Heroes" and Indian Corn

It is November, and Dan, now a veteran nursery-school student, arrives at the school without his mother via his neighborhood car pool. When he enters, only a few children have arrived. The teacher is placing on the snacktable aluminum pans holding Indian corn cobs, dishes of glue, and squares of cardboard. Mark is dashing around excitedly, humming "Batman" music and talking to anyone who will listen about "Super Heroes." He runs up to Dan and shows him the "Spiderman" tee-shirt that he is wearing under his sweater. Dan is impressed, and, stimulated by Mark's activity, joins him in his frenzied run through the rooms of the school.

Meanwhile, other children have been arriving at the nursery school, primarily in car pool groups, each escorted by the mother-driver of the day. The children greet one another, show the teacher treasured possessions brought from home, and begin to take up various toys, puzzles, and books to play with individually or in small groups.

Mark and Dan now have several followers—two or three "Spidermen," two "Supermen," and one "Luke Skywalker"; they race through the nursery rooms and beg the teacher to help them make "Super-Hero" capes. After most of the children have arrived and the mothers have departed, the teacher leads the "Super-Hero" group into the workroom, sets on the workbench a big bag of fabric remnants, and suggests that each boy choose the piece he would like for a cape while she helps some children begin on another project at the snacktable. Three or four girls are also in the workroom now; they sit at the low worktable drawing, printing, and coloring. The "Super-Hero" group begins to pull fabrics out of the bag, rejecting and selecting various pieces.

When the teacher returns to the workroom, she shows each boy how to make a cape by weaving ribbon through the top of a fabric piece to form a tie and pasting a red fabric "S" on the back. As each cape is completed, its wearer rushes out of the workroom into the large general purpose room, and joins in impromptu and continuous "Super-Hero" play, composed of pretend battling, shouted directions and admonishments, flights to and from various treacherous locations, and self-produced musical accompaniment and sound effects.

Meanwhile, the helping mother and the teacher, who hurries back and forth between workroom and snacktable, help a small group of boys and girls make "Indian corn messages." Kernels of Indian corn are glued to cardboard squares randomly or in various designs captioned by the adult with the creator's interpretation of the "message" (e.g., "Indian corn secret message: It tells where the corn is," or "Indian corn secret message: It tells where the train is"). Throughout most of this period the small group of girls have remained at the table in the workroom, talking to one another, drawing and coloring pictures, making geometric-like designs, or practicing printing with brightly colored markers.

Participants in all three of these activities come and go as they desire; some drift in and out of various activities, moving quickly from "Batman" play to Indian-corn-making. Intermittently, various children stop and do other individual activities—look at books, put together puzzles, build with blocks, or play the piano by following color-coded musical sheets. During this time, the children talk freely to the adults and to one another. Although there is a great deal of adult assistance and direction for both the capemaking and Indian-corn projects, there is little adult interference with the children's actions, and two of the three major co-occurring activities are initiated by the children. These activities continue, simultaneously, for more than an hour until all of the boys who want them have capes and the Indian-corn-makers are finished.

Then the teacher stands at the piano and plays the "rug-time" song, singing out directions to the children to put away their toys and come to the rug. As most of the children slowly gather on the rug, three girls announce to the teacher that they would like to sing songs for the group. They sit side by side on the bench facing the children. While some children are still coming to the rug, two of the girls sing and one picks out the notes to "Snack Song" on the piano by following the color-coded music sheet. When the musical performances are over and all the children have settled on the rug, the teacher reads aloud. The first story is quite lengthy, and when many of the children become inattentive, the teacher puts the book aside and reads a second book that is simpler and shorter. All the children are involved in the second book, listening and laughing together.

Following the second reading, all the children go outdoors to play. They swing, play in the sandbox, climb trees, and ride wheeled toys. Their play is monitored but not organized or directed by adults. After approximately 30 minutes of outdoor play, the children are called indoors.

The teacher plays "Snack Song" on the piano, reminding the children musically to wash their hands and get their juice cups. She tells them they will have "rug" after "snack." One child brings a book to the table, and the teacher reads a few pages from it. Then the teacher leads the children in a group-participative song with hand motions. During the snack, the children talk to one another and to the adults around them. When they finish, the children place their cups in the kitchen sink; several immediately return to the rug and begin, independently, to look at books.

When most of the children have gathered on the rug, the teacher continues reading the long book that she began earlier. When some children become restless and leave the rug to play in other areas, the teacher does not insist that they return, but continues reading to the small group of children that remains attentive and interested. By the time the reading is over, several mothers have already arrived to take their children home.

Dan and three other children stay at the nursery school for lunch and other activities until they are picked up at 3:00.

Unlike the first day of school described in Narrative Segment 1 in the previous chapter, the November nursery-school morning described in Narrative Segment 2 was typical of nursery-school days observed over a period of 18 months. It was like other days in several ways: few whole group, organized activities were required; the children themselves initiated many activities; the schedule for the day was flexible and continuously modified; adults monitored but did not dominate activities; children were relatively free to come and go as they wished; and a variety of activities and materials were available and in use simultaneously. The day was not structured in the formal and orderly manner that we often expect of organized school events. Indeed, as several nursery-school parents confided during interviews, nursery-school days like the one described in Segment 2 often seemed rather chaotic to outside observers.

Despite initial impressions, and despite the flexibility of routine, nursery-school days were not, as I explain below, either unorganized or disordered. On the contrary, underlying the considerable diversity of materials and activities was an orderly structure based primarily on consistent ways of organizing and using time, space, and materials. These patterns of organization form the structure of the nursery-school environment and illuminate the net-work of activities that surround and support nursery-school bookreading.

Nursery-school structure is described in the pages that follow according to: physical plant, material culture and organization of space, and organization of time. The November morning described in detail in Narrative Segment 2 serves both to introduce these aspects of nursery-school structure and to provide a sense of the ways its various parts were related to one another.

Physical Plant

Physically, Maple Nursery School forms a stubby "L" shape, composed of four rooms and a hallway that connects the nursery rooms to the reception hall, sanctuary, and offices of the church building in which it is located. The front entrance to the nursery school is through a large fully-equipped kitchen with a long table in the center. Adjoining the kitchen is a spacious square room with wide window ledges and built-in closets, cabinets and shelves along its two exterior walls and entrances to two other rooms along its interior walls. On each side of this large room are two smaller rooms, each with two exterior walls that face the back church property and two interior walls. Three of the four exterior walls have tall, wide windows with built-in shelves below. The fourth exterior wall features large double doors leading to a grassy tree-lined play area with permanent swings and sandbox and several stone walks and paths.

Material Culture and Organization of Space

The physical space described above was organized into a number of smaller spaces primarily according to the ways that these spaces could be used by the children. Uses of space varied according to the kinds of activities, the material items that were located in or could be taken into and out of the areas, and the kinds of peer participation that occurred there. Distinct uses of space were marked by the language employed by children and adults to refer to the spaces, and by the degree and kind of adult direction and supervision imposed in each area. Description of how the two small rooms that adjoined the main nursery-school room were used serves as an introduction to the way space was divided and organized at the school.

The two small rooms were "the doll room" and "the workroom." These designations were used by both adults and children when referring to the rooms and on printed label cards posted on the doors. In the dollroom were dolls, carriages, beds and other doll furniture, a small table with chairs, a play sink, stove and cupboards, doll dishes, doll and child-sized clothing, and a long mirror. In this room the children played "house" and "dress-up." Girls more commonly participated in these activities than boys, although boys played both "house" and "dress-up" at times. The activities in the dollroom were always unsupervised and usually unobserved by adults.

Except when invited occasionally, adults were regarded by the children as intruders in the dollroom. Children costumed in various combinations of dress-up items often paraded their creations into the workroom or the large general-purpose room to be admired and enjoyed by others. They also frequently wore costumes for shows, plays, and dances that were shared with group audiences at "rug." The activity of dressing-up, however, almost always occurred in the dollroom itself, and costumes were always eventually returned to that room by either children or adults. Similarly, a "mother" might stroll with her "baby" and baby carriage through several of the nursery rooms and then return to the dollroom, but mostly "playing house" or "playing baby" were confined to the dollroom.

Just as the dollroom was equipped for children's role-playing, the second small room, the workroom, was equipped for working and playing with various kinds of tools and media. Two easels were located along one wall of the workroom ready with paint and brushes. A low round table with several chairs was located in front of permanent shelves filled with various sizes and kinds of papers, pencils, markers, crayons, scissors, tape, glue, staplers, and paperpunches. A low workbench held two vice-grips and adult-size tools—hammers, drills, saws, and wrenches—next to boxes of scrap wood, nails, screws, bolts, and other items of hardware.

Like dollroom play, activities in this room—painting, coloring, drawing, printing, pounding, sawing, drilling—were usually initiated by children; unlike dollroom play, workroom activities were usually, but not always, monitored by adults. Adult assistance was offered in response to children's requests for help.

The goals of many workbench and worktable activities were process rather than product-oriented. That is, children drilled holes or painted papers because they wanted to feel the power of drilling or see color drip down a page, rather than because they wanted to make finished products. However, like the "Super-Hero" cape project in the November day described earlier sometimes children wanted to make specific items. At these times, adults usually suggested approaches or provided materials to help children create their projects. Woodworking and painting tools were used exclusively in the workroom for woodworking and painting activities; they were not carried from room to room. Some general materials, such as scissors, tape, pencils, and markers could be carried out of the workroom and used for large-group activities, but these were always returned to the workroom.

The kitchen was a fully-furnished and functional room, used primarily by the church members. Nursery-school adults used the kitchen to store, prepare, and clean up the children's daily snacks. When nursery-school children occasionally participated in adult-initiated cooking projects, the children were closely supervised by adults and did not have access to materials or utensils. Usually, however, the kitchen was used by the children only for entering and leaving the building. The exception to this limited access was the long adult-sized table in the middle of the kitchen. This was referred to by children and adults as the "going-home-table." Finished art projects. treasures found outdoors, notes to parents, and items to be borrowed from the nursery-school were all placed on this table at various times during the nursery-school day. When children left for the day, they were reminded by parents or teacher to check the going-home-table to reclaim their possessions.

No specific term was used by nursery-school participants to describe the large general-purpose room as a whole. Sections of the room, however, were differentially used and referred to by participants. The most important section of the general-purpose room was "rug." This space-designation did not include only the actual green rug located in one corner of the room; rather the term "rug" referred to an area of the floor covered by a rug and large pillows and bounded by shelves built into the wall, a bookcase against another wall, and an upright piano.

Several relatively quiet activities occurred at various times of the day in the rug area. The material items needed for these activities were stored in shelves and cabinets around the rug. These included, most importantly, a large collection of hardback and paperback books, stored in either the wall bookcase or on a sandwich-style book display whose contents was frequently changed. Books were secured from several sources: the teacher regularly borrowed a collection of books and book-based filmstrips from local public libraries, nursery-school families donated books to the collection, and the nursery-school organization added to its own materials with paperbacks from the nursery-school-sponsored book club.

Many manipulatable materials were also used in this area (picture puzzles, shape-, color-, letter-, and number-matching devices, small plastic attachable blocks), as were card games and boxed games. These materials were used by individuals, as well as by pairs or small groups of children. Activities were initiated by either children or adults, and small groups often included an adult as leader/player. Several small groups of children often played on the rug beside, but not with, one another. These materials were not taken away from the rug area or used in other areas. The most important activity in this spatial area was "rug-time," which is discussed in detail in Chapter 7.

Two long, low snacktables with many child-sized chairs were located and frequently rearranged within an area along the street-side wall of the all-purpose room. The tables were used primarily for group snacks or teacher-directed art and cooking projects. Materials needed for such activities were brought to the tables from other locations. The teacher and adult helpers supervised these activities, and the children themselves had somewhat limited access to materials.

Other locations in the general-purpose room were designated and labeled as receptacles for certain items (e.g., "Lego cupboard," "big-block cupboard"). Toys were always kept in their own places and were normally used in nearby open areas of the general-purpose room. These materials included sets of small plastic and rubber animals, large wooden building-blocks, large geometric shapes, and plastic bowling pins and balls. The children had free access to these materials, and played with them in both small and large groups, usually within sight of adults, but without adult supervision.

In addition to the corners and areas of the general-purpose room already described, the room had a large open area that was used for a variety of different activities. These involved active play with large pieces of equipment or toys, set out by adults and often requested by the children—indoor sliding board, rubber inner tubes, climbing bars, and a three-sided wooden stage and playhouse. Such materials were brought out for limited periods of time and then returned to cupboards or other storage spots. The children also used the open area for large-group spontaneous dramatic play at games such as spaceship travel, "Super-Hero" battle, or cowboys and Indians. Play of this sort required few props but lots of space.

As the above description suggests, many items were consistently used by the children in particular ways and in particular spaces. Others were not associated with specific areas and were not directly used by the children, but were, nonetheless, part of the material culture of the nursery school. For example, many of the display items on the walls, windows, and bulletin boards were photographs of previous nursery-school activities, children's artworks (paintings, drawings, hangings, pictures, cut-outs), and children's print works (stories, booklets, signs, letters, and print practice). Other things on display were commercially-produced arithmetic or reading posters, nature or science prints, charts, maps, and calendars. In addition, there were many three-dimensional pieces of equipment that were not played with or regularly used by the children; these included a large thermometer, a dry measure scale, a manipulatable cardboard clock, a spring scale, a tripod with magnifying glass, a terrarium, an aquarium with fish, an animal cage, and live plants. When these materials were used, they were usually introduced to the whole group under the direction of the teacher.

Organization of Time

As I have pointed out, Maple Nursery School, although unstructured by certain standards, was spatially structured in a way that was consistent with material items, types of activities, and degree and kind of child-adult and child-child interaction. The temporal structure of the nursery school was somewhat more flexible than the spatial structure, but it was also consistent with materials and activities and with various kinds of interaction. The temporal structure also paralleled in many ways the school's spatial structures.

The three-hour morning session, which included as many as 16 children and one volunteer mother, in addition to the teacher, was more planned and more adult-directed than the twice-a-week, three-hour afternoon session which included as few as four children and no adult assistants. Both these sessions, however, were organized around a series of "times."

The daily morning session revolved around four time periods, three of which were referred to by children and adults as "rug-time," "snack time," and "going-home-time," plus one "time" that was not specifically labeled—a period of outdoor play. Neither these routine times nor other nursery-school events were scheduled or discussed according to clock-time. In fact, most events were referred to in terms of their relationships to the major time periods mentioned above. For example, a child was promised he or she could have a certain item "after rug-time" or "right before going-home-time," instead of "at ten o'clock" or "in half an hour."

Rug-time was pivotal to the organization of the morning session; it was one of the few activities that all the children did together and was the most formally organized event of the nursery-school day. Rarely omitted, although sometimes abbreviated, rug-time provided a significant physical and psychological framework for interaction around and interpretation of storybooks. Because rug-time is particularly important in this monograph it is treated in detail in Chapter 7.

Although less formal than rug-time, snack-time also occurred during every morning session and frequently served as a time and sequence marker for other nursery-school activities. It provides a good example of the consistency between temporal organization and other features of nursery school life. Snack-time was always introduced with the "snack song," played on the piano by the teacher. The children knew the significance of this song, and usually responded by completing activities, as necessary, before eating. During snack-time, but before the food was served, the teacher sang songs or did brief finger plays with the children. While eating, the children spoke freely with other children and adults.

Consistency between temporal and spatial organization, type of activity, and type of interaction during snack-time were striking: children were never served food at the nursery school at any time other than snacktime; snack-time always occurred at the snacktable and children were not allowed to carry their food away from the table; during snack-time, activities other than eating did not occur at the table, although at other times the table was used for art projects and games; the children used their cups only at snack-times and were discouraged from bringing any other items to the table. When they had finished eating, the snack-time routine was completed as the children took their cups and placed them in the kitchen sink.

Unlike rug-time and snack-time, periods of outdoor play were not ritualized or formal. Outdoor play was boisterous, child-directed and non-routinized. Children played on swings and in sandboxes, climbed trees, and raced on wheeled toys. Adults observed, and when requested to do so, helped children. They seldom interfered to settle children's squabbles, and they did not organize and direct games except on the infrequent occasions when children requested such assistance. During outdoor play periods, both children and adults went back and forth between the play area and the nursery-school building. Indoor toys, however, were seldom brought outdoors, and outdoor riding toys were not permitted inside the nursery school except to be stored in the workroom.

Going-home-time signified the end of the morning session when children claimed artwork, printed works, and other possessions from the going-home-table. During this time, there was more adult-to-adult than adult-to-child interaction. Going-home-time was frequently mentioned to indicate the order of activities and to mark off time during the morning.

The beginning of afternoon sessions at the nursery school was marked by the going-home-time of the morning session. Afternoon sessions were very loosely structured; most of the time was spent in child-initiated group or individual play that was unsupervised by adults. These informal sessions were, however, organized around two "times"— lunch-time and quiet-time. Lunch-time was similar to snack-time; it always occurred at the snacktables, children were discouraged from handling items other than food and were encouraged to stay at the table until lunch was over. Relaxed, informal conversation among the children and between children and teacher was common.

Although it often featured storyreading and always occurred in the rug area, afternoon quiet-time was much less ritualized and routinized than the morning rug-time. During quiet-time, the teacher encouraged the children to participate in a group sedentary activity, such as tracing pictures, playing or creating a board or card game, looking at or talking about books, or listening to stories. The purpose of this activity was for the children to rest and calm down; it frequently occurred after rough, physical play when the children were especially stimulated.

As these descriptions indicate, the nursery school, while flexible and relaxed, was characterized by an extremely consistent organization of time, space, materials, activities, and personal interactions. This organization was accepted and referred to by children and adults, and it was established very early in the nursery school year. The description of the first day of school in Chapter 4 reveals that this spatial and temporal organization was introduced immediately to new nursery-school children by printed labels, the teacher's language, and the sequence of activities. Also, because of the age range at Maple Nursery School, each September about half of the children were new and half were veteran nursery-school students. The more experienced children taught the routines to the younger children, both through their actions and through explicit admonishments or reminders. The nursery-school teacher was always consistent in both the language she used to describe the division of times and spaces and in suggesting rules for behavior in particular places and at particular times. She frequently talked with the children about the schedule of nursery-school events and explained the sequences that would occur.

Summary

Analysis of the organization of time and space at the nursery school contributes significantly to an understanding of the children's literacy and literary experiences there. Most important, this organization needs to be understood in terms of its support of storyreading events "on-the-rug" (see Chapter 7). As I show in Chapter 7, the temporal and spatial designation, "rug-time," provided the children with an orientation for bookreading. Like the other spaces and times that structured the nursery school day, it framed the activity as one with specific interactional norms and as a time and place to use particular kinds of materials.

The children came to expect a particular set of rules for each kind of activity at the nursery school, and became accustomed to using different interactional and interpretive norms for different activities. As Chapter 7 makes clear, during "rug-time" the degree and kind of child participation and direction, the nature of physical and verbal interaction, the extent of adult-child interaction, and temporal and spatial stipulations were different from the rules for other nursery-school activities. Despite differences, however, certain kinds of nursery-school activities did require particular norms, and the children learned to function more or less according to these norms, listed below.

1. Large spaces were permanently segmented into smaller spaces:
   (a) Spaces were labeled, both orally and in writing, according to the language used to describe them (e.g., "dollroom," "rug").
   (b) Certain activities occurred only in certain spaces (e.g., hammering was done at the workbench, sandplay occurred inside the sandbox).
   (c) Some spaces were defined and labeled according to their functions as receptacles for specific material items (e.g., "block cupboard," "book shelf").
   (d) The degree and kind of adult direction and supervision varied according to spaces.

2. The nursery school day was organized into periods of activity often called "times":

   (a) Times acted as sequential and temporal markers for other activities and were consistent with norms for interaction and behavior (e.g., "put the box back on the table until it's lunch-time").

   (b) Times consistently occurred in particular spaces (e.g., "rug-time" occurred on the rug, "snack-time" occurred at the snacktables).

   (c) Particular materials were used during particular times (e.g., cups were used only at snack-time, wheeled toys were used only during outdoor play time).

   (d) Particular times determined the extent of ritualized and routinized behaviors (e.g., rug-time was more formal and ritualized than quiet-time, even though the same kind of activity often occurred in both).

   (e) Times determined rules for interaction between children and adults and among children (e.g., rug-time was a time for sitting and listening to the adult in charge, while snack-time was a time for talking with peers).

   (f) Sequence of times was not standardized, but the nature of activities that occurred during specific times was extremely consistent (e.g., snack-time might follow either rug-time or outdoor play, but snack-time itself was always the same.

CHAPTER 6

Are You Sure the Pen is Mightier Than the Sword?: Reading and Writing off the Rug

The major focus of this monograph is bookreading. As I have mentioned, nursery-school bookreading almost always took place within a psychological and physical framework called "rug-time," which signalled the interpretive and interactional orientation of its participants. Nursery-school reading, however, did not occur only on the rug. Reading and writing were interwoven with many nursery-school activities and occurred in many different situations throughout the school day. Some occurrences were "literacy events," that is, events in which the production and/or comprehension of printed materials were central to participants' interactions. At other times, print was not necessarily produced or comprehended, but was simply part of the material culture of the nursery school (e.g., bulletin board displays, posters, signs). The children were exposed to such print, but it was not necessarily brought to their attention.

Both kinds of print—print that was central to literacy events and print that was simply part of the material culture—were part of the nursery-school environment. Both were involved in the children's initiation into the community's patterns of reading and writing. Looking carefully at these contributes significantly to understanding the children's literary and literacy socialization.

There were many different situations in which reading and writing occurred off the rug. All of the reading and writing activities that included the nursery-school children in some way, even indirectly, had something to do with their literacy socialization. Therefore in this chapter on uses of reading and writing in the nursery school, I have included those situations in which adults were the primary users of printed materials, but children were direct observers of the use of the materials. For example, a child observed as an adult noted on the "Things Borrowed" list that he was taking home a particular item; or a child participated in discussion of a note which was delivered by the child to the teacher. Because children participated in them, literacy events like these are included in this chapter. On the other hand, I have not included in this chapter situations in which adults were exclusively the producers and consumers of printed materials.

Through many literacy events, nursery school children were exposed to two major aspects of reading and writing: (a) ways in which reading and writing could be used for various purposes and goals, and (b) the mechanical competencies involved in the processes of encoding, decoding and printing written language. At the nursery school, formal, direct instruction in the uses of literacy was virtually non-existent and was very infrequent in the skills of literacy. The teacher did not plan formal lessons on how reading and writing could be used, and only infrequently gave direct instruction in how to encode, decode, or print. Rather, learning about reading and writing was the result of a gradual process of socialization that was indirect, informal and embedded into the routine social interactions of adults and children. Indeed as we saw earlier in adult interviews, neither the teacher nor the parents of the community considered literacy development as a nursery-school goal for children. In fact, academic instruction in reading and writing skills for preschool children was either de-emphasized or criticized by nursery school adults. That all sorts of school activities included literacy events, and that the material culture of the school was heavily print-oriented were unremarkable from the perspective of the adults. Rather reading and writing were integrated in the routine social exchanges of adults and children.

Uses of Reading and Writing

Although some of the nursery-school children could read and write their own names and recognize some environmental print, they could not, for the most part, decode and encode words that were decontextualized from the environment. All of the children, however, were

⌐regular participants in situations where adults used reading and writing for and with them for a variety of purposes. As they did so, adults and children moved along a continuum of participation in literacy events. At one endpoint of this continuum were situations in which uses of reading and writing were completely initiated, directed, and accomplished by adults *for* children. At the other end were situations in which children themselves initiated, directed, and accomplished the reading and writing.

Two examples illustrate these endpoints. In Narrative Segment 3, the adult used print *for* the child; in Narrative Segment 4, the children used print for themselves.

Narrative segment 3
let me put your name on that

Alice is painting a picture at the easel in the workroom. The teacher walks by and says, "Here, Alice, let me put your name on that so that you'll know it's yours at going-home-time". Alice looks up as the teacher prints her name in a corner of the picture. At noon when her mother arrives, Alice tells her she has painted a picture. Via the name label on the painting, Alice's mother verifies that the picture is Alice's and takes it home.

Narrative segment 4
is this your name

It is snack-time, and the children are finding places at the table. There is an argument between Linda and Jeffrey over a juice cup. Both children claim that the cup is theirs. Jeffrey will not give in until Linda demands that he look at the name printed on the cup. "Is this your name?" When Jeffrey admits that the writing does not seem to say "Jeffrey", Linda triumphantly announces that it says "Linda," which is her name and (which) means that it's her cup.

In Narrative Segments 3 and 4 the use of print as a name label to show ownership was identical; there was considerable difference, however, in the extent of the children's participation in the use of print. In Narrative Segment 3, although the child was directly involved, adults dominated the literacy event; they initiated and controlled both the mechanical processes of encoding and decoding the name and the use of print as a label to signify ownership and later to re-claim ownership. Narrative Segment 4 was quite different. Here the actions of both children indicated that they understood the use of name labels to show ownership; Linda's actions also indicated that she could initiate and control both this use of print and the decoding it required.

Another way to think about the nature and extent of adult-child

Figure 6.1 Literacy events controlled by adults

Literacy Event Is
Controlled by Adult(s)

participation in literacy events is to view these schematically. We can begin wih a horizontal line that represents adult-child participation in literacy events (see Figure 6.1). At the far left is an endpoint that signifies literacy events that are completely controlled by adults. Like the literacy event in Narrative Segment 3, literacy events placed at this left endpoint are those that are initiated, guided, and terminated by an adult *for* a child. At this endpoint, the adult functions as an intermediary between child and print by carrying out for the child all the steps needed in order to use print in a particular way. In Alice's case in Narrative Segment 3, Alice did little except to observe. Both adults involved, however, behaved *as if* Alice intended to use print as a way to show ownership and acted *as if* she herself had used the printed name label in this way.

At the far right of the continuum of adult-child participation in literacy events is an endpoint that signifies literacy events controlled by children themselves (see Figure 6.2). Like the literacy event in Narrative Segment 4, a literacy event that is placed at this right endpoint is one that is initiated, guided, and terminated by the child. At this endpoint, the child himself or herself carries out the steps necessary to use print in a particular way. In Linda's case in Narrative Segment 4, Linda herself did everything: she called Jeffrey's attention to the name label on the cup, required that he attempt to read the label, verified the label herself, and announced the outcome of a situation in which a name label is used to establish ownership. Of course, a prior literacy event had occurred when adults labelled juice cups for the children, but in the literacy event described in Narrative Segment 4, there was no adult participation or intervention.

There are many points between the two ends of this continuum of adult-child participation. Situations vary according to the degree, more or less, of adult-child initiation, guidance, control, verification, and termination of uses of print and adult-child decoding and encoding. It is not important to try to identify specific points along the continuum, but only to know that many exist. Narrative Segment 5 illustrates one of the many points between adult and child control of print in literacy events.

Figure 6.2 Literacy events controlled by children

Literacy Event Is
Controlled by Child(ren)

Narrative segment 5
between the boats

Susie and I (the researcher) have been trying to make a sailboat out of half a walnut shell. We get the sail on but can't get the boat to balance—it keeps tipping and then sinking into the water. We finally make a second boat that looks like the first, but will float. At about the time we finish, the children all go outdoors to play. Susie hurriedly brings me a scrap of paper and asks me to write her a little note to place between the boats. She directs me: "it will say, 'this one will go in the water and this one will not,' so that no one will put the wrong one in the water and it will sink."

In this example, Susie herself completely controlled the literacy event; she stipulated the exact message to be written down, the context in which the message was to be used, and the way that the message was to be interpreted by passers-by in relation to the nearby water table and the two little boats. Susie's actions indicated that she clearly understood that print could be used in place of an oral message. An adult did act as an intermediary in this event—but only as encoder, as an instrument for the child's use of print.

In Susie's case, described in Narrative Segment 5, and in many other situations where both adults and children participated, more or less, in literacy events, we can see that the continuum has an almost limitless number of intermediate points. Each of these represents a literacy event accomplished through joint adult-child participation, with the adult acting in some way as intermediary between child and print (see Figure 6.3).

Daily, there were dozens of literacy events at the nursery school, with adults and children taking greater or lesser roles as participants and adults taking greater or lesser roles as intermediaries. From these events eight major ways that print was used by and for the children emerged.[1]

Figure 6.3 Continuum of Adult-Child Participation in Literacy Events

Literacy Event	Literacy Event	Literacy Event
Is Controlled	Is Jointly Con-	Is Controlled
by Adult	trolled by Adult	by Child
	and Child	

[1]Four of the eight uses of print that emerged from the nursery school observations were similar to those in Heath's (1980a) analysis of functions and uses of literacy in a southeastern American community; Heath's category names have been used for these four categories.

These were in addition to the many ways that books were used "on-the-rug" in the nursery school. (On-the-rug uses of books are discussed in detail in Chapter 10.)

In the following description of the eight ways print was used, there are many examples that fit at various intermediate points along the continuum. There are fewer examples of literacy events that fit at the endpoints of the continuum. In other words, there were few literacy events that were controlled exclusively by children or exclusively by adults. Rather, most of the literacy events involved joint adult-child participation. This pattern points up the need to look carefully at who participated in literacy events, how they participated and interacted with one another, and what kinds of social situations encompassed these literacy events.

The most significant characteristic of these eight ways of using print is that the nursery-school children were exposed to them on a daily basis, and as the examples below will reveal, they acquired great facility with many of them. For the most part, the children did not know how to encode or decode, but they did know a great deal about contexts in which print could be used, purposes for which print could be used, strategies for interpreting print in various contexts, and relationships between oral and printed language.

• *Oral message substitutes.*   On many occasions, reading and writing were used at the nursery school in place of oral communication. Sometimes, written messages were used because direct oral communication was not possible (e.g., a parent's note to the teacher, a parent's note to a child tucked inside a lunchbox to be found and read at lunchtime, or Susie's note in Narrative Segment 5 informing passers-by about her walnut-shell boat while she herself played elsewhere). At other times, written messages were simply more convenient than oral ones. This was especially true of messages concerning current nursery-school business. At the beginning and end of each nursery-school day, the teacher was very involved with the children and with preparations or clean-up of the day's activities, and had little time to speak with each individual parent. Messages were, therefore, posted on the front and back doors of the nursery school, so that parents would see them when arriving and departing with their children (e.g., "October tuition now due," or "Trip to Aquarium on Friday"). Although these messages were produced by and intended for adults, they were also noticed by the children, as Narrative Segement 6 indicates.

Narrative segment 6
the sign on the door

It is a few minutes after 9:00. Children are busily looking at books about fish and drawing fish pictures. Brad and his father arrive and greet the teacher. The parent asks the teacher what time the group will leave for the aquarium. At this point, Brad excitedly breaks into the conversation to inform the teacher that his dad knew they were going on the trip because he read the sign on the front door. The teacher and parent smile and nod, confirming that this is a good way to get information.

At times, written messages were preferred over oral ones, even though oral messages were possible. Written messages seemed to carry more power and authority than the spoken word. Narrative Segment 7 indicates that some of the children themselves acknowledged the superiority of the printed word over the spoken word in certain situations. At least one of them, however, was not convinced that the written word could also be "mightier than the *sword.*"

Narrative Segment 7
the pen and the sword

It is late in the afternoon. Mark and Nat are playing "Super Heroes" outside in the courtyard. In need of enemies to foil, they decide that the passers-by walking on the courtyard paths between the parking lot and nearby buildings can be the bad guys. The boys have difficulty, however, attracting the attention of the passers-by and provoking them into a battle. Mark and Nat come into the nursery and ask the teacher to write down, "Don't come here anymore." She does, and each boy laboriously copies the message onto a tiny scrap of paper. When their courtyard game continues, Mark and Nat rush up to passers-by, thrust the notes in front of them, giggle, and then stand, "Super Heroes" poised and ready for battle. Now they get a bit of response—a few friendly people people talk to them and ask what they're doing, but no one engages them in battle. Frustrated, the boys re-enter the nursery. Mark is carrying a stone and wants something real like a broomstick, that he can use for a sword. When the teacher denies the request, Nat suggests that they continue their play just using the notes as weapons, but Mark is disgruntled. Without him the "Super-Hero" play fizzles out.

Narrative Segment 7 offers a particularly clear example of how the nursery-school children used print for their own social purposes. In this example, the two boys themselves initiated a literacy event in order to enliven their "Super-Hero" play. The printed messages that the boys planned and copied were not effective in supplying them with enemies to battle. Nevertheless, the example makes clear that for these boys, print was something that could connect them with other people and could help them to do things in their daily lives. For them, using print was very much a social action that had a place within many of the significant contexts of their everyday experiences.

• *Sources of information.* Reading and writing were often used as sources of information concerning everyday situations, both within the nursery school itself and in the many outside locations to which the nursery-school group travelled on frequent trips. During the first school day, as we saw earlier, the teacher introduced this use of reading and writing as a primary way of finding out about the practicalities of the nursery school itself. The children were invited to look at the labels on the bathroom door or the snack cupboard in order to learn about locations: "Now we'll know where snacks go! We'll read this sign." Similarly, the children were encouraged to notice and use the information on street and traffic signs, advertisements, posters, billboards, and placards. Uses of reading and writing for information were context-specific. When adult intermediaries participated in events of this kind, they emphasized the contexts in which the print occurred and demonstrated to children that they could understand practical events by relating print information to the situations in which it occurred. Narrative Segment 8 illustrates adult-child participation in a literacy event where print was used as a source of information.

Narrative segment 8
just read this sign

The nursery-school group is going on a trip; they will travel about three miles by trolley to the library. They have waited on the street corner for a few minutes when a trolley approaches. Although the teacher raises her arm and signals that they are waiting, the vehicle passes by without slowing down. Several children remark that the driver must be mean. The teacher disagrees and carefully explains that as he passed the driver pointed to the "out-of-service" sign posted across the trolley windshield. The driver told her to read the sign, just read the sign, the teacher explains, then she would understand why he didn't stop. After an explanation of "out of service," the children decide that the driver wasn't mean after all; they look carefully for signs on the next approaching trolley.

There can be little doubt that the children themselves understood and controlled this use of print. In buses and trolleys, at curbside parking spaces, in museums and other educational sites, they referred to the information on signs and asked adults to read the information to them. They seemed to expect adults to know the answers to their questions, not so much because they were adults with more experience, but because they knew that adults could decode. Although there were many degrees of adult-child participation, in many cases, adult intermediaries were needed by the children only as decoders; the children themselves controlled the use of print, as Narrative Segment 9 demonstrates.

Narrative segment 9
ordering books

It is the afternoon session, and a very relaxed lunch-time is almost over. The teacher and I (the researcher) are looking at a paperback-book-club advertisement and discussing the merits of the various books offered. The order form has pictures of the covers and descriptions of each book offered. Several children become interested and run to get order forms of their own. Brad identifies several titles from the cover pictures and then asks me to read the descriptions of certain books to him. He nods as I read and ask him whether these are the books he wants. Then he points to the order form and asks me to show him which boxes to "X" in order to designate the books he has selected. He carefully marks three boxes, then asks about the rest of the form. I show him the space for his name; he prints it in. Then he asks the price of the books, which is also printed on the form. We discuss the total cost and whether or not he will have enough money. Later, he takes the form home for approval by his mother.

As Narrative Segment 9 and many others indicate, uses of print for information required users to integrate contextual and written information in order to understand practical situations in the world around them. Maple Nursery School preschoolers filled this requirement quite competently, not only by understanding some environmental print and many of the contexts in which print was used to convey situational information, but also by controlling some of the interpretive strategies needed to process the relationship between environmental print and context.

• *Social interactions.* Reading and writing also affected personal relationships and social interactions among the children and between children and adults. Social messages were frequently printed on items of children's clothing and toys (e.g., comic strip figures' names and faces, college names, phrases in other languages, signs, letters of the alphabet, numbers, initials, manufacturers' names). In many cases these messages simply became part of the material culture and were not specifically commented upon by either children or adults. At other times, it was clear that the children themselves were aware of the print messages and their potential significance for social relations. Narrative Segment 10 indicates that some of the children were interested in and had control over these social messages.

Narrative segment 10
'cause I'm the DA

Mark comes to nursery school wearing a baseball cap that has the initials "DA" on the front. He seems to feel very powerful with this hat on; throughout the morning he touches his hand to the cap's visor and boasts in a gruff voice, "I'm the DA and you better watch out 'cause I'm the DA!" Mark's tone of voice and scowling face are intimidating to some of the children, but most do not understand what he's talking about. At one point, Mark demands that the teacher verify that his cap says "DA" for "District Attorney's Office". The teacher verifies the message, but Mark's attempts at authority are generally unsuccessful.

Print was also frequently used to convey social messages in greeting cards. The children made Valentines and Christmas cards that included their messages to parents and grandparents. The children also received greeting cards, which they frequently brought to school to show to others. As Narrative Segment 11 reveals, the children were shown that pat, non-individualized messages could become significant for particular social relationships when tagged with information regarding sender and receiver roles.

Narrative segment 11
I love you

Three little girls are at the snacktable making rubber-print pictures. The picture is created when heavy rubber cut-outs glued to a pegboard are sponged with paint, then inverted and printed onto a clean paper. Each girl makes her own picture, using the rubber cut-outs—the words, "I love you," in fat, capital letters. The teacher asks whom they want to say this message to and prints at the top of the picture exactly what each girl says (e.g., "for my mommy"). Independently, two of the girls sign their own names at the bottom of the pictures and read their messages aloud with satisfaction.

Like uses of reading and writing for information, social-interaction uses depended for part of their meaning on the contexts in which they occurred. However, for informational uses of print, the relationship between the printed message and its environmental context *determined* meaning; for social-interactional uses, meaning came from the act of giving the message a context. Hence, in Narrative Segment 11, the "I love you" pictures became messages, instead of pictures, when the teacher and children established a context by designating senders and receivers for the sentiment. Social-interaction uses of print make clear that literacy was relevant and meaningful in the lives of Maple Nursery School children. For them, reading and writing were not isolated sets of skills used only at school. Rather, reading and writing were part of both a larger educational context and an almost limitless number of social contexts.

• *Memory-supports.* Reading and writing were often used by nursery-school adults as aids to memory (e.g., records of tuition paid, names, addresses and telephone numbers of nursery-school families, birthdates of the children), but the children were not involved in any of these matters. Occasionally, however, through almost complete adult intermediation, the children were exposed to the use of reading and writing as a memory support. Narrative Segment 12 illustrates this use of print.

Narrative segment 12
ask me to read it to you

It is the second day of school, and the children are having snack-time. The teacher asks if anyone remembers my (the researcher's) name. No one does. I introduce myself again, and the teacher asks me to print my name on a label card. When I do, she takes the card and hangs it on the wall. "Marilyn. Her name is Marilyn. If you forget, ask me to read it to you."

There were no examples in my data of children themselves initiating or controlling this use of reading and writing. This may have been related to the fact that the use of print as a memory aid is not context-dependent. That is, there are few environmental or situational cues that aid comprehension of this kind of print. This is the case precisely because the use of print as a memory aid occurs after the fact. Memory of information comes after the situation in which the information is originally conveyed; therefore, when print is used as a memory aid, the situational cues are gone. The name label placed on the wall in Narrative Segment 12 had few features that supported the reading or use of the print. On the other hand, name labels used informationally to show location (e.g., "bathroom" on the door of the room, "snacks" on the closet that contains such foods) had many supporting contextual and environmental features.

• *Self-expression.* Reading and writing were frequently used at the nursery school for the expression of feelings and emotions. When the children verbally or nonverbally expressed strong emotions, such as anger, fear, sorrow, or pride, adults often wrote down their words, or encouraged the children to join them in a cooperative writing session wherein adults transcribed as children dictated. Adults used print in this way to reflect the children's feelings, that is, to acknowledge and give credibility to their emotions. Various pages of writing of this kind were often collected into booklets and preserved; adults would later read the pages of the booklets back to their child authors and invite discussions of the messages. There were many instances of this expressive use of reading and writing. When Anna talked repeatedly and longingly of family summers spent in Maine, for example, her comments were written down by the teacher and eventually collected into a Maine booklet[2] whose text appears in Narrative Segment 13.

Narrative segment 13
up in Maine

When we first got to Maine, I got to swim.
We had chicken soup with rice.
Then we had pork chops./
We swam in a pool.
It was really fun. It had a shallow part, and I could swim all the way around it.
'Mommy, look I can do it by myself!'
But not in the deep part./
Up in Maine I saw a baby puppy./
Up in Maine we cut down trees and pulled them to our house and cut them up for firewood./

The nursery-school teacher believed that writing down the children's feelings was very important; it could be "therapeutic," she felt, and could "help get things out in the open." It also helped her to get to know the children better. Narrative Segment 14 is particularly revealing of the way reading and writing were used for self-expression in the nursery school.

---

[2]Slashes indicate individual utterances shared on separate occasions; each utterance was printed by the teacher on a different page and then eventually collected into a booklet.

Narrative segment 14
I hate some kids

Mark has many strong feelings. He often explodes and lashes out angrily at other children. For several days he has been particularly angry with Alice, who wants to do what he does. After an episode that ends with Mark hitting and Alice crying, the teacher talks to Mark quietly. She suggests that he seems very angry with Alice. He agrees and elaborates. As he does so, the teacher reaches for a pencil and paper and, without comment, begins to transcribe:

I want some kids to follow me around, all except Alice. I want to show these notes to her.

(Teacher: You want her to see these notes. You want her to be upset?)

I want to upset her. I'm not going to be her friend. Her sister can be my friend.

(Teacher: You feel very angry with her?)

I feel angry. I hate some kids. She always wants to be in the same room with me.

(Teacher: She follows you and you don't like that?)

And she follows me around. I like a two-headed monster. I'd like to have a wrecking truck to wreck Alice's house and furniture.

There were frequent episodes like this one with the teacher helping the children use writing as a way of expressing strong emotions. Often, the teacher read their words back to the children at times after the incidents had occurred. As she did so, child authors nodded emphatically to confirm and relive their feelings.

In these examples, the teacher used print as a technique for effective listening; the primary underlying message was the acknowledgement of feelings: "I hear you, I accept your strong feelings. You are permitted to have strong feelings here." There is little doubt that nursery-school children understood this message and came to expect the adults around them to be sensitive and accepting of their feelings. It is also significant, however, that nursery-school adults elected to use *print* to convey this message about the legitimacy of children's feelings. There are, of course, many nonverbal and verbal non-print alternative ways for dealing with children's feelings. However, at Maple Nursery School, print was chosen consistently as an effective way to deal with feelings. The two incidents described in Narrative Segments 15 and 16 were directly related to one another; the first occurred two weeks after the second. Narrative Segment 16 illustrates dramatically that the child himself understood both the affective message underlying expressive writing and the power of the print medium in which that message was expressed.

Narrative segment 15
"I want my mommy"

The children are playing outside. Alice crashes her "Big Wheels" into the wall of the building and hurts her hand. She is crying, sobbing that she wants her mother. The teacher picks her up, hugs her: "Of course you do. Would you like to write her a note?" Alice is crying too hard to respond. The teacher carries her inside where they sit down at the worktable. As Alice continues to sob, the teacher transcribes:

A: I want my mommy. (crying)

(The teacher asks something about whether her own mother or a car-pool mother will pick her up today.)

A: Grandma and Grandad are moving their clock today. It's a big clock. (crying)

(Long pause for more sobbing and tear-wiping.)

A: Mommy, come get me!
I want to go home. (crying)

The teacher makes an envelope for Alice and addresses it to "Mommy." By the time the writing and envelope-making are completed, Alice has stopped crying. Still sniffling, she goes back outdoors to play, clutching the letter in one hand and the envelope in the other. Later in the day when all the children have gone home, the letter is still lying on the table.

Narrative segment 16
let's write a note

The small afternoon group of children are playing indoors on the big sliding board. Mark falls and hurts his head. He begins to cry and goes to the teacher for comfort. He climbs into her lap, but immediately jumps up and says, "Let's write a note to my mother." He brings paper and pencil from the workroom, hands them to the teacher, and dictates without elicitation or interruption:

Dear Mom and Dad:

I fell down on a very hard place.
It hurt a lot.
And I love you, Mom and Dad.
I bumped my head.

Marilyn would like to come over soon, and I'd like her to (referring to plans for researcher-parent interviews).

When the teacher is finished writing, she reads the letter to Mark. He points to the first few sentences of the letter with a circular gesture, "Now this is the part about the fall, right?" The teacher replies, "Yes, and this (pointing to third sentence) says, 'I love you.' Then this (pointing to the fourth sentence) says you bumped your head, but it should be up here (drawing an arrow connecting the fourth sentence to the first two)." Satisfied, Mark nods and rolls the letter into a scroll, whch he deposits in his lunch box to take home later. His hurt is apparently forgotten.

In the incident in Narrative Segment 16 the adult was an intermediary only as an instrument for the child; she encoded and helped to revise the organization of the child's letter. The child himself, however, controlled the expressive use of reading and writing. He himself initiated, directed, and concluded the entire literacy event. His actions indicate that, to a certain extent, he had internalized the use of reading and writing as a way of expressing strong emotions; when he fell he immediately sought comfort in writing a note to his mother. Although related to using reading and writing as substitutes for oral messages, the expressive writing used by the child seemed to substitute more for the comfort Mark would have received from his mother, if she had been present, than for the oral message he might have conveyed to her. In many examples of using print for self-expression, the written message was never delivered. Rather, it was the act of writing, the literacy event itself, that was important.

Narrative Segment 16 makes it clear that the role of the nursery-school child in literacy events was not a passive one. Rather, the child was actively involved in employing print for his own social purposes and, in the process of doing so, sorting out the rules for using and interpreting print in various situations. In this instance, Mark was particularly interested in the organization and content of his note to his mother. He independently composed the note and then questioned the teacher about its organization and form. In many similar situations, children were actively experimenting with various uses of print to fulfill their own needs effectively.

• *Presentations.* Reading and writing were also used at the nursery school to organize and present information efficiently and clearly. All of the examples in the data of this use of print were initiated and controlled by adults,and were very simple. Through presentational uses of print the nursery-school children were introduced to the print convention of relating the spatial arrangement of written words (or figures and symbols) to the lexical meanings of written words, in order to present and organize information efficiently. Narrative Segments 17, 18 and 19 illustrate three presentational uses of print: the first and simplest presents a single vertical list of words; the second presents an equivalence relationship between three vertical lists; and the third presents pairs of items along corresponding vertical and horizontal axes.

Narrative segment 17
naming the guinea pig

It is the first day of school, and the children are sitting on the rug in front of a large movable blackboard. The teacher invites them each to suggest a name for the new nursery-school guinea pig. As they make suggestions, she writes down all the names in a vertical list. After the names are printed on the board, the teacher points to each one and reviews them, asking various children about there favorites.

Narrative segment 18
learning Arabic

Ris, who is Egyptian and verbal in Arabic but not in English, is accompanied to the nursery school by her governess. The teacher asks the governess to share with the children some Arabic words, so that they can all talk to Ris more effectively. As the governess explains a few Arabic words, the teacher prints them on a cardboard chart in three vertical columns, containing the Arabic word, the English word, and a small picture or symbol, if appropriate. She reviews these with the children by pointing to the first column and pronouncing the word, then sliding her finger over to the next column and pronouncing the word there, and then pointing to the picture. She suggests that the children refer to this chart later when they are communicating with Ris.

Narrative segment 19
favorite colors

At the snacktable, the teacher asks the children their favorite colors. As they respond, she places each child's name in a vertical column along the left edge of a cardboard chart and then makes an ''X'' in the appropriate box along a horizontal row headed by circles of various colors across the top of the chart. As she does so, she pronounces the child's name and traces with her finger a horizontal line from the name to the box with the ''X,'' then names the color and traces a vertical line from the color label down to the ''X.''

The cardboard charts described in Narrative Segments 18 and 19 were hung on nursery-school walls, but were later referred to, if at all, only briefly and informally. Although the children probably did not use the charts for later reference (whether through an adult intermediary or independently), they were nonetheless exposed to the possibility of organizing print for this purpose.

• *Knowledge acquisition.*   Print at the nursery school served as an important source for the acquisition of knowledge. Reading and writing were used in this way both to ground the children's knowledge by introducing or following up on direct experiences and to broaden their knowledge by providing information in areas where they had no direct experience. As discussed in Chapter 10, many cases of this use of print occurred in bookreadings "on-the-rug."   Print materials other than books and literacy events "off-the-rug," however, were also used to provide new knowledge. In Narrative Segment 20, print was used to offer the children knowledge about an experience they were about to have.

Narrative segment 20
honey bees

Tomorrow the children will visit a man who keeps bees in his backyard. They will see the bees and bee hives, touch honeycomb, and taste honey. Today the teacher shows the children a commercially-produced chart about bees; it features drawings of various types of bees with labels and brief descriptions of each. The teacher points out several pictures and reads the labels and descriptions to the children; then she emphasizes the specific kind of bee that they will see on their trip and suggests things to to look for based on the information on the chart.

Unlike the example in Narrative Segment 20 where print was used to introduce a new experience, Narrative Segment 21 illustrates how print was used to review and frame an experience immediately after it occurred.

Narrative segment 21
a walk in the park

The children have returned from a long walk of several blocks from the nursery school around and through the northern tip of a large city park. The teacher shows several boys a local map of the area. She points out the places that the children saw during their walk and invites them to identify nearby places—the creek, the railroad tracks, and the street where the nursery school is located—by using the symbols and words on the map. As the children and teacher identify various spots, the teacher points to the written label for each and encourages discussion that relates those spots to the route and events of the walk.

The entrance to the park, for example, is identified not only according to the map conventions of the printed label and heavy boundary line, but also according to its status as the spot where the children saw a dead squirrel on the ground.

In both Narrative Segments 20 and 21, reading and writing were used to ground direct experiences by providing information that introduced, supplemented, supported, or contextualized the information embedded in actual experiences.

Reading and writing were also used as substitutes for direct experiences. That is, as Narrative Segment 22 reveals, reading and writing provided primary, rather than supplementary, ways of acquiring new information and having new experiences.

Narrative segment 22
around the world

The children are looking at a large map of the world. They have been introduced to the map before: they have matched continent-shaped cutouts to the continents on the map; they have made their own world maps by arranging, tracing, and labeling the cut-outs on large papers; and they have discussed foreign places and events in terms of the map. Now the teacher holds up *National Geographic* pictures of children from various places in the world and asks the children where the boys and girls in the pictures might live. The children point to the map and call out the names of various places in response. The teacher confirms or supplies each location by reading the caption below the picture, pointing to the appropriate spot on the map, and showing its relationship to the Philadelphia area.

In Narrative Segment 22, a literacy event provided the children with new knowledge of people from other places. New places were discussed in relation to places and people the children already knew; but their experience with Hawaiian or Japanese or African children was primarily through the labeled pictures and their corresponding locations on the world map. This literacy event and other similar events became important frames of reference for the children's understanding of the world. In examples like this one, it is particularly clear that literacy was a social phenomenon in this community. At school, literacy was something that could be used to connect the children to other places, people, and things.

• *Status clarifications.* The authority of print at the nursery school was particularly clear when reading and writing were used to establish, confirm, or clarify the status of various material items. Print was frequently used in this way to confirm the children's ownership of pictures, art projects, toys, and other possessions. Children themselves often initiated and controlled this use of print, and as Narrative Segment 4 (p. 74) has indicated, invoked the authority of print to settle ownership disputes.

Print labels were also used to confirm the lexical identity of items that were represented in pictures or other art work created by the children. When children drew or painted, their creations were often blobs or dribbles of various colors. In discussions with adults, or through direct elicitation by adults, children frequently labeled their dribbles and blobs, "balloon," or "sun," or "Mommy". These lexical labels were printed by adults on the children's pictures and connected with arrows to the colored shapes to indicate the identity of these images. Subsequently, the labels were used by other nursery-school adults as points of reference when discussing or admiring artwork with the children.

Printed labels to confirm lexical identity were primarily used for the children by adult intermediaries who initiated and controlled the process. In several cases, however, children themselves used labels to establish the status of items in imaginative play, or to legitimate their rights and privileges in social interactions with other children. For several of the children, the rule seemed to be, "if it says so in print, it *is*." Hence, children who could use print in this way could control a rather influential source of nursery-school authority. Narrative Segment 23 illustrates this use of print.

Narrative segment 23
this is a fire station

Nat and Davey are busily working at the worktable. Copying from a model made by the helping mother at their request, they are laboriously printing, "fire house" and "fire station" on label cards. They tape these labels to the large refrigerator box that the children helped paint and carve out—to make doors and windows—earlier in the week. With the signs, Nat and Davey dub the box a fire station, insist to other children that the box is neither a playhouse nor a doll house, and claim the box exclusively for their own fire-station enactments. Their adamant assertion is based primarily on the labels.

Nat (insisting, pointing to the sign):
"This is *not* a house! This is a *fire station!*"

> Although not happy with the situation, Linda and Susie temporarily abandon their plans to use the box as a doll house.

In this example, it was not only the label that helped establish the box as a fire house. The boys also *used* the box as a station: they made appropriate fire-engine sound effects; they pantomined climbing ladders and spraying jets of water at burning buildings; and they told people verbally that the box was a fire house. It is significant, however, that all of their play was preceded by the placement of a written label, and that when the status of the box was disputed, the boys expected others to defer more to their label than to their oral pronouncements or to their play.

The following incident (Narrative Segment 24) gives similar testimony to the children's belief in the power of print to legitimate social interactions.

Narrative segment 24
no girls allowed

Official rug-time has ended and the teacher is informally reading a story to a small group of children. Other children are playing noisily in the dollroom, and it is clear that there is some sort of argument taking place. The reading continues and the arguing grows louder until Susie and Linda suddenly burst out of the dollroom and into the reading group. Linda is very upset, because Mark has put a sign on the dollroom door that says, "No Girls Allowed." Several other children run out from the dollroom arguing.

The teacher intervenes: "See what gets people upset? We need to talk about this." She gathers the rest of the children from the dollroom and explains that putting up a sign like that hurts people's feelings and it's not nice not to share.

Mark has been growing increasingly impatient during the teacher's talk. Suddenly, he angrily stomps out of the group and into the dollroom. He returns, forcefully crumpling a piece of paper in his hands. He interrupts the teacher, announcing in a loud demanding voice, "*That* settles *that*! I took down the sign!" Then he stomps away. There is a bit more discussion, but the children begin to drift away.

Whether or not the problem was really resolved, it is interesting that at least for some of the children, the problem was the sign itself and not the actions that surrounded it. These children had a somewhat confused concept of the power of print to establish status or legitimate authority in their community. However, many of them had been exposed to the idea that the printed word did carry authority, and they were beginning to deal with this idea.

Contexts for Reading and Writing

As we have seen in the preceding descriptions and narrative segments, nursery-school reading and writing were used in many situations
by both adults and children for different purposes and goals. Each of the
eight uses of print involved specific strategies for relating written words
and their spatial configurations to the oral language and situational
contexts that surrounded them. Part of learning to use reading and
writing for various purposes involved learning whether oral or written
language took precedence, whether paginal arrangement was to be
taken into consideration, and whether the meaning of print was more or
less context- and situation-dependent.

As the narrative segments imply, nursery-school children were exposed to and involved with these uses of reading and writing apart from
involvement with the more or less mechanical skills of encoding and
decoding print. Their control and understanding of the uses of print did
not depend on their control of these mechanical skills. Although Maple
Nursery School preschoolers knew a few of the rudiments of encoding
and decoding, they could not read and write print that was decontextualized. Nevertheless, all of the children had some control over uses of
reading and writing.

It is important to note that the contexts in which print was used in
these eight ways at the nursery school were never instruction in the use
of reading and writing; rather, the contexts were everyday situations
into which these uses of print were routinely interwoven. For example,
the context of incidents in which reading and writing were used for
children's self-expression was not instruction in this purpose so that
children would learn that written words could be helpful in sorting out
feelings. Rather, the context was always a situation in which there was
an angry or confused child, and the goal was to help the child deal with
his or her emotions. Reading and writing were used in these situations
because adults saw them as effective ways for people to deal with their
feelings, not because adults felt obligated constantly to instruct children
in the development of literacy skills.

Although children were being oriented to a kind of literacy that
included using print for a wide range of purposes—as oral substitutes,
as sources of information, for social interactions, as memory-supports,
for self-expressions, presentations, knowledge acquisition, and status
clarifications—the children were exposed to all of these purposes within
the everyday environment of the nursery school, rather than within
contexts constructed for instructional purposes. These preschoolers

were not so much surrounded with print as they were surrounded by people who chose to use print because it was effective in many aspects of their everyday lives.

In the children's own lives too, literacy was meaningful and relevant—it could help them claim ownership, establish their pretend play settings, and celebrate their important occasions. There were, therefore, many reasons for the children to be interested in print: it functioned effectively in many different ways in their lives and was not restricted to any single context. As Schieffelin and Cochran-Smith (in press) point out, a prerequisite for literacy seems to be that literacy is functional, meaningful, and relevant both to individuals and to their larger social groups. The children of Maple Nursery School had no difficulty meeting this prerequisite, and they were, indeed, acquiring facility with literacy at a very early age.

The nursery-school children participated with adults in countless interactions in which literacy events were embedded or interwoven. An important part of what was going on in these daily interactions was a gradual process of socialization into a particular kind of literacy. In other words, through their everyday experiences and interactions, the nursery school children were being socialized into the ways of using reading and writing that were taken for granted by the adults around them. Many paired examples like the notewritings in Narrative Segments 15 and 16 (p. 85) provide us with evidence that the nursery-school children were indeed involved in a process of socialization. They were beginning to internalize the ways of using reading and writing that were modelled by the adults around them.

Adults played very important roles in the literacy socialization process of the children by acting as intermediaries for the children's uses of print. They took larger or smaller intermediary roles, depending on the needs and skills of individual children. With very young children, who seemed to have little control over the uses of print, adults used print *for* them by initiating literacy events, encoding or decoding the necessary printed words, and following through for or with the child with the appropriate response or interpretation of the print.

Adults initially played all the parts in literacy events, completely producing and comprehending print for the children and behaving as if children were using the print themselves. Little by little, the children took over the various roles in these events, with control of the uses of print preceding control of the mechanical skills of decoding and encoding. However, even in situations where adults completely controlled the uses of print, children were not merely observers but in a sense, consumers or users of print. The purpose of literacy events initiated by adults for children was in most cases to fulfill the perceived or anticipated needs and wishes of the children themselves. Through adult intermediaries, for example, children's possessions were retrieved, artworks identified, or feelings expressed.

Instruction and Practice in Reading and Writing

The literacy socialization process of Maple Nursery School included experiences not only with many different ways that reading and writing could be usefully organized, but also with the more or less mechanical skills of reading and writing. The tools and materials needed for reading and writing surrounded the nursery-school children. Papers, cards, cardboards, blackboards, chalk, markers, pens, pencils, and crayons were available in the workroom at all times. Books, booklets, posters, signs, charts, labels, advertisements, and calendars were on the walls, doors, bulletin boards, and the furnishings of every nursery-school room. The children used these materials whenever they wished. They had a great deal of interest in print, and they frequently practiced on their own the skills needed for reading and writing. Furthermore, although unlike rug-time and snack-time, there were no regular nursery-school times for learning to encode and learning to decode, there was both direct and indirect instruction in reading and writing skills.

Direct instruction in encoding, decoding, and printing

The nursery school teacher and other nursery-school adults occasionally instructed the children in the mechanical aspects of encoding, decoding, and printing. Instruction of this kind was not systematic or regular and usually occurred at the request of individual children themselves. Individual instruction was informal and occurred almost in passing when, for example, a child requested an adult's help in printing his or her name on a picture. Incidents of this kind were different from occasions where children asked adults to print messages *for* them; in incidents identified as instruction, children asked for adult assistance in doing their own printing. As Narrative Segment 25 indicates, the teacher also occasionally instructed a group of children in reading and writing skills; incidents of this kind, however, were rare.

Practice in encoding, decoding, and printing skills

Nursery school children were generally quite interested in the skills involved in reading and writing. They were particularly interested in printing; both individual children and small groups often spent long periods of time experimenting with and practicing the various skills involved in printing. These practice sessions were initiated by the children themselves. They picked up pencils and printed, just as they picked up brushes and painted, or picked up tools and drilled or hammered. Sally, for example, printed an entire page of left-to-right rows of "P's" in a variety of bright colors; when she finished, she started a new page. Dan ran through the workroom and decided to stop and paint; he made three round shapes with red paint and then ran off. Mark spent 20 minutes drilling two holes in a block of wood; when he finished, he left the block on the workbench and went on to other activities.

In none of these activities were the children very interested in products. Rather, in their experimentations with paint and with tools, as in their printing practice, the children's involvement was process-oriented. They were much more interested in the process of shaping letters than they were in using those letters for specific purposes. Narrative Segment 27 provides a typical example.

Narrative segment 27
copying

The teacher invites the children to make pictures on invitations to a potluck dinner for the nursery-school parents. The message is already printed inside. Anna decides, instead, to copy the writing. She works independently for 15 minutes, laboriously copying the first three lines of the invitation onto a blank sheet. Then she joins some other children to watch a filmstrip. The invitation lies, forgotten, on the table.

As we have seen earlier, some of the children's printing practice was more product-oriented than in the examples above. Most often, however, the children were interested in printing, and to a much lesser extent, in attempting to encode and decode words, because these activities were challenging and enjoyable. They wanted to experiment with the various manipulable modes and media available to them in the nursery-school environment. It is not surprising that these children would express an interest in print. As we have already seen, print was very meaningful and functional in their nursery-school lives and their home lives. They also regularly saw the adults around them using print and its accouterments for various purposes.

A few of the older nursery-school children also showed interest in practicing the skills of encoding and decoding. Susie, for example, announced that she could spell "Don" and "open"; she then spelled them out and laughed with satisfaction. As he helped to paint a playhouse, Brad wanted to leave unpainted the advertising on a refrigerator box; as he painted, he haltingly sounded out "Whirlpool" and "refrigerator." Davey worked for 10 minutes at the worktable finding the correct rubber stamps to spell out his name. Davey brought an old datebook his father had given him and, with help, read aloud the names of the months. Like their printing practice, the children's encoding and decoding practice was more process- than product-oriented. Narrative Segment 28 illustrates this pattern.

Narrative segment 28
lunchbox notes

It is 9:00. Only a few children have arrived. Mark's mother is sitting at the worktable writing a note to leave in his lunchbox. Mark decides to reciprocate. He leans on the workbench with a piece of paper and pencil. Unaided, he prints:

"MOMMY I LOYE"

At his request, his mother spells "much," which Mark adds to his note. The teacher asks whether he would like to add "you" and points out where the word is needed. Mark adds the word.

While his mother goes into the kitchen to leave her note in Mark's lunchbox, he decides he wants to mail his note "in the real, *real* mail." He prints "MOMMY" and his phone number on the front of an envelope and begs the teacher for a stamp. His mother tries to discourage him—he's printed his phone number instead of his address, the envelope is too big, postage would be too expensive. Adamantly Mark insists. His mother sits down and prints the correct address on the envelope while Mark watches. Suddenly Mark turns and runs into the next room; his friend has just arrived with a new toy. The forgotten envelope lies on the worktable all day.

As these examples indicate, Maple Nursery School preschoolers were being exposed to literacy skills as well as uses. Instruction in literacy skills was informal, nonsystematic, and irregular; it was often given at the request of the children themselves. Practice in literacy skills was initiated and controlled by the children, and was process-rather than product-oriented. Practicing these skills was simply one of the ways children experimented with the materials that surrounded them.

Summary

The foregoing description of the reading and writing that occurred off the rug at Maple Nursery School was based on direct observation of literacy events over an 18-month period. As we have seen, the preschoolers who attended the school were exposed to a specific orientation to literacy via consistent adult and peer models, adult intermediaries, self-practice and experimentation, and adult instruction. This literacy orientation was compatible with the ideas about books and bookreading to which the children had been previously and were still being exposed at home. The following general concepts about literacy seemed to operate at the nursery school.

1. Both children and adults were appropriate producers and consumers of print.
2. Reading and writing were effective means by which both children and adults could accomplish a variety of specific goals.
3. Reading and writing played important social, transactional and informational roles in the lives of children and adults, specifically the following:
    (a) Print messages substituted when direct oral communication was inconvenient, impossible, or less authoritative than written communication.
    (b) Print provided information about everyday transactions.
    (c) Print could be used to influence social relationships and interactions.
    (d) Print aided memory.
    (e) Print helped express personal feelings and emotions.
    (f) Print presented and organized information efficiently.
    (g) Print was useful for the acqusition of knowledge.
    (h) Print provided information about the status of items, people, and events.
4. Different uses of print were determined and affected by the nature of relationships between print and speech, between print

and its immediate environment, and between print and its situational context.

5. Print carried a certain amount of authority:

   (a) In many situations, written language took precedence over oral language.

   (b) Print often established the validity or invalidity of personal knowledge.

6. Adults relied on print as sources of information and authority in many situations.

7. Adults had control over information (at least partially) because they could read and write.

8. Important events, personal expressions or experiences were often recorded in print.

9. Print provided a primary way of knowing:

   (a) Print provided a way of extending knowledge beyond the realm of direct experience.

   (b) Print grounded knowledge by both introducing and following up on primary experiences.

10. Written materials were appropriate items to look at, discuss and share with others in almost any situation.

11. Literacy tools and materials were permanent features of the environment:

    (a) It was appropriate for children to experiment, play, and work with these tools and materials.

    (b) Literacy tools and materials could be used in almost any nursery-school time and space.

12. It was desirable for children to develop literacy skills:

    (a) Adults were interested in children's attempts at reading and writing and encouraged children to experiment with, practice, and display literacy skills.

    (b) Adults willingly gave instruction, guidance and coaching in literacy skills, when requested.

    (c) Children were pleased by their progress in literacy skill development.

In the foregoing list of notions about literacy, the authority and predominance of print in the children's lives is striking. Equally striking, and perhaps even more important to the eventual development of the children's adult orientation to literacy, is the fact that these children were by no means intimidated by the power of print. They were both readers and writers, both consumers and producers of print. They utilized print as tools for their own purposes. Furthermore, as many of the preceding narratives testify, although these young children were not yet able to encode and decode, they were quite capable of using reading and writing in many aspects of their lives. They were gradually acquiring the skills of encoding, decoding, and printing and learning the uses of print. Their exposure to and involvement with uses of print, however, generally occurred apart from their involvement with the mechanical skills of literacy. Consequently, the nursery-school child who could successfully identify only his own name in print could, nonetheless, request that an adult transcribe an oral message to be used for the child's own purpose and in a particular social context stipulated by the child. Many instances like this provide evidence that the children's acquisition of the *uses* of literacy preceded their acquisition of its skills.

The children's knowledge and experience with so many ways of using reading and writing provided them with a ''readiness'' for the technical skills of decoding and encoding that is outside of the meaning of the term as used in educational contexts. Maple Nursery School preschoolers were not ''ready'' merely by virtue of appropriate developmental levels in auditory and visual discrimination and memory, oral language use, and fine motor coordination. Although, as their self-practice sessions indicate, many of the children were considerably developed in these areas, they were also ''ready'' with knowledge of various kinds of reading—knowledge of appropriate ways print could be used in various situations to achieve specific goals in their community. Literacy skills—proper ways to form letters, put word parts together, use punctuation marks—are meaningless without knowledge of the ways reading and writing function in a particular social group. Maple Nursery School children had an abundance of such knowledge and had had many experiences with the ways reading and writing functioned in their community.

CHAPTER 7

Rug-Time, Framework for Storyreading: Sitting, Listening, and Learning New Things

The printed materials used during on-the-rug literacy events at the nursery school were almost always children's storybooks. These storybooks are examples of what researchers have called "decontextualized" written language. Decontextualized print is quite different from the contextualized print that was used in most off-the-rug nursery-school literacy events. Contextualized print, such as labels for containers, signs on the doors to cupboards and rooms, notes from parents to children, and captions to accompany pictures, derives some of its meaning from the context in which it occurs. With contextualized print, relationships between print and its environment and its situation function as significant interpretive cues for the reader.

The decontextualized print of storybooks, on the other hand, is written language for which meaning depends on the lexical (or definitional) and syntactical (or word order) features of the print itself and on the conventions of the institution, "literature". For decontextualized print, meaning is independent of the particular context in which the print occurs. The strategies needed by the nursery-school children in order to interpret decontextualized print, therefore, were quite different from those needed to control contextualized or environmental print.

The rug-time framework set off on-the-rug literacy events from all other nursery-school literacy events. There was a highly consistent distinction between them; on-the-rug literacy events were nearly always bookreadings, while off-the-rug events were almost never bookreadings. The rug-time framework, therefore, signalled to the children that a different kind of print—decontextualized print—would be used, and that different interpretive strategies would be needed on the rug. Essentially, the underlying message was this: while you are on the rug, do not rely for meaning upon the print environment (the physical format of the picture book) or on the literacy situation (nursery-school adults and children seated on a rug); instead, focus on the information contained in the specific text that is being shared.

Chapters 4, 5, and 6 described several aspects of the context in which nursery-school storyreading occurred. Much of this context had to do with children's exposure to, and experience with, contextualized reading and writing. Chapters 7, 8, and 9 examine group storyreading, the nursery-school children's major experience with decontextualized print.

Storyreadings were the most frequent, most prominent, and most consistent formally organized literacy events at Maple Nursery School. As such, storyreadings were pivotal to the children's literary socialization as well as to their larger literacy socialization. Many early notions about appropriate reading and reading-related behaviors were introduced and developed within the patterns of verbal give-and-take that surrounded storyreadings.

As we have seen in Chapters 4, 5, and 6, nursery-school storyreading was embedded within three concentric outer layers of context: the belief system of the adult community, the organization of the nursery-school environment, and a network of off-the-rug literacy events. All of these surrounded and supported storyreadings. The most directly influential and conspicuous layer of storyreading context was a fourth inner layer—the event called "rug-time" within which bookreadings almost always occurred. This event served as a framework that physically and psychologically set bookreading apart from other nursery-school activities and literacy events. Rug-time structured for the children the experience of listening to books and provided an important interactive and interpretive orientation to bookreading.

Rug-Time as a Speech Event

Rug-time was a nursery-school activity during which children and adults gathered at a rug- and pillow-covered corner of the room surrounded on three sides by bookshelves, cabinets, and a piano; this area was known spatially as "rug." At rug-time sessions, the teacher (and occasionally individual children) sat on a wooden bench facing the children with back against a bookshelf while the children sat, knelt, or lay down on pillows and rug facing the teacher. Other adults present sat with the group, holding their own or other children on their laps.

Although many activities occurred within the actual rug area at various times of the day, only specific activities occurred when the event was framed as rug-time: individual children showed items brought from home; the teacher discussed and verbally shared art, craft or story projects made at the nursery school; she led discussion of past or future nursery-school events, showed sound-filmstrips, or read stories aloud to the children. Verbal sharing, discussions, and other activities varied from day to day; storyreadings, however, always occurred and served as the major rug-time activity. In fact, storyreading was often the only activity during daily rug-time sessions. Many of the rug-time activities that were not storyreadings were directly based on or related to story-readings, such as a filmstrip based on a picture-book already familiar to the children, or a discussion of a real wolfskin pelt in comparison to the pictures of wolves in "Little Red Ridinghood".

Interactional and interpretive norms

Rug-time was pivotal to the organization of nursery-school days. Like free play outdoors and snack-time, rug-time was never omitted from the nursery-school day; some nursery-school sessions even included two rug-time events. Although clock time was never mentioned, rug-time occurred consistently between 10:00 and 11:00 a.m., usually following indoor activities and preceding either outdoor play or snack-time. It served as an important temporal and sequential marker for other nursery-school activities and events. "Rug-time," a phrase consistently used by nursery-school adults and children alike, was perceived by participants as a discrete event within the nursery-school day. It was initiated ritually by the teacher, who played a few introductory piano chords and then sang the "rug-time song." Together, the ritual of the rug-time song, the physical location of activities on the rug, and the temporal location of rug-time after a period of child-initiated project work and indoor play signalled the beginning of the speech event known as rug-time. When these three features did not occur together, participants were sometimes confused.

In Narrative Segment 29, for instance, we see that a child was uncertain about what was going on because rug-time was already in progress when she arrived at school a few minutes after 9:00 a.m. Rug-time rarely occurred prior to indoor play, and although the space, the activity, and the physical configuration of participants told her it was rug-time, the child had not heard the rug-time song and the temporal cue was misleading.

Narrative segment 29
at rug-time

Rug-time is early today because Dori's father has come to play his guitar for the children. Children and adults are all seated on the rug. The teacher has just finished showing the children a wolfskin pelt and comparing it to the illustrations in two different versions of "Red Riding Hood" read earlier in the week. The children are now resettling in their places for "Jingle Bells" and then a Christmas storybook.

Susie arrives and sits down on the rug next to me. She shows me two carrots that she has brought from home; they have grown together, completely twisted around one another.

Marilyn (Researcher): Do you want to show them to the other children?

Susie: Yes, but I want to do it on rug-time.

Marilyn: That's what this is.

Susie: Yeah, but I wanna do it later.

Susie's confusion about the status of rug-time was clearly related to the lack of the usual temporal indicator. Her desire to show the carrots at rug-time and not at any other time also indicated that she was aware that rug-time was uniquely appropriate for showing and verbally discussing concrete items with the group. During rug-time, all nursery-school participants gathered together, and one person (almost always the teacher, but occasionally a child) had the floor. The children were expected and encouraged to attend visually to the item being shown and to direct relevant comments to the person who had the floor.

In this way and in several other ways, rug-time was unlike other nursery-school activities: all children were required to participate; verbal rather than nonverbal interaction was expected; the children were physically passive rather than active; they were expected to be present throughout rug-time and were not free to come and go as they wished; and rug-time was teacher-initiated, teacher-controlled, and teacher-dominated. The oral-language rules and strategies of rug-time further set it apart from all other nursery-school activities. During rug-time, all the children were to listen to one person, and they were discouraged from having individual conversations with other children. Rug-time was the only activity that required this sort of attention and selective verbalization. During this time the children were, in one sense, learning to be a class, to listen and respond within the framework of whole-group activity. Even more important, during rug-time they were learning to be "readers" and were being instructed in behaviors that accompanied and supported the activity of reading.

Verbal sharing

Verbal sharing occurred during rug-time when children brought items from home to show to their peers, or when the teacher called on individual children to show projects made at the nursery school. Sharing occurred rather casually, and often spontaneously, when the teacher learned during the larger rug-time episode that children had things to share. Sharing Segments 1 and 2 illustrate the range of formality among verbal sharings. Sharing Segment 1, which continued from Narrative Segment 29 (p. 105) illustrates an informal verbal sharing. The group had sung "Jingle Bells", and the teacher had just finished reading a picture book. Susie was then convinced that it was indeed rug-time and had crawled up to sit next to the teacher.[1]

The verbal sharing in Sharing Segment 2 was more formally organized than the previous sharing example. In Sharing Segment 2, the teacher had just finished reading a book to the children. The children began to disperse when Davey told the teacher he had brought from home a little musical instrument. The teacher played a few notes of the rug-time song to call the children back to the rug. In the informal sharing of Segment 1, Susie showed the carrot with no preamble except for "Look, what!"; based on the teacher's expressions of interest, a brief interaction followed. Part of this interaction was playful, and although the interaction ended with a remark about carrots, it also included a riddle-like sequence initiated by Anna and having nothing to do with the topic. In contrast, Sharing Segment 2 was more formal. The teacher played a very active role in the sharing process by modeling sharing behavior and structuring Davey's oral sharing by asking specific questions about the harp.

The type of sharing represented by Sharing Segment 2 resembles the "topic-centered" discourse required of primary-school children during

---

[1]The transcription conventions used in Sharing Segments 1 and 2 and in the Storyreading Segments throughout this monograph are described in detail in Chapter 3, pp. 30–36.

Sharing Segment 1: Carrots and Pigs

	Readers		Listeners	
Focal Points	Verbal	Nonverbal	Verbal	Nonverbal
	Amy: AND IT'S CALLED "FA-THER CHRISTMAS!"	holds up cover of book		Susie on knees, leans against teacher, taps teacher
	ALL RIGHT, NOW . . . OH! (very interested)	puts book in lap	Susie: Amy! Look, what!	holds up two carrots twisted together
	THAT IS THE MOST . . . DID YOU BUY A BAG OF CAR-ROTS AND IN IT CAME THAT?	holding car-rots with Susie		Susie nods, giggles
	WOW! OH ME! (impressed) LET'S HOLD 'EM UP.	holds carrots up so all can see		
	DID EVERYBODY SEE THIS?		Nat: I did! Alice: It's a carrot!	several laugh
	A CARROT ALL WOUND AROUND (delighted) . . .	traces path of carrots with finger		
	LOOK! WHERE DOES IT START, AND WHERE DOES IT END?	points to top, bottom of carrot	Ris: (Egyptian girl, does not speak English): Ga-zar! Ga-zar! Ga-zar!	pointing to car-rot, calling out, excitedly
			* * *	
			Anna: I know what makes car-rots! (excited, playful)	
	WHAT?		Anna: (pause)	
	PIGS! (mock astonishment)	laughs	Pigs! (playful, laughing)	
			Alice: Hey Amy, guess what? Anna: I know what makes ham.	
			Alice: Hey Amy, guess what? Anna: I know what makes ham. (louder)	
	What?		Anna: Pigs! (gruff voice, playful)	

(continued)

Sharing Segment 1 *Continued*

Focal Points	Readers		Listeners	
	Verbal	*Nonverbal*	*Verbal*	*Nonverbal*
			Alice: Hey, Amy, guess what?	
			Anna: I know what makes milk, I know what makes milk! (fast repetition, silly voice)	rises to knees
			Alice: Amy, Amy, Hey Amy, guess what?	taps Amy
	WHAT?			
			Anna: Co-ow-ows! (very gruff, silly voice)	
	YES?		Alice: Amy, guess what?	
			Alice: Amy, guess what?	
	WHAT?			
			Alice: I have ate carrots before, and they're good	
	YES, AND THEY'RE DELICIOUS.		(several children talking to each other)	
	ALL RIGHT, WE HAVE A SPECIAL TREAT TODAY. DORI'S DAD CAME AND HE'S GONNA PLAY WITH US.			
	(leads into singing of Christmas carols and other songs with guitar)			
	* * *			

"sharing circle" or "show-and-tell" activities in many schools (Michaels, 1981). Both informal sharings and more formal ones were common during rug-time. When nursery-school newcomers brought items to show to the group, they were encouraged by the teacher to wait until rug-time. The older, more experienced nursery-school children had already learned that rug-time was the appropriate setting for this sort of activity, and—as Susie did above—usually saved their sharing items for this time. However, verbal sharing at Maple Nursery School was not a discrete event to which the children were consistently exposed as part of their literacy orientation. Rather, verbal sharings occurred as more or less spontaneous fillers between major rug-time events, which were almost always literacy or literacy-based or related events.

Sharing Segment 2: Something to Show

Focal Points	Readers		Listeners	
	Verbal	*Nonverbal*	*Verbal*	*Nonverbal*
	Amy: TAKE YOUR SEAT AGAIN, CLAY!			many children moving around on the rug
	DEARIE, COME SIT WITH ME	motions to Clay that he can sit be- side her		Jeffrey plunking on piano
	OKAY . . . DAVEY HAS SOMETHING HE'D LIKE TO SHOW YOU.			Davey comes and stands by Amy at bench
	YOU KNOW WHAT THIS IS? ANYBODY KNOW WHAT THIS IS THAT DAVEY BROUGHT?			Davey holds up little harp-like instrument
			Lyn: (helping mother): Oh boy! A harp. ?: Harp	several children yelling, fussing with toys
		* * *	Davey: Amy, Amy, I need this because my uncl--	Ris pulling on harp; Davey doesn't let go
	OKAY, GIVE IT TO DAVEY. GIVE IT TO DAVEY.	mimes action for Ris		
				Ris lets go
	WHAT IS IT CALLED, HONEY?		Davey: A harp.	
	IS IT?	puts arm around Davey		Mark runs back in and yells loudly; tries to get others to come with him
	AND WHERE DO YOU GET IT?		Davey: Um, um, my next door neighbor got it.	
	AND GAVE IT TO YOU?			Davey nods
			Lyn: That's real- ly nice, Davey.	Dan runs out to join Mark
	YOU'RE VERY LUCKY. YOU'RE LUCKY TO HAVE THAT.	pats Davey		
		picks up book from lap		
				Davey sits on rug

Rug-Time as Preparation for Reading

Although there were ostensibly no rules for storyreading that were separate from rules for rug-time as a whole, the rules of rug-time were most often explicitly introduced and restated when the teacher was preparing for or attempting to read aloud to the children. Furthermore, when the rug-time rules broke down, as they frequently did, they were most often repaired when storyreading was in preparation or in progress, but often not repaired during other rug-time activities.

The rug-time framework, in other words, was generally synonymous with preparation for reading. It provided guidelines for the nonverbal behavior that was to accompany bookreading and helped to structure for the children the experience of reading. Storyreading Segment 1 is composed of chronological excerpts from one storyreading event. In it you will see many examples of the storyreader's reminders of the norms of storyreading behavior, including rules for: appropriate seating arrangements, listening and behaving attentively, paying exclusive attention to the book being read, and not interfering with the attending habits of others. Interactions during storyreadings that centered on the norms of storyreading behavior are what I have called Type I "Readiness interactions." (Types II and III are introduced in Chapter 8 and discussed in detail in Chapters 9 and 10, respectively.)

Storyreading Segment 1: Christopher Columbus (McGovern)

The teacher has played the rug-time song and has begun to gather the children on the rug. Mark asks what book they will hear, and the teacher holds up a biography of Columbus. Several children, however, are still not settled on the rug.

	Reader		Listeners	
Focal Points	Verbal	Nonverbal	Verbal	Nonverbal
→	Amy: ALL RIGHT, DAN? (two-second pause) DAN? DAN, COME ON, DEARIE. I WANT YOU TO SIT NEXT TO ME WHILE WE READ. HERE, DEARIE. DAN?	goes toward work-room motions for Dan	(many children are getting settled on the rug, talking, playing)	Dan and Jeffrey racing from rug to workroom Dan looks over, keeps running

Storyreading Segment 1 *Continued*

Focal Points	Reader		Listeners	
	Verbal	*Nonverbal*	*Verbal*	*Nonverbal*
	DAN, COME ON OVER, DAN. COME ON OVER SO YOU CAN BE MY HELPER.	to come points to seat on bench for Dan		
→	COME ON, DEARIE. I WANT YOU TO BE THE LEADER.	walks toward Dan	(many children talking to each other, looking at books, toys)	Jody comes to Amy, wants to be cuddled, to sit on Amy's lap Dan starts toward rug
→	(to Jody) SIT DOWN, SWEETIE. I'LL HUG YA LATER. ALL RIGHT, WE'RE NOT GONNA HAVE MUCH TIME.			
→	COME ON OVER HERE.			Jody sits beside Amy on one side of bench
→	HERE, DAN, ROUND THIS SIDE. SIT RIGHT OVER HERE.	guides Dan to spot beside her on other side of bench		
				Jeffrey runs in, has been racing around in workroom
→	OKAY, JEFFREY, WHERE WOULD YOU LIKE TO BE?	looks around		

(*continued*)

Storyreading Segment 1 *Continued*

Focal Points	Reader		Listeners	
	Verbal	*Nonverbal*	*Verbal*	*Nonverbal*
	THE NEXT HELPER?	for a spot	Dori: I wanna be . . . there	points to general area in front of bench
→	OKAY, WOULD YOU LIKE TO BE THE NEXT HELPER?		Dori: Can I be there?	
→	OKAY, YOU SIT RIGHT THERE	points to spot		Dori nods yes Dori sits on rug directly in front of Sally
		turns to shelf, starts to get book		
	WE GOTTA . . . WE GOTTA HAMMER THAT NAIL PRETTY SOON (murmurs more to me than to the children)	taps nail sticking out of book-shelf		
		looks up at chil-dren, stands		
→	OKAY, I'D LIKE TO HAVE ALL THE BOOKS. I'LL PUT THESE ONES AWAY AND YOU GUYS CAN HAVE THEM LATER.	holds up hand, gathers up books	?: Amy, can I . . .	Jeff gets up, starts to run

Storyreading Segment 1 *Continued*

Focal Points	Reader		Listeners	
	Verbal	*Nonverbal*	*Verbal*	*Nonverbal*
		children have been looking at; puts books on shelf; holds out hand for Mark's book		toward doll- room again
→	MARK? HAND ME OVER YOUR WHALE BOOK. WOULD YOU LIKE TO LEARN MORE ABOUT WHALES ONE TIME SOON? YOU KNOW WHAT'S THE BIGGEST OF ALL?		Mark: Blue!	Mark nods, gives Amy his book
	THE GREAT BLUE WHALE? THE GREAT BLUE WHALE'S IN THIS BOOK MMMMMMMM, HMMMMM, HE'S IN THERE TOO. OKAY . . .	patting book		
→	JEFF! JEFFREY, COME ON, DEARIE, WE'RE WAITING FOR YOU.	turns toward doll- room sits on bench	several children talking, looking at small toys on rug	Ris runs into dollroom

(continued)

Storyreading Segment 1 *Continued*

	Reader		Listeners	
Focal Points	Verbal	Nonverbal	Verbal	Nonverbal
		stands, quietly takes toys from children		
			Mark: Amy, call Brad (referring to fact that Brad is sitting way at back of rug)	
→	BRAD, COME ON OVER! (inviting) CAN YOU HEAR FROM THERE, HONEY? CAN YOU HEAR VERY WELL?	sits on bench gets up, goes over to Jeff	Brad: Yes, I can	Jeff comes back from dollroom riding horse; Ris comes pushing doll carriage
→	WAIT A MINUTE, RIS. RIS, ALL RIGHT. LOOK, JEFF, JEFF (calling to him)			Jeff starts to ride away
→	JEFF, WHEN WE HAVE RUG-TIME, THESE THINGS GO IN THE DOLLROOM.	goes over to Jeff takes carriage and horse, puts in dollroom		
→	COME ON, JEFF. JEFF, WE'RE GOING TO PUT THESE THINGS IN THE DOLLROOM, 'CAUSE WE CAN'T HEAR.	at door of dollroom		Jeff follows her into dollroom to retrieve horse

Storyreading Segment 1   *Continued*

	Reader		Listeners	
Focal Points	Verbal	Nonverbal	Verbal	Nonverbal
→	YOU MUST LEAVE IT IN HERE. COME ON, HONEY.	 * * *	children playing and talking on rug while waiting	Jeff gets horse

Interactional and interpretive norms for reading

As this storyreading segment indicates, appropriate reading behavior for Maple Nursery School children demanded more than the use of specific language strategies. It also involved specific nonverbal behavioral norms for seating arrangements, posture, visual attention, and listening patterns. Negotiation of seating arrangements was quite elaborate at times. Children were to sit on the rug in such a way that they did not block the view of others. Although sitting up was preferred, standing and kneeling were permitted at the back of the rug, and lying down was allowed when only a few children were present. The children were not supposed to play with toys, look at other books, or play with one another during storyreadings. The large plastic barrels that sat in the corners of the rug area could be climbed on and into at any time of the day except during rug-time; large wheeled toys (e.g., riding-horse, doll carriage, train) could be brought from the dollroom into the general-purpose room except during rug-time. Children were supposed to be quiet during rug-time and listen to the storyreader.

The actions of the storyreader were highly predictable during rug-time storyreadings, and there is little doubt that the children knew both what to expect of the storyreader and what was expected of them. Key illustrations of the predictability of storyreading behavior were those occasions when children themselves took over all or part of the storyreader's role. (Three such instances occurred in my data, and two others were reported to me.) The following instance is unique in that it was completely unelicited. The teacher did not plan ahead for the child to share her book, nor did the child's parent practice with the child, as was true of three of the other four instances. Instead, sharing the book in Storyreading Segment 2 was completely spontaneous. Pay particular attention in this sharing to the little girl's knowledge of the proper orientation for bookreading—how to hold the book, how listeners ought to be attending to the book, how to relate pictures to the discussion around them, and how to pace the turning of the pages. Behaviors that indicate knowledge of a bookreading orientation are marked with arrows.

Storyreading Segment 2: The Little Golden Book of Dogs (Jones)

The teacher has played several rug-time song chords on the piano, and the children have gathered on the rug. At one child's insistence, the group plays a boisterous charades-type game, following which the teacher replays the rug-time song to call the group back to order. Voluntarily, Anna perches on the storyreader's bench. As she does so, she draws a stuffed Babar the Elephant toy from her bag. The teacher sits on the piano stool and interviews Anna about the toy as Anna pretends to be the toy in her answers. (Note: The listener named Lyn is an adult, the helping mother of the day; she is sitting with the children on the rug. The listener, Amy, is the nursery-school teacher who sits on the piano bench throughout the storyreading. The reader, Anna, is a child.)

	Reader		Listeners	
Focal Points	*Verbal*	*Nonverbal*	*Verbal*	*Nonverbal*
→		Anna pulls dog book out of her bag, holds it up	Lyn: Dogs! Wow!	
→		Anna holds up the book to show all the children	Amy: Dogs! This is good! (excited) We needed that book because we needed to show the kids about all the	
→		Anna turns to first page and shows picture	different kinds of dogs.	
→	[PIC: cocker spaniel]	Anna points to picture	?: I know! (calling out)	

Storyreading Segment 2 *Continued*

	Reader		Listeners	
Focal Points	*Verbal*	*Nonverbal*	*Verbal*	*Nonverbal*
			Amy: What's that? That's . . . a cocker spaniel. What kind of dog is that?	
			(Lyn is explaining something about dogs to several other children—indiscernible)	
			Nat: Cocker spaniel! (in loud, silly voice)	
	Anna: (looks pointedly at Nat): YES!			
			Amy: A cocker . . .	
			Several children: Amy! Amy! (yelling)	
			Amy: . . . spaniel!	
			Amy: See, there's a black cocker spaniel.	points to PIC
				Mark climbs into barrel in the corner, calling out to others
			(several children yelling)	
			Amy: Okay . . . tur-ur-urn. (to Anna in drawn-out voice)	
→		Anna turns page, holds LP out to children		
	[LP: girl hugging collie] [RP: boy telling Scottie dog to sit up]			

(continued)

Storyreading Segment 2 *Continued*

	Reader		Listeners	
Focal Points	Verbal	Nonverbal	Verbal	Nonverbal
→		Anna holds out the LP, emphasizes it, points to it	Amy: What kind of dog is that? You saw that one on television. What kind is that? ?: I don't know	nods toward picture of collie
			Davey: Amy, Amy (calling out), can you . . . (breathless)	is at other barrel in corner, wants to get in
			Amy: What kind is Lassie?	
			Amy: What kind is Lassie?	
			Lyn: Ahh! (breathless) Lassie's a collie! My favorite.	
→	[LP: Irish setter] [RP: Saint Bernard]	Anna turns page and holds out LP, (skips RP on previous page)	Lyn: Uh oh, and there . . . is an Irish setter, that red one.	points to LP
→		Anna points to LP	Amy: And what kind is that? That red one?	looks up at book
			Lyn: An Irish setter. Amy: An Irish setter?	

Storyreading Segment 2 *Continued*

	Reader		Listeners	
Focal Points	*Verbal*	*Nonverbal*	*Verbal*	*Nonverbal*
→		Anna points to RP	Amy: How 'bout this kind? This great big one that can pull sleds if you want? (several children talking to one another in loud voices—indiscernible)	
→		Anna closes book and holds it in her lap	Amy: Let's clap for Anna, very nice! Lyn: Very nice, thank you, Anna. Amy: (to Lyn and to me, [the researcher]): Very nice pacing, I think.	starts to clap several children clap
→		Anna leaves bench, takes place on the rug		Lyn and I nod

In Storyreading Segment 2, no one actually read or decoded, the text; rather, the teacher and, to some extent, the helping mother talked with the children about each picture. Anna took on many of the story-reader's duties, and in doing so, indicated her knowledge of what was involved in storyreading. She sat in the teacher's spot on the bench and held the book at shoulder height, facing the children. She turned each page individually and held the picture on the page being discussed in a more prominent position than its opposite page. She moved the book slowly from side to side in a kind of arc so that the children on all parts of the rug could see the pictures. Anna pointed to the dog pictured on a particular page at precisely the time when the breed of the dog was being discussed and identified.

Except for the first page of the book where she was prompted, Anna, unprompted, turned to each new page of the text after allowing a period of time for discussion. She had clearly internalized a reading orientation—she knew that attention sould be focused on the book, that pictures should be studied in relation to the discussion about them, that participants had to be able to see the appropriate pages, and that ample time had to be given for processing each page. From her many experiences as a listener in group storyreadings, she had extracted the patterns of behavior that accompanied reading. Her actions are good evidence for an image of the child as active learner, working to sort out the rules for approaching and interpreting print.

Rug-time rules for storyreading were frequently in need of repair. As Storyreading Segment 1 (p. 110) indicated, some children consistently did not sit quietly and listen. Rules were by no means rigidly enforced; the teacher's treatment of disruptions varied according to the situation and according to the needs of the disrupting child. Behavior that was in keeping with rug-time rules was more consistently demanded of five-year-olds than of three-year-olds. When the rules broke down, the teacher usually initiated Type I Readiness Interactions that reminded the children of rug-time rules. Sometimes, she also physically managed children by seating them next to her, interrupted rug-time to put away distracting toys or games, or required that some children leave the rug-time group. At other times, she ignored behavior that deviated from rug-time rules or tried to distract disrupters by drawing them into the story being read: she would call on specific children to answer a question, label a pictured item, or imagine themselves in the place of storybook characters. The use of any of these techniques depended upon the situation, the needs and abilities of particular children, and the needs of the group as a whole.

Most children, however, did follow rug-time rules and did conform to expectations of appropriate reading behavior. In preparation for storyreadings and during storyreadings, the children were expected to:

1. Sit on the rug facing the storyreader.
2. Visually attend to the book being read, and look carefully at the pictures.

3. Listen to the words being read.

4. Pay attention to relationships between words and pictures.

5. Listen to the words and look at the pictures for *every* page (not give intermittent attention).

6. Remain quiet and avoid distracting others by talking or making noise. (Certain kinds of talk *were* allowed and very much encouraged during storyreadings; these are discussed in Chapters 9 and 10.)

7. Attend to the nonverbal actions of the reader. Notice especially the pictured items that the reader pointed to or emphasized. Watch the reader pantomime actions, make gestures, or change facial expressions.

8. Attend to the verbal actions of the reader. Listen carefully when the reader read softly or loudly. Notice inflectional or intonational variations.

9. Attend to the world created symbolically in the book and not to the immediate real situation of the children or objects nearby.

10. Concentrate only on the book being read. Avoid extraneous matters that could distract.

11. Avoid interfering with other listeners' abilities to follow these rules.

By teaching them a reading orientation, this set of behavioral norms framed for the children the experience of getting information from decontextualized print. This experience was different from other nursery-school activities and also from reading and writing events that occurred during activities off-the-rug. As described in Chapter 6, in off-the-rug reading and writing, the children were generally encouraged to interpret print in relation to the context in which it occurred. They were exposed to the idea that part of the information about the meaning of print was in its environment and purpose. In on-the-rug storyreading, on the other hand, the children were encouraged to attend only to the book itself. The rug-time activity within which storyreading occurred was an important interpretive cue only insofar as it signalled the listening and looking bookreading orientation. Likewise, the physical environment of the print (a paper and cardboard object) was not helpful in interpretation. Rather, all of the information for interpretation had to come from the book itself. The children were oriented in this direction by following the rug-time rules.

Consistency of interpretive and interactional norms

Many rug-time rule-messages underlay the teacher's actions and responses to the behavior of the children. In addition to the rules that were implicit in her responses, the teacher also explicitly stated norms for rug-time in Type I Readiness Interactions during or before story-reading. The following summary of rug-time is pieced together from several different storyreading events; all of the words, however, are verbatim quotations from the teacher:

> This is rug-time, a quiet time. . . . This is a place for sitting. . . . It's a time for sitting and looking and listening. . . . When it's rug-time, you need to keep your voice quiet so you can hear. . . It's not a time for playing with other things. When Amy (the teacher) is reading to you at rug-time, that's a time for you to leave all other things alone. Otherwise you miss the story, and then you'll come back and say, "Amy, I didn't hear that part," or, like Susie, "Wait a minute, I missed that page" because you were busy doing something else. . . . This is rug-time, a quiet time, a time for learning new things.

Preschoolers entered Maple Nursery School with many experiences in listening to and getting information from storybooks and other printed materials. The consistent rug-time framework of the nursery school seemed to further contribute to the children's literary socialization by teaching them a set of behaviors for group attention to textual materials. The only other group bookreading experience that these pre-schoolers had was at storyhours provided periodically for the nursery-school group at local public libraries.

Library storyreading: a contrast

The children's experiences with library storyhours were quite different from their nursery-school storyreading experiences. At the libraries, rules were precisely stated and uniformly and strictly enforced; no allowances were made for the special needs of particular children. Even more significant were differences in the nature of storyreading interaction. Nursery-school storyreadings were interactive reader-listener negotiations based on the sense-making of the audience. Library storyreadings, on the other hand, were one-sided performances of set texts within which the children's participation was not encouraged and, in most cases, not permitted. In library storyhours there was little or no negotiation of text and little mediation between text and listeners. Despite these differences, which made for two strikingly contrasting kinds of storyreading experiences, the nonverbal behavior required of the listeners in preparation for and during storyreadings was essentially consistent at both nursery school and libraries. The following example illustrates this consistency:

Narrative segment 30
at the library

The nursery-school group arrives at the public library a few minutes after their scheduled time. The librarian quickly herds them into a straight line and takes them to the reading room. Carpet-square mats are already laid out in a triple semi-circle on the floor. The librarian directs each child to sit on a mat on the floor; she sits on a chair facing them. She instructs the children that they are to sit with legs crossed ''Indian style''; everyone is to behave in the same way and remain quiet throughout the storyreading time. This way, they are told, they will listen better, hear the story better, and see the pictures better. During the storyreadings, when individual children rise to their knees or begin to lounge down on their mats, the librarian immediately asks them to sit up ''like everyone else.''

Interspersed with the stories that the librarian reads aloud to the children are little rhymes and finger plays intended to ''get all the wiggles out of you, so you'll be ready to be quiet.'' When children call our responses or comments during the readings, the librarian puts her finger to her lips and sharply reminds, ''Sh!''

As can be seen, the rules of library storyreadings were much more uniformly and strictly enforced than they were for nursery-school readings. Nevertheless, the messages in both settings were consistent: first, children had to sit in proper upright posture, direct visual, aural and mental attention at the book held up by the storyreader, and remain silent; then they could have a bookreading experience.

The children's behavior during nursery-school and library bookreading sessions indicates that in at least these two settings, the children were expected to, and for the most part did, adopt a specific set of nonverbal behaviors in preparation for and during bookreadings. Despite frequent disruptions and breakdowns of bookreading behavioral norms, the majority of storyreading events were strikingly uniform in terms of the children's behavioral patterns. Thus, group bookreading was consistently associated with this particular set of expectations for behavior.

Although we have evidence that the nursery-school children were internalizing a particular set of rules for group storyreading, we can only speculate on the extent to which they might have internalized and applied this bookreading orientation to other group reading situations. It seems worthy of speculation, however, to consider the possible implications of such a preschool bookreading orientation for school reading instruction, which is almost exclusively located within teacher-dominated reading groups of one kind or another.

Educators have long claimed that preschool experiences with books are correlated with early school success. It may be that an important part of what preschool children who have had group reading experiences bring to their school reading groups is a knowledge of the nonverbal behavior that many teachers expect to accompany reading. Such nonverbal behavior may indicate to teachers that children are prepared for and attentive during reading lessons. Maple Nursery School children, for example, might appear to exhibit certain reading and prereading skills by sitting up properly, looking at reading materials, listening carefully to teachers' words, associating words and pictures, and concentrating only on textual materials rather than on extraneous factors in the environment. None of these nonverbal behavior patterns have directly or necessarily to do with strategies for interpreting (decoding, making sense of, and using) written language. They may, however, help to provide for children a significant frame within which bookreading occurs and, to similarly-oriented adults, signals that "appropriate" reading behavior is occurring.

CHAPTER 8

What Do You Say Dear?: Storyreading as Interactive Negotiation

Storyreading was the only literacy event in which the nursery-school children were required to participate; it was also the most frequently and regularly occurring literacy event. As such, storyreading provided valuable insights into the literacy and literary orientations of the nursery-school community.

As we have seen, storyreading was surrounded and supported by: (a) a physical and behavioral framework, called rug-time, that served to structure the bookreading experience for the children by providing an interpretive and interactional orientation; (b) a wide variety of off-the-rug non-reading and non-writing activities within which literacy events were embedded and to which many different uses of reading and writing were integral; (c) a general nursery-school environment in which time and space were consistently organized and correlated to types of activities, uses of materials, and interactional norms; and (d) an adult belief system in which literacy was both a primary method of access to knowledge and a major source of solitary and social pleasure.

To study storyreading, it was necessary to describe each of these concentric layers of the context of storyreading. Together they provided a background against which the process of storyreading could be analyzed as one of the keys to the literary orientation of the nursery-school community.

One Storyreading Event: An Example

Following is the transcription of one nursery-school storyreading event in its entirety. Although a single storyreading does not convey the richness and variety of more than 100 storyreadings recorded, it does provide a sense of the general nature of these events. As such, this storyreading helps to convey the two major and closely related characteristics of Maple Nursery School storyreadings that will be discussed in this chapter: (a) storyreadings were socially interactive events that included active participation by both adult reader and child listeners, and (b) storyreadings were joint ventures in which the "meanings" of storybooks were cooperatively negotiated.

The book that was read in Storyreading Segment 3 is Maurice Sendak's well-known *In the Night Kitchen* (1970). It uses many cartoon conventions to tell the story of a little boy's dream—how he went into the kitchen after everyone was asleep to see what the bakers did there. In the kitchen, he was mixed into batter, then flew into the sky in a dough-airplane to bring Milky Way milk back down for the bakers. The book's illustrations are in the art deco style of the 1930's and 1940's; much of the kitchen is drawn to resemble a New York skyline with labeled food packages, cans, and boxes becoming buildings, towers, and trains. That the little boy's adventure in the kitchen is a dream is metaphorically rather than explicitly conveyed. All of the listeners in this storyreading had heard the book read at least once before. As you read through this transcription,[1] you will see that storyreading was characterized by what I have called, "interactive negotiation." That is, both reader and listeners *interactively* participated in order to build jointly or *negotiate* a meaning for the story (See also Cochran-Smith, 1981).

Social Interactional Aspects of Storyreading

The most immediately striking feature of Storyreading Segment 3 is the socially interactive nature of the event, with both adult reader and child listeners playing very active verbal roles. There was no way to consider separately what the children were saying and what they were understanding of the text, in isolation from the interaction itself. That

---

[1]The transcription conventions used in Sharing Segments 1 and 2 and in the Storyreading Segments throughout this monograph are described in detail in Chapter 3, pp. 30–36.

Storyreading Segment 3: In the Night Kitchen (Sendak)

	Reader		Listeners	
Focal Points	Verbal	Nonverbal	Verbal	Nonverbal
	Amy:			
		picks up book from shelf		
	JEFF WANTED TO HEAR THIS BOOK	holds up "In the Night Kitchen" puts book down, goes over to Mark		Mark is yelling, runs toward pyramids
	MARK, MARK, SHH! IF YOU CAN'T BE A LIT-TLE QUIETER, I'M GONNA ASK YOU TO . . . (quiet conversation continues with Mark—indiscernible, but point is that Mark will choose between listening to story and going into workroom alone)	comes back over to rug, picks up book		Mark reluctantly comes over to rug, sits down
	OKAY . . . NOW, UH . . .	looks up to see where Mark is		
	MARK, WOULD YOU LIKE TO DO WHAT YOU DID YESTERDAY AND TRY TO GET THE LINES ON THE BOOK? (referring to large print in the book			

(continued)

Storyreading Segment 3 *Continued*

	Reader		Listeners	
Focal Points	Verbal	Nonverbal	Verbal	Nonverbal
	that indicates character's speech)		(children resettling on the rug; some individual conversation)	
	WOULD YOU LIKE TO BE THE ONE WHO DOES, WHO SAYS THE LINES?			Mark shakes his head
			Alice (jumping up, excitedly): I will! I want to! I want to!	
	OKAY, ALL RIGHT . . . STAND RIGHT OVER HERE.	guides Alice to stand beside her at bench		
				Alice stands at corner of bench, facing listeners
		holds up book to first page		
	[LP: Mickey (M) in bed, sitting up—hears noises] "Did you ever hear of M, and how he heard a racket in the night?"			
	[RP: M standing on bed, yelling, 'quiet down there,' in very large type]			
	"And he shouted . . ."	points to type, turns	?: I can't see	

Storyreading Segment 3 *Continued*

	Reader		Listeners	
Focal Points	*Verbal*	*Nonverbal*	*Verbal*	*Nonverbal*
		to Alice, nods	Susie: Quiet!	
			Alice: Quiet down there!	
		nods head	Brad: Quiet down there!	
	REALLY LOUD, HE SHOUTED THAT, DIDN'T HE? SO BIG! IT'S AS BIG AS THE PAGE! OKAY, SIT NEXT TO LINDA, JEFF, AND YOU CAN SEE BETTER.	points to large type	Anna: I can't see!	Jeff stands in front of book to see picture, blocks others
		points to space on rug for Jeff	Susie: I can't even see!	
			Dan (echoing Susie): I can't even see!	
	SIT DOWN, SO YOU CAN SEE BETTER AND YOU CAN REST WHILE YOU'RE WATCH-ING. ALL RIGHT?	motions to Jeff to sit TP	Dan: I can't even see.	Jeff moves slightly, but returns to front place
	[LP: M falls through his room, past the clock and out of his clothes] "And he fell through the dark, (right) out of his clothes . . ."			
	WHOOPS! THEY FELL RIGHT OFF?	hand to mouth in surprise		
	[RP: M falls past moon at open window and past parents' room]			

(continued)

Storyreading Segment 3 *Continued*

		Reader		Listeners	
Focal Points	Verbal	Nonverbal		Verbal	Nonverbal
	And he fell ''past the moon and his mother and father sleeping tight.''			Dan: I can't see . . . (whining)	
	WHAT'S HE SAYING? (to Alice)	points to speech balloon beside M			
				Dan: I can't see.	
	REALLY LOUD, YOU SAY IT!	nods to Alice			
				Alice: Mommy . . . Mama! Papa!	
	YEAH! (in awe) IS HE SCARED? IS HE SCARED WHEN HE'S GOING AWAY FROM HIS HOUSE? (eyes wide, breathless)			Alice: Ye-ah.	
				Susie: Mmmm hmmm.	
	IS HE? HE'S GOING STRAIGHT DOWN DOWN DOWN, BUT WHERE'S HE FALLING INTO?	points in sequence to each of four pictures of M falling nods, TP		Linda (to me): He's dreaming (matter-of-factly) . . .	nods head knowingly
				?: A ho— Brad: Into the night kitchen. (softly)	
	[LP: M falls into mixing bowl] [RP: 3 bakers come toward him]				
	''Into the light of the night kitchen.'' (with finality)	TP		(total silence)	

Storyreading Segment 3 *Continued*

Focal Points	Reader		Listeners	
	Verbal	*Nonverbal*	*Verbal*	*Nonverbal*
	[LP: bakers mix with M's head sticking out of batter] "Where the bakers who bake till the dawn so we can have cake in the morn . . . (they) mixed M in batter, chanting . . ." (emphasizes 'chanting' with pause for what's to come) [RP: bakers stirring, M's head sticks out of batter] OH, IT SAYS . . . ALL, RIGHT HERE YOU CAN PLAY IT ALL OF YOU.	points to speech balloon at specific words within it	Alice: Mickey cake! (excited) Brad: Mickey cake!	pointing to RP
	"Milk in the batter! Milk in the batter! Stir it! Scrape it! Make it! Bake it!" (very rhythmical, deep voice— chanting)	pointing to words as she chants	Children: Milk in the batter! (in same chanting pattern as reader) (children get confused after first line, stop chanting)	
	ALL RIGHT? "Milk in the batter! Milk in the batter! Stir it! Scrape it! Make it! Bake it!" (very slowly, but in chanting rhythm, exaggerates each	pointing to each individual word as she chants	Children: (chant with reader as much as possible, some drop out) Milk in the batter . . .	

(*continued*)

Storyreading Segment 3 *Continued*

	Reader		Listeners	
Focal Points	Verbal	Nonverbal	Verbal	Nonverbal
	word of chant) CAUSE YOU'RE ALL THE BAKERS NOW, AREN'T YOU? [LP&RP: baker carries bowl, other two bakers look on]	TP	Brad: Uh huh.	

	"And they put that batter up to bake a delicious Mickey cake."
	BUT WHERE'S MICKEY?
	
	FOR REAL?
	
	[LP: bakers look worried, steam fills the kitchen]
		
		TP
			Alice: He's inside it!
			Dan: He's inside it!
			Alice: Yeah . . .
			  Several: Uh huh.
			Dan: Can't see, I
			  can't see!	

	"But right in the middle of the steaming and the making and the smelling and the baking, M (popped out) (t: poked through) and he said" (emphasis on 'Mickey,' pauses to anticipate M's speech) [RP: M pops up out of cake] "and the milk's	 points to speech balloon, holds book toward Alice, nods	 Alice: (hesitates at first, can't remember) I'm not the milk, and the, uh . . .	

Storyreading Segment 3 *Continued*

Reader			Listeners	
Focal Points	Verbal	Nonverbal	Verbal	Nonverbal
	not . . ." (quietly, to Alice, coaching her)	points, shows there are more words	Alice: Milk's no . . . milk's not me!	
			Alice: I'm Mickey! (loud)	
	AND I'M MICKEY! SO THERE! (with finality)	shakes finger, nods head		
			Linda: So there! (same intonation)	
		TP	Several others: So there! So there!	
	[LP: M falls from oven, past moon, into pile of dough] "So he skipped from the oven and into (the) bread dough. (T:All) ready to rise in the night kitchen."	points to each of three picture frames		
	[RP: four frames, M kneads dough into shape of airplane] And "he kneaded (it) and (he) punched it and (he) pounded (it) and (he) pulled (it) . . ." (emphasizes each 'p')	pantomimes each action		
				Mark, Alice mime kneading, punching, etc.
	AND WHAT WAS HE MAKIN'?	TP		
			Jeff: A airplane!	
			Several: Airplane!	
	[LP: top-M looks proudly at plane; bottom-M turns propellers]			Jeff stands directly in front of book, to get better

(*continued*)

Storyreading Segment 3 *Continued*

Focal Points	Reader		Listeners	
	Verbal	*Nonverbal*	*Verbal*	*Nonverbal*
	"Til it looked okay."		(All listening intently)	view of pictures
	[RP: M flies off into night kitchen in plane, past jars, etc.]			
	"Then M in dough was just-on-his-way." (each word separately emphasized)	TP		
	[LP: M flies by baker holding measuring cup]			
	[RP: two bakers look distressed, with spoons, all calling for 'milk!']			
	Then "when the —" "ran up with the measuring cup . . ."		Clay: I can't see! Anna: I can't see, and neither can Clay! (annoyed)	
	WOULD YOU SIT DOWN SO THAT . . . JEFFREY, 'CAUSE OTHER CHILDREN CAN'T SEE. THEY'RE HAVING A REAL PROBLEM SEEING. CAN I HOLD THE BOOK LIKE THAT? IS THAT ALL RIGHT, SO THEY CAN SEE BETTER?	holds book back further	Dan: No, and then I can't see . . . (whining)	Jeff sort of kneels right where he is in the front; he is soon standing again

Storyreading Segment 3 *Continued*

	Reader		Listeners	
Focal Points	*Verbal*	*Nonverbal*	*Verbal*	*Nonverbal*
			Jeff: I can't see!	
	WELL, THEN, CAN YOU SIT DOWN SO THAT EVERY-BODY CAN SEE? IF YOU STAND SMACK IN FRONT OF THE BOOK, NOBODY CAN SEE EXCEPT YOU.			stays by bench, blocking others
	HERE, TAKE THIS PILLOW, THIS FLOWERY ONE . . .	picks up pillow puts it right at her feet		
	AND YOU'LL BE VERY CLOSE. THAT'S IT, RIGHT THERE, HONEY, AND THEN I'LL HOLD THE BOOK RIGHT LOOKING AT YOU. OKAY? DOWN LIKE THAT. SIT DOWN, THOUGH, SO THAT I CAN HOLD IT NEARER TO WHERE YOU ARE.	holds book down	Brad: I can't see, Dan! Brad: Hey, move out! (angry at Jeff) Linda: I can't see! (very annoyed) . . . 3 other children: I can't see! I can't see! Brad: I can't see! So	crouches where he is Jeff kneeling, still blocking others

(continued)

Storyreading Segment 3 *Continued*

| Focal Points | Reader | | Listeners | |
	Verbal	Nonverbal	Verbal	Nonverbal
			get down! (yelling)	
	SIT DOWN HERE, HONEY.	moves pillow a little		
			More children: I can't see (annoyed) . . .	
	THE KIDS ARE AN-GRY AT YOU (to Jeff). SIT DOWN HERE.	moves pillow again	Anna: Yeah, sit down! Several: Sit down!	Jeff looks around an-grily at other children
	ALL RIGHT, THEN, I'M SORRY, I'M GONNA HAVE TO HOLD THE BOOK UP OVER HERE.	turns back to book, holds book over Jeff's head so others can see		Jeff won't come over to pillow
	SO . . . WHAT THEY CAME UP WITH THIS MEASUR-ING CUP, "howling:"	points to words in speech balloons		
	"Milk, milk milk for the morning cake!"			Jeff stands in front of bench
	NOW WHERE THEY GONNA GET MILK FROM OUT OF THE SKY? Up, up . . .	TP	Brad: Ah-hah! ?: I can't see! ?: Move!	
	[LP: M over baker's heads, smiling down at them]			

Storyreading Segment 3   *Continued*

	Reader		Listeners	
Focal Points	*Verbal*	*Nonverbal*	*Verbal*	*Nonverbal*
	"What's all this fuss? I'm M the pilot! I get milk the M way!" (emphasizes 'I') [RP: M with cup on head flies upward]	points to self		
	"And he grabbed that cup as he flew up" [LP: M going higher]	TP		
	"and up and up . . ." [RP: M goes past moon, comes to giant milk bottle]	points to RP		
	"And over the top of the milky way."	points to picture		
	IS THERE MILK UP IN THE SKY?			
			Chorus: Yes! No!	
	SO IT'S CALLED THE MILKY WAY, WAY UP HIGH WHERE YOU CAN SEE LOTS OF TINY STARS ALL TO-GETHER, IT'S CALLED THE MILKY WAY. YOU LOOK OUT-SIDE AT NIGHT AND YOUR MOMS AND DADS WILL SHOW YOU WHERE THE			

(*continued*)

Storyreading Segment 3 *Continued*

Focal Points	Reader		Listeners	
	Verbal	*Nonverbal*	*Verbal*	*Nonverbal*
	MILKY WAY IS UP IN THE SKY. IT'S VERY BIG, LOTS OF . . . VERY, VERY FAR AWAY . . .	TP	(several children start to talk at once—indiscernible, but they are trying to get the teacher's attention to say something about making things out of dough)	
	DOUGH?		Dan: Out of, out of, out of airplane . . .	
	AN AIRPLANE?		Jeff: I can't see!	
	YOU CAN MAKE AIRPLANES OUT OF DOUGH . . .	turns back to book	Jeff: I can't see!	
	LOOK, HE FLEW RIGHT OVER THERE . . . [LP&RP: bakers below, M over bottle; background NY skyline via kitchen]	points to RP & LP	Jeff: I can't see!	
	TO WHERE THE GIANT MILK BOTTLE WAS. [LP: M jumps into bottle; M falls down] "M the milkman (he)	points to RP&LP TP	(several children still talking)	

Storyreading Segment 3 *Continued*

	Reader		Listeners	
Focal Points	*Verbal*	*Nonverbal*	*Verbal*	*Nonverbal*
	dived (right) down to the bottom''			
	[RP: M falls, beginning to lose clothes; M floats down, naked]			
	"singing: I'm in the milk, and the milk's in me" (quietly, coaching Alice)	pointing to words, nods to Alice	Alice: I'm in the milk and the milk's in me!	
	"is in me!" "God bless milk and God bless me!"		?: I can't see! Jeff: Look, he's all bare!	
	SAY THAT (to everyone).	pointing to words	Jeff: He's all bare! (louder)	standing in front of book again, points to M, looks at other kids, smiles
	"God bless milk and God bless me!" (chanting rhythm, leading the children)	pointing to words	Children: God bless milk and God bless me! (with teacher) Jeff: He's all bare! (louder)	
			Several children: I can't see!	
			Anna: I can't see, I can't even see! (annoyed)	
	WELL, ANNA . . .		Anna: I can't even see. I can't even see!	starts to stand
	SIT DOWN ANNA. YOU CAN ALL			

(continued)

Storyreading Segment 3 *Continued*

Focal Points	Reader		Listeners	
	Verbal	*Nonverbal*	*Verbal*	*Nonverbal*
	SEE, DEARIE.	holds book up higher TP		
	[LP: M floats up in bottle; pours milk down to bakers below]			
	"Then he swam to the top pouring milk from his cup into the batter below."		Jeff: He's all bare!	pointing
	[RP: bakers mix batter, put it in oven]		Anna: I can't see cause he's putting his hand . . .	
	"And they (t: so they) mixed it and beat it and baked it."		Jeff: He's all bare! (yelling loudly)	pointing
	IS HE? WHAT HAPPENED TO HIS CLOTHES?			Jeff nods
			Jeff: It dried way?	
			Anna: No they're not, they're . . .	
	ISN'T HE GONNA GET COLD IN THAT MILK?	pointing to M in bottle	Several: Yeah, no . . .	
	DOES IT FEEL GOOD THERE?		Brad: Yes (very quietly) . . .	
	AND THEY MIX IT AND THEY BAKE IT.	points to RP again		
	THEY HAVE PLENTY OF MILK NOW. AREN'T			

Storyreading Segment 3 *Continued*

Focal Points	Reader		Listeners	
	Verbal	*Nonverbal*	*Verbal*	*Nonverbal*
	THEY CATCHING THE MILK?	pointing back to LP	?: Yeah.	
	THEN IT SPILLS DOWN INTO THEIR BOWL?	points	(several children start to talk at once Mark: _____ _____ _____ _____ and they put it in the batter . . .	
	YEAH, AND THEN THEY DUMP IT INTO THE BAT-TER AND MIX IT AROUND. DID YOU HAVE, HAVE MILK IN YOUR MORNING CAKE? [LP&RP: 3 bakers happy, mixing bat-ter, all talking]	TP	Chorus: Yeah! No!	
	"Milk in the batter! Milk in the batter! We bake cake! And nothing's the mat-ter!" (same chant-ing intonation as before) [LP: on top of bottle, proudly crowing] "And now M in the night kitchen cried . . ."	points to speech balloons TP	(several children join in)	

(*continued*)

Storyreading Segment 3 *Continued*

Focal Points	Reader		Listeners	
	Verbal	*Nonverbal*	*Verbal*	*Nonverbal*
	MARK? (quietly, prompting)	pointing to words	Brad: Cock-a-doodle-doo!	
	GOOD, BRAD, SO LOUDER?	points to words	Jeff: I was trying' to find that picture . . .	points, standing again
			Chorus: Cock-a-doo-dle-doo! (yelling) Jeff: I was trying to find that picture!	
	RIGHT, CAUSE HE REALLY YELLED IT, DIDN'T HE?	points to words		
			Jeff: I was tryin' to find that picture!	
	YOU WERE?			
	DOES THAT LOOK FUNNY WITH MICKEY STAND-ING ON THE EDGE OF THE BOTTLE, HOL-LERING, 'COCK-A-DOODLE-DOO!' (yells in higher, louder voice)		Linda: It's as big as the page! (excited)	pointing
				Jeff nods
	[RP: M slides down bottle, falls back through house] "And he slid down the side"	TP	Dan: Cock-a-doodle-doo! (yelling)	
	[LP: M falls toward bed, stands in bed, laughs]			
	"and straight into bed."			
	[RP: M yawns, sleeps]		(some children talk-ing, still crowing)	

Storyreading Segment 3 *Continued*

	Reader		Listeners	
Focal Points	*Verbal*	*Nonverbal*	*Verbal*	*Nonverbal*
	"cakefree and dry."	TP	Anna (singing): Cock-a-doodle-doo!	
	[LP: M with bottle in sunshine, writing goes around in a circle]			
	"And that's why, thanks to M, we have cake every morning."			
	SEE HOW THEY MADE THE WRIT-ING GO RIGHT AROUND? (laughs) IN A CIRCLE?		(several children laugh)	
			?: Am-, Am-, can I look?	reaches for book
			(several children start to talk)	
	THAT'S FUNNY, ISN'T IT? HE GOT RIGHT BACK INTO HIS BED ALL SAFE AND SOUND, DIDN'T HE?	turns back a page	Alice: Hey, Amy my mom . . .	
		points to pic-ture of M in bed	Linda: (to the re-searcher) That's cause it was only a dream . . . (several chil-dren talking)	
		looking for another book on shelf	Alice: Hey Amy, guess what? Uh, uhm, gue-- Uh, last night, I was down in my,	

(continued)

Storyreading Segment 3 *Continued*

	Reader		Listeners	
Focal Points	*Verbal*	*Nonverbal*	*Verbal*	*Nonverbal*
			uh, my, uh, house, house, and I didn't see any of that.	gestures toward book
	YOU NEVER DID?			Alice shakes head solemnly
	BUT SOMETIMES WHEN YOU'RE ASLEEP, YOU CAN DREAM A LITTLE BIT, AND YOU CAN THINK ABOUT THINGS, YOU KNOW? AND SOMETIMES YOU CAN DREAM FUNNY THINGS THAT YOU GO DIFFER- ENT PLACES. DID YOU EVER DO THAT?			Alice nods
			Jeff: I can say . . . I can say that word . . .	
	COCK-A-DOODLE- DOO?	picks up an- other book	(several children talking)	Jeff nods
	YOU COULD SAY COCK-A-DOO- DLE-DOO.			
			Jeff: a-doodle-doo (humming)	

is, the children's experience with the book could not be studied as a product after the reading was over or apart from the reading itself. Rather, the children's experience occurred *within* social interaction with the adult storyreader. Much of the children's experience had to do with what the reader was saying and doing as she guided the verbal interaction around the text and pictures, so that it became a dialogue in form and shape. Much of the dialogue was patterned by reader-questions and listener-answers and was underlaid by the norms of conversational turn-taking. The dialogic pattern of storyreading emphasizes the fact that storyreading events were social and interactional.

The interactive nature of storyreading necessitated a social-interaction framework for both studying and understanding such events. This sort of framework accommodates a key to understanding nursery-school storyreadings: finished stories were neither adult performances nor child products. Rather, they were cooperative ventures shaped by a conversational network of adult-child verbal give and take.

There are several differences between the social-interaction framework that was necessary to understand the storyreadings I observed and a performance-oriented framework that views literary understanding as a product. Some of these differences are pointed up in the two following examples (Storyreading Segments 4 and 5) featuring children who were about the same age looking at the same wordless picture-book. The story, told completely through the pictures, is about a bird and a fish who became friends after sharing a worm together. The first example is from a study of individual nursery-school children who were invited to look at the book and tell a story to the researcher (Whalen-Levitt, 1977). The second example is taken from the storyreadings observed for this study; the nursery-school teacher was sharing the book with a group of eight nursery-school children ranging in age from three years, three months to four years, nine months.

The important thing to notice about these two storyreading segments is their striking contrast. The first (Storyreading Segment 4) was taken from a child who was asked by the researcher to "read" a storybook alone. Underlying this research approach is the assumption that we can get some insight into children's competence at interpreting stories by asking them to interpret or comprehend storybooks *independently*. The result of this request by the researcher was a cataloguing by the child of the separate items pictured on the individual pages of the book. The second storyreading segment (Storyreading Segment 5) was embedded within the social interaction of an adult and several children. The adult storyreader "read" to and with a group of children, as she did every day. Underlying the second approach is the assumption that we can best understand storyreading and its meaning for a given social group by studying it as it occurs naturally for that group. The result of this second approach was the joint construction across utterances of a thematically and narratively connected story about a bird and a fish.

The point of this comparison is that very different pictures of story-reading emerged when it was investigated within the social setting where it normally occurred, rather than within a situation constructed specifically for research purposes. To understand storyreading within the social group studied here it was necessary to identify social interaction as a key feature. Likewise, to study storyreading within this group, it was necessary to adopt a social-interaction framework. Note the contrast of Storyreading Segments 4 and 5.

Storyreading Segment 4:
A Child's Version of The Good Bird (Wezel)[2]

> A bird. A tree./1 A bird on a tree./2
> A fish and a bird./3 A fish and a bird./4
> A bird and a fish./5 A bird. A tree and a
> Christmas tree./6 A bird and a fish./7
> A big fish and a big bird./8 A big fish and
> a big bird./9 A bird and a fish./10 A
> brown fish and a purple bird and a yellow
> sun./11

Storyreading Segment 5: The Good Bird (Wezel)

Focal Points	Reader		Listeners	
	Verbal	*Nonverbal*	*Verbal*	*Nonverbal*
	Amy: ALL RIGHT . . . [PIC: bird flying downward toward evergreen tree] ONCE UPON A TIME . . . THERE WAS A . . .	holds up book opens to first page pats picture of bird	(many children talking) Mark: Once upon a time . . . (exact intona- tion as reader) Curt: Birdie! Mark: Birdie Susie: Birdie	

---

[2]This telling was taken from a child, age three years, nine months. Slashes and numbers were used by Whalen-Levitt (1977) to indicate pagination.

Storyreading Segment 5 *Continued*

Focal Points	Reader		Listeners	
	Verbal	*Nonverbal*	*Verbal*	*Nonverbal*
			Curt: Flying! (excited)	points to picture
	THIS IS CALLED THE . . .	turns back to cover,		
	good . . .	points to		
	/beh/ . . .	words of title	Susie: I want a scary, scary	
		TP	story.	on knees
	[PIC: bird sitting on tree; house with fishbowl in window off to side of picture]			
	AND HE FLEW . . .	makes downward motion with hands, tracing path of bird		
			Curt: To a tree!	
			Andrew: De tree, and then he flew to a house!	
			Mark: A house!	
	NEAR A HOUSE . . .			
			Susie: With a fish!	pointing to fishbowl
			Mark: With a fish	
			Andrew: With a fish . . .	
		TP	(louder)	
	[PIC: fish lands on windowsill of			

Storyreading Segment 5 *Continued*

	Reader		Listeners	
Focal Points	*Verbal*	*Nonverbal*	*Verbal*	*Nonverbal*
	house, sees fish swimming in bowl]			
			Curt: And *then,* the bird flew in the, to from the window open, yeah! Shshpish!	makes flying noise and motions flying with arms
	[PIC: close-up, bird looks at fish through glass, fish is sad]	TP	Andrew: The fi--, fib . . . I cannot tell a fib, I __ __ name in the contest . . .	
			Curt: Do you hafta figure out what . . .?	
			Mark: And water . . .	
	AND WHAT DID HE DO?	points to fishbowl	Curt: Peck, peck. He pecked on the glass . . .	
	AND THE LITTLE FISH . . .	points to fish's frown	Curt: Was afraid. Mark: Scared.	
	[PIC: bird is right beside fishbowl	* * *		

Storyreading Segment 5 *Continued*

Focal Points	Reader		Listeners	
	Verbal	*Nonverbal*	*Verbal*	*Nonverbal*
	with worm in mouth]			
	AH, CUTE . . .			
	RIGHT OVER TO THE . . .	points to fish	Mark: Fish Susie: Fish	
	his friend, the . . .	TP	?: Fish	
	[PIC: bird perches on edge of fish-bowl and gives fish worm]	* * *		
	AND WHAT DID HE DO WITH THAT WORM? MARK, WHAT DID THE BIRDIE DO WITH THAT WORM?			
	HE GAVE . . . HALF OF IT TO HIS . . .		Susie: Half Susie: friend	
	THE FISH. AND HE KEPT HALF OF IT . . .		Curt: For hisself . . . Bobby: Half for hisself . . .	
	[PIC: night comes, fish and bird asleep]	TP		
	AND THEN . . .			
	WHAT IS IT?	points to picture	Mark: Them sick? Curt: Well . . . it was the *night* time!	

(*continued*)

Storyreading Segment 5 *Continued*

		Reader		Listeners	
Focal Points	*Verbal*	*Nonverbal*		*Verbal*	*Nonverbal*
	THE MOON CAME OUT . . .			Mark: night time, and then, and then, and . . . (Andrew making loud noises)	
	AND IT WAS NIGHT . . . THEN THE . . .			Mark: And then the bird and the fish were all alone.	
	ALONE, ASLEEP QUIETLY, THE BIRD OUT IN THE AIR AND THE FISH IN HIS WATERY TANK.	TP			
	[PIC: bird on plain white background]				
		closes book		Curt: That's . . . Mark: And then . . . Curt: Good night, little birdie! Goodbye, little birdie! (singing)	
	DO YOU THINK HE WAS A GOOD BIRD, MELISSA?	turns back to front cover		Melissa: Yes. Curt: Goodbye, little birdie.	

Although the second, socially interactive telling of Storyreading Segment 5 is clearly more narratively sophisticated than the telling in Storyreading Segment 4, the point of this comparison is not to judge or evaluate the quality of the picture-book readings. The point is that, unlike the first reading that was staged in a quasi-experimental setting, the second occurred spontaneously in a natural setting wherein picture-books were shared on a daily basis. In the second example, even though there was no printed text that had to be decoded for the children, the storyreader did not simply show the pictures on each page of the book. Instead she took an active role and aided the reading so that it became a cooperative venture.

Unlike the first reading of *The Good Bird* where the child was completely on his own, the second bookreading was framed within the rug-time setting that signalled to the children the interactional and interpretive strategies discussed in detail in Chapter 7. The bookreading experience was further framed as a story by both the words of the formulaic story opener, "once upon a time," and the prosodic features that marked these words (a rising and falling intonational pattern that was followed by a pause to allow the children to fill in the blanks: ónce ūpōn ā timè).

The interaction was framed as a story about a bird by both the reader's continuation of the phrase, "there was a . . . ." while patting the picture of the bird and her emphasis on the book's cover picture and title, *The Good Bird*. These were the only words in the book; they reinforced the idea that a bird would be the main figure in the story and also told the listeners how they should evaluate this figure. As the telling progressed, the adult storyreader provided connectives between characters and events, supplied temporal markers, and offered cues to help the children evaluate particular outcomes. She also kept them on the track of the "plot" of the story by asking, "and then what did he do?"

Unlike the child in Storyreading Segment 4 who was asked to tell the story unaided, the children in Storyreading Segment 5 *had little chance to view the pictures in the book as a series of items unrelated to one another temporally, spatially, or thematically.* Rather, the story-reading *participants together constructed the story* of the good bird via a reader-guided interactional sequence of both questions-and-answers and phrase completions. The finished story was clearly a cooperative venture, a network of verbal give-and-take, rather than either an adult performance or a child product. Neither the adult storyreader's or the children's utterances made sense apart from one another or apart from the text.

Those who write children's storybooks operate according to conscious or unconscious generalized expectations concerning their readers and the ways that their books will be read. It was a stylistic feature of many of the picture-book texts shared during group storyreading to directly address the reading/listening audience with open-ended questions (e.g., "Do you know what you like?" or "What makes you mad?"). Such questions in these texts apparently anticipate that some adult reader would address "you" phrases to child listeners, and invite audience response through verbal participation.

As the Storyreading Segment 6 illustrates, the conversational style of picture-book texts fed directly into a dialogic, socially-interactive

Storyreading Segment 6: What Do You Say Dear? (Joslin)

	Reader		Listeners	
Focal Points	Verbal	Nonverbal	Verbal	Nonverbal
	Amy: [PIC: man with elephant under arm; children walking away, carrying elephant] "You are downtown and there's this gentleman giving baby elephants to people. You want to take one home because you've always wanted a baby elephant, but first the gentleman introduces you to each other.			
→	What do you say dear?"			
			Ben: Thank you.	
→	WHAT DO YOU SAY, DEAR?			

Storyreading Segment 6 *Continued*

Reader			Listeners	
Focal Points	*Verbal*	*Nonverbal*	*Verbal*	*Nonverbal*
			Kris: Thank you. Curt: Thank you.	
→	WHAT DO *YOU* SAY?	nods toward Andrew		
			Andrew: Thank you.	
→	IF HE'S INTRO- DUCING YOU . . . HE'S GETTING YOU SO THAT YOU KNOW . . . WHAT DO YOU SAY . . .		Ben: Thank you. Andrew: Thank you.	
→	WHEN YOU FIRST MEET SOME- BODY, YOU SAY . . .	mimes shak- ing hands with someone	Ben: Hello. (in rapid succession) Kris: Hello. Curt: Hello. Andrew: Hello.	
→	INTRODUCING A PERSON, YOU SAY . . . [PIC: boy and ele- phant bow to one another] "How do you do?"	TP	Ben: How do you do, mister!	
→	HOW DO YOU DO, SIR? SHAKE MY HAND, THAT'S VERY POLITE	shakes hands with Ben		
→	Shake your hand. How do you do, sir.	mimes shaking		

(*continued*)

Storyreading Segment 6 *Continued*

Focal Points	Reader		Listeners	
	Verbal	*Nonverbal*	*Verbal*	*Nonverbal*
			(Ben is making swishing noises) Ben: How do you do, sir? (in silly, mimicking voice) Andrew: Smack!	mimes sword fight roughly shakes hands with Andrew; slaps hands with Ben instead of shaking
→	HOW ABOUT YOU SIR?	holds hand out to Kris		
→	HOW DO YOU DO, SIR?			Kris holds left hand out to Amy
	OTHER HAND, KRIS.			
		* * *		

pattern of storyreading. The book that was shared in this example was a comical play on both books of politeness and parental reminders to children to use politeness formulas. The conversational text of the book, which was directly addressed to the audience, invited listeners to participate by repeating the correct formulas and, at the same time, laughing at the absurd situations posed by pictures and text. The arrows indicate examples of the stylistic feature of direct address and how it helped the storyreader invite listeners to become verbally involved.

Many interesting things happened in Storyreading Segment 6. However, the point to be stressed in describing storyreading as social interaction is the relationship between the verbal style of the text and the conversational style of the storyreading. The stylistic feature of direct address used in the text invited the audience to become involved with the book and to participate actively in creating its meaning. It also assumed a conversational relationship between adults as storyreaders and children as listeners and responders (Cochran-Smith, in press). This conversational pattern is correlative with and supported by the oral-language patterns revealed in many studies of children's early language acquisition and development in white, Western, literate societies. As much of this research has pointed out, children in these situations learn to make sense of oral language in dialogue with adults. In such dialogues, adults shape and guide both the meaning of children's speech and the interpretation of others' speech through a process of oral turn-taking (Ochs and Schieffelin, in press). At Maple Nursery School a similar pattern of conversation characterized storyreading.

Ochs and Schieffelin have argued that all theories of children's language acquisition are essentially cultural theories, that both patterns of development of children's language and our explanations of those patterns are not universal but embedded within cultural assumptions about the nature of language and learning. A similar perspective is needed in considerations of the ways that children are initiated into the literary and literacy patterns of their communities. Although supported by the verbal style of many children's picture-books, the socially interactive conversational pattern of storyreading that I have described cannot be claimed as universal.

We need many more case studies of children's initiations into literacy patterns before we can determine the cultural and community settings within which conversationally interactive literacy patterns exist or do not exist. Some recent research provides a few clues in this area. For example, a Chipewyan girl teaching her younger sister to "read" a picture book initiated a liturgy of verbatim repetitions of single words of the text (Scollon and Scollon, 1981); although this verbatim repetition certainly involved both reader and listener as participants, it was not conversational or socially interactive in the sense that I have described. Similarly, in neither of two Piedmont Carolina communities did adults have socially-interactive bookreadings with children (Heath, 1982b). In one community adults did not read to their children at all; in the other, even though children had numerous experiences with bookreadings and bedtime stories, they were expected to be quiet listeners rather than active participants in reading. They were, however, encouraged to respond to stories by retelling them on a verbatim basis. These reports of storyreading practices do not include the social interactional dimension I have been describing.

Conversational social interaction is one dimension of adult-child storyreading. It can provide part of a comparative framework for looking at storyreadings within various social groups. In some social groups, storybooks are regularly shared with young children and interaction does exist as part of the taken-for-granted way that they are shared. In these cases, children's understanding and sense-making of books need to be investigated as part of that interaction and as part of the larger social context within which it occurs.

We have seen in previous chapters that Maple Nursery School story-reading took place within a very meaningful and socially relevant context that featured an approach to bookreading for entertainment, access to knowledge, and problem-solving. In other social groups, however—even where bookreadings appear to be socially interactive—they may *not* be embedded in larger contexts where literacy is socially relevant and meaningful. For example, the form of book-looking activities of one Kaluli mother and child in Papua New Guinea was found to resemble the form of Maple Nursery School bookreadings. However, for the Kaluli mother, book-centered conversation was "talk to no purpose," as it had no relevance or meaning in the larger social context (Schieffelin and Cochran-Smith, in press). This comparison reminds us of the importance of not only investigating book experiences in terms of the social interactions within which they occur, but also of understanding their meanings *for the participants* themselves.

The Negotiation of Storybook Meaning

As we saw in the reading of *In the Night Kitchen,* in Storyreading Segment 3, nursery-school storyreading was highly interactive and listener-participative. The listeners were verbally responsive to what the reader was saying and doing; aloud and very actively, they answered and asked questions, made comments, and offered interpretations of the text. The storyreader's role was also active. This presents a striking contrast to other oral readings we can envision (e.g., a professor delivering a paper at a conference, a minister reading a Biblical passage to his or her congregation, a Congressman presenting a statement to the legislature) wherein there is usually little or no commentary or glossing on the text while it is being read. During such oral readings, even if the reader is the author of the text, he or she seems to function primarily as spokesperson for the text by translating from the written to the oral channel. Reader-as-spokesperson for the text was *not* the case in the storyreadings I observed; on the contrary, the storyreader almost never functioned simply in this role. In fact, as many as 80% of a reader's utterances during a single storyreading were commentary and annotation rather than direct reading.

The texts of stories were not simply read to the children; nor did the children respond as passive listeners or participants via ritualized responses. Rather, nursery-school storyreadings were based on cooperative negotiation of textual meanings by the reader and the listeners

(Cochran-Smith, 1980). The storyreader was very much aware of the responses of her particular group of listeners, and individuals' responses influenced the storyreader's guidance of interaction around the text. Again, this contrasts with other oral-reading situations, such as responsive readings or church prayers where the congregation reads ritual phrases at specific times. These are socially interactive (i.e., both readers and listeners actively participate) but are not cooperatively negotiated since readers' and listeners' utterances are *not* mutually dependent. In responsive readings and the like, standard phrases are uttered by both readers and listeners; neither is free to deviate from the text. In nursery-school storyreadings, however, just the opposite was true. Both readers and listeners deviated from the texts, and the responses of each depended to a great extent on the responses of the other. Especially for the storyreader, who dominated the interaction, the sense that the listeners seemed to be making of texts directly shaped her own role in the storyreading.

Storyreading as focused and non-focused interaction

In their comparison of bard and formula oral narratives with Athabaskan oral narratives, Scollon and Scollon (1980) have suggested a distinction between "focused" and "non-focused" interactions. Focused interactions like the performance of bard and formula oral narratives "force(s) the adoption of some non-negotiated way of making sense" (p. 27) and allow for little repair or recycling. Non-focused situations, on the other hand, are interactive and "mutually negotiated . . . [they] emphasize respect for the sense the other is making of the situation. . ." (p. 27). Scollon and Scollon argue that essayist literacy necessitates focused situations because writers know little or nothing about their distant audiences and hence must "assume responsibility for unilateral sense-making" (p. 28).

The arguments posed by Scollon and Scollon help to point out an interesting and significant aspect of nursery-school storyreading: it involved both the reading of essayist literacy (Scollon and Scollon's focused interaction) and cooperative negotiation of the story by reader and listeners (non-focused interaction). While this may present a contradiction in Scollon and Scollon's terms, it provides some insight into the nature of nursery-school storyreading and its role in children's literary socialization.

The books shared during nursery-school rug-times are examples of what historians have called essayist literacy. That is, the books were received by audiences for whom their authors/illustrators were completely anonymous. In turn, the authors/illustrators who create children's books do not intend them for any particular child audience; rather, like adult works of fiction, children's storybooks are directed to a more or less general child reading public, and readers are fictionalized or implied within the works themselves (Booth, 1961; Iser, 1974, 1980). The choices that authors/illustrators make depend, in part, on their conceptions (whether conscious or unconscious) of some generalized child and the experiences and knowledge of that child. The reader/listener of the book must make sense of language that is decontextualized or not dependent for its meaning on a particular writing or reading context. In this respect, Scollon and Scollon's focused-interaction category applies to nursery school storyreading materials.

Equally clear from the many examples of storyreading I collected over 18 months, however, was the fact that nursery-school storyreadings were also negotiated or non-focused interactions. The storyreader was very much aware of the sense-making of the particular groups of listeners who sat before her. Two readings of the same book by the same storyreader, therefore, did not call forth the same interactive patterns; storyreading was not a recitation of set reader-questions and listener-responses. Rather, the cooperative negotiation of the story depended on what listeners noticed in the text and pictures, what they understood or were confused by, and how they were interpreting the story—in short, the sense that the listening group seemed to be making of the picture-book.

In Storyreading Segment 7 parts of two readings of the same picture-book by the same storyreader are juxtaposed. The excerpt to the left (Reading A) is taken from a storyreading to three children during quiet-time in an afternoon nursery-school session; none of the three children had heard the story before. The excerpt to the right (Reading B) occurred one week after Reading A; the story was read to a group of 12 children, including all of the listeners in Reading A. All of the children had heard the story at least once before. Arrows indicate differences in the two storyreadings.

Although they represented interactions that occurred around the same two double-page spreads in the same picture-book, these two interaction sequences were quite different. The interaction in Reading A was considerably longer than that in Reading B. The sequence in Reading A centered around the listeners' fascination with the fact that the New York City skyline was made from kitchen items. The sequence in Reading B focused on clarification of the phenomenon called the

Storyreading Segment 7: Two Versions of In the Night Kitchen (Sendak)

	Reader		Listeners		Reader		Listeners	
Focal Points	Verbal	Nonverbal	Verbal	Nonverbal	Verbal	Nonverbal	Verbal	Nonverbal
	Reading A: Amy: [LP: Mickey (M) going higher and higher (two vertical frames: M flying straight up into dark sky over kitchen; M looking down into skyline)] "And up! And up!" (voice rises at end of each 'up') And . . .	points to picture	Clay: And there was it! (excited)	points to giant milk bottle in RP	Reading B: Amy: [LP: Mickey (M) going higher and higher (two vertical frames: M flying straight up into dark sky over kitchen; M looking down into skyline)] "And up! And up!"	points to RP		
↑	[RP: Two panels: M goes past moon, high in air over kitchen; M over large bottle of milk]				[RP: Two panels: M goes past moon, high in air over kitchen; M over large bottle of milk]			

(continued)

159

Storyreading Segment 7 Continued

160

Focal Points	Reader		Listeners		Reader		Listeners	
	Verbal	Nonverbal	Verbal	Nonverbal	Verbal	Nonverbal	Verbal	Nonverbal
	"And over the top of the Milky Way in the Night Kitchen."	points to two frames			"And over the top of the Milky Way."	points to picture		
↑	TO WHERE THE GREAT BIG GIANT BOTTLE WAS? IS IT BIGGER THAN THE . . . WHOLE . . . CITY?		Sarah: Yeah		IS THERE MILK UP IN THE SKY?		Chorus: Yes! No!	
↑	IS IS BIGGER THAN THE TRAINS?	points to L-like train made in picture with loaves of bread	Susie: Yeah, lookit! Lookit! (excited) Everything, look-it! See, that's, that's a . . . See it's all wrong 'cause every-	points excitedly to background of city (real-izes the	SO IT'S CALLED THE MILKY WAY, WAY UP HIGH WHERE YOU CAN SEE LOTS OF TINY STARS ALL TO-GETHER, IT'S CALLED THE MILKY WAY. YOU LOOK OUTSIDE AT NIGHT AND YOUR MOMS AND DADS WILL SHOW YOU WHERE THE MILKY WAY IS UP IN THE SKY." TP			

						(several children start to talk at once—indiscernible, but they are trying to get teacher's attention to say something about making things out of dough)
↑ IT'S . . .						
↑ RIGHT, FOOD . . .	nods	thing's made out of foo-ood and like that . . .	skyline is made of kitchen & food items)	IT'S VERY BIG, LOTS OF . . . VERY, VERY FAR AWAY.		
↑		Susie: Lookit! See! See! That's made out of a . . . um, thing.	points to building made out of bottle	DOUGH?		Dan: Out of, out of, out of airplane . . .
↑		And that's made out of a thing that you put, you, uh, put lemon it, and . . .	points to lemon squeezer on end	AN AIRPLANE?		Jeff: I can't see!
↑ THAT'S RIGHT, THAT'S A LEMON SQUEEZER . . .		Susie: Yeah, and that . . .	points to box in picture, looks	You can make airplanes out of dough.	nods turns back to book	

(continued)

Storyreading Segment 7 Continued

Focal Points	Reader		Listeners		Reader		Listeners	
	Verbal	Nonverbal	Verbal	Nonverbal	Verbal	Nonverbal	Verbal	Nonverbal
↑	THAT SAYS 'OATS' . . .	points to picture	Susie: That says . . .	toward Amy points to cream pitcher, waits for Amy to read				
↑	C-R-EAM (sort of sounding out the word)		Susie: Hey, lookit! What's that made out of?	points to jar, looks like tomato				

162

↑	THAT SAYS, "150 MEALS FOR $1.00."	points to tiny printing	Susie: And lookit, that's . . .	points to nut-cracker
			sauce with tiny printing at top
↑	WHAT IS THAT? IT'S NOT A NUT CRACKER, IS IT?		Susie: Yeah! It is! (excited)	Susie is going directly across skyline, from left to right, pointing out each item
	(laughs)		Susie: And this is a teapot . . .	points to pot;

(continued)

Storyreading Segment 7 Continued

Focal Points	Reader		Listeners		Reader		Listeners	
	Verbal	Nonverbal	Verbal	Nonverbal	Verbal	Nonverbal	Verbal	Nonverbal
↑	A KETTLE, A LITTLE POT . . .		and what is this?	points to pan				
			Susie: And what is this?	points to bag of flour				
↑	UMMM . . . LOOKS LIKE A BIG BAG, LOOKS LIKE A BAG OF FLOUR OR SOMETHING.		Susie: Or sugar or something					
↑	THAT, LOOK AT THAT SIGN. THAT FLAG SAYS, "FOOD" . . .FOOD FOOD.	points to banner on top of roof	Susie: And what, what is	Susie nods				

164

			that made out of?	points to bottle with "berries" printed on label
↑	BERRIES IN THERE . . .		Susie: And lookit! (delighted) Lookit what that's made out of, *BREAD!* (yelling, laughing)	points to Wonder Bread train
↑	GARLIC BREAD, IT SAYS, THAT'S A LOAF OF BREAD. THE TRAIN IS A LOAF OF BREAD. (chuckles)	points to tiny print on bread	(Dan laughs)	
↑	THAT'S VERY GOOD-LOOKING.	nods to Susie	Susie: Hmm . . . everything's cuckoo (very quietly)	
		TP		
	[LP&RP]: single picture		[LP&RP]: single picture	

(*continued*)

165

Storyreading Segment 7 *Continued*

Focal Points	Reader Verbal	Reader Nonverbal	Listeners Verbal	Listeners Nonverbal
↑	of M above milk bottle, bakers at bottom of kitchen city; skyline behind them] AND THEY ARE . . . LOOKIT! THERE'S MICKEY UP BY THE MILK! (laughs)	points to M in picture	Dan: Yeah! Hmmmm . . . (excited)	
↑	IS ANYTHING IN THAT BOTTLE?		Susie: And look what else! Look what else!	points to upside-down egg-beaters that form top of
	of M above milk bottle, bakers at bottom of kitchen city; skyline behind them] LOOK, HE FLEW RIGHT OVER THERE!	points to LP & RP TP	Jeff: I can't see!	

166

		* * *	
		buil- dings	
		(Dan laughs, points to the picture, acting silly)	
↑ OH YEAH! EGGBEATER! — points to egg-beaters

↑ Eggbeaters on . . . (laughs)
EGGBEATERS ON THE TOP OF THE BUILDING! (laughs)

↑ YOU'RE DYING WITH LAUGHTER! — TP   * * *

"Milky Way." The interaction in Reading A was initiated by a child listener, while in Reading B it began with a question posed by the reader about the listeners' understanding of a phrase used in the text.

The differences between these two excerpts were certainly related to differences in the sizes of the two groups, the children's familiarity with the book, the relations of the listeners to one another and to the reader, the physical proximity of the listeners to the book, and the nursery-school frameworks within which the readings occurred. That all of these factors influenced the verbal interaction is precisely the point to be emphasized—storyreadings were negotiated according to the listeners' direct indications of their understanding of the book and the reader's inferences and assumptions about the listeners' understanding.

Interactive negotiation is not a function of all oral storyreadings any more than, as Scollon and Scollon (1980) argue, non-focused interaction is a function of all oral narratives. The storyhours conducted for the nursery-school children at local libraries offered a striking contrast to the storyreadings at Maple Nursery School. As we saw in Chapter 7, library storyreadings were very different from nursery-school storyreadings, even though the same group of children participated as listeners and many of the same texts were used in both settings. Unlike the nursery-school readings, library readings were characterized by neither social interaction nor negotiation. On the contrary, at library storyhours the nursery-school children were discouraged from speaking, and their responses, questions, and comments were cut short by librarians' reminders to be quiet. The library storyreader rarely deviated from the text or commented on the stories. In fact the readings were usually verbatim recitations of the texts. Furthermore, librarian storyreaders did little pointing, gesturing, or miming story actions.

What took place in library storyhours was unilateral sensemaking of decontextualized storybooks. What took place in the nursery school, on the other hand, was negotiated, interactive sensemaking of decontextualized storybooks. Making sense of decontextualized print is usually an activity which is essentially solitary. Indeed, school literacy progress and reading success are especially marked by children's abilities to read and understand independently. For Maple Nursery School preschoolers, the negotiated, socially interactive, and oral aspects of early storyreadings helped to introduce and allow opportunities for practice in the solitary, unilateral, and silent process of decontextualized bookreading. To see how this happened, it is necessary to look more closely at the nature of the negotiated interactions.

Types of storyreading interaction sequences

The storyreader played the key role in making nursery-school story-reading a process of interactive negotiation. Let us take a closer look at the kinds of interactions the reader initiated or guided during storyreadings (Cochran-Smith, 1981).

In preparation for and during the storyreading, the reader guided the children in a series of interaction sequences. Some of these sequences were initiated by the children with their questions, comments, facial expressions, or gestures; many were initiated by the questions, explanations, incomplete statements, exclamations, or actions of the story-reader. Interactions were primarily verbal, but included nonverbal behavior as well. Three broad types of interaction sequences emerged from the data and accounted for nearly all of the verbal interactions in the 100 storyreadings I studied: (a) Type I "Readiness" interaction sequences helped to establish or maintain norms of appropriate reading and reading-related behavior; (b) Type II "Life-to-Text" interaction sequences helped listeners make sense of the events, characters, action, and information in the particular books being shared; and (c) Type III "Text-to-Life" interaction sequences guided listeners in their application, extension, or use of the information, themes, or messages in the books being shared. Most storyreadings, but not all of them, had interaction sequences of all three types. The three types of sequences did not, however, occur in a particular order.

Type I Interactions: Readiness for Reading. Many storyreading interaction sequences centered around appropriate reading behaviors, which were essentially the norms of rug-time. As we saw in Chapter 7, these norms were related primarily to the listeners' seating arrangement, posture, visual and aural attention to the text, pictures and storyreader, and mental concentration. Another of the ostensible rules of rug-time was listener silence. Silence, however, was not as important as non-interference in the good reading behavior of others. Furthermore, listeners were encouraged to indicate their involvement, interest, and attention to the story by participating in interactive sequences related to their making sense of books (Type II Life-to-Text interaction sequences) or applying the information in books to events and situations outside of books (Type III Text-to-Life interaction sequences).

The majority of Readiness interaction sequences occurred just before or at the beginning of storyreading events. The storyreader frequently spent a great deal of time talking about appropriate behavior during storyreadings and encouraging individual children to behave accordingly. The message underlying reminders of this sort was clear: *first* you indicate that you are ready to be "a reader" by sitting, listening, and looking appropriately, *then* you may begin to read (or listen to) a book. Once the reading of a specific text had actually begun, the storyreader sometimes overlooked inappropriate reading behaviors, unless these began to interfere seriously with other listeners trying to follow the rules and attend to the story. The incident in Storyreading Segment 8 was typical; readiness sequences are marked by arrows.

The children themselves frequently interrupted storyreadings to complain of interference with their reading behaviors. The primary reasons for disruptions were seating arrangements that interfered with the looking and attending of other children who frequently initiated Readiness interaction sequences by demanding visual access to the book being shown.

Storyreading Segment 8: Fish Is Fish (Lionni)

	Reader		Listeners	
Focal Points	Verbal	Nonverbal	Verbal	Nonverbal
	Amy: FIRST, I'LL DO ONE MORE.	picks up book		
→	ANDREW, COME ON DEARIE. THIS IS NOT, THIS IS RUG-TIME. YOU HAVE MOST OF THE TIME YOU GET TO PLAY ALL BY YOURSELF.	motions for them to re-join the group on the rug	Andrew (to Ben): Let's go __ __ __	Andrew and Ben go and stand at back of group at rug
				boys stay at back of rug
	NOW . . . THIS IS . . .	holds up	Anne: "Fish Is Fish"	

Storyreading Segment 8 *Continued*

	Reader		Listeners	
Focal Points	*Verbal*	*Nonverbal*	*Verbal*	*Nonverbal*
		book, points to words of title	(reading title)	
	FISH IS FISH.	nods at Anne points at words		
		TP		
	[PIC: fish and tadpole underwater talking]			
	Now "at the edge of the woods there was a pond, and there were a minnow and a tadpole. They swam among the weeds. Why they were inseparable friends."	TP		
			* * *	
				Ben and Andrew want to leave rug; start to play; put hands over ears and talk to one another in loud voices
	"They argued and argued until finally the tadpole said, 'Frogs are frogs and fish is fish and that's that!'"			Mark goes and stands with them at back of rug and starts to imitate them
→	LOOK ANDREW, BEN, BEN, BEN, BEN . . .			
			Andrew: What? (loud)	
		puts book	Ben: Can't hear you!	

(continued)

Storyreading Segment 8   *Continued*

	Reader		Listeners	
Focal Points	*Verbal*	*Nonverbal*	*Verbal*	*Nonverbal*
		in lap		Boys still with hands over ears
→	I DON'T WANT YOU TO DO THAT. THIS IS THE TIME . . .		Ben: What? (very loud)	
				takes hands down
→	THIS IS THE ONLY TIME I GET TO READ TO YOU, AN- DREW; THIS IS THE ONLY TIME I GET TO READ TO YOU. I WANT YOU TO LISTEN THIS TIME. A LOT OF TIMES I LIKE TO LISTEN TO YOU, BUT THIS IS A TIME WHEN YOU GET TO HEAR NEW THINGS.	turns atten- tion back to book * * *		Ben and Andrew sit down at back of rug

The storyreader encouraged children to assume appropriate reading behaviors by setting the stage for rug-time prior to reading and by interrupting the storyreadings to remind some children of the rules or to respond to the complaints of other children. She also used the technique of calling upon specific children and inviting them to participate in Life-to-Text or Text-to-Life interaction sequences. This strategy was intended to distract children from inappropriate reading behavior and draw them back into the group of "readers" who were attending properly to the book.

Type II Interactions: Life-to-Text.   The largest number of story-reading interaction sequences was aimed at helping listeners make sense of particular texts. The direction of this type of sequence was outside-in. That is, within Life-to-Text sequences, the storyreader was teaching the listeners how to make sense of text by bringing to light the extra-textual information they needed in order to make inner-textual sense. Extra-textual information came from broad areas of knowledge, including knowledge of lexical labels, literary and cultural heritage, narrative structure, human nature, and literary conventions. Life-to-Text sequences seemed to be the most important type of interaction around storyreading. A detailed analysis and description of such interaction sequences follows in Chapter 9.

Type III Interactions: Text-to-Life.   Many reader-listener interaction sequences centered around helping the children discover the meaning that a book's message, theme, or information might have in their own lives. Unlike Life-to-Text sequences, in which the reader focused on extra-textual references in order to illumine textual materials, in Text-to-Life sequences almost the opposite was true. Textual references were used to throw light on extra-textual matters. Text-to-Life interactions involved the application of book information or material to real life, including the direct application of book knowledge to the ongoing events of nursery-school life. Type III Text-to-Life interaction sequences are discussed and analyzed in Chapter 10.

CHAPTER 9

What is Given is No More Than a Way of Taking: Life-to-Text Interactions

In his preface to *S/Z*, Barthes' (1974) seminal work on ways in which readers read, Richard Howard argues that "we require an education in literature as in the sentiments in order to discover that what we assumed—with the complicity of our teachers—was nature is in fact culture, that what was given is no more than a way of taking" (p. ix). What Howard is suggesting is that we tend to consider our ways of reading as "given" or "natural" rather than learned. Barthes' analysis urges us to examine the givens in literature as learned and culture-specific "ways of taking" from texts. This idea is especially helpful in examining Type II Life-to-Text interactions in nursery-school storyreading.

Making sense of the uncomplicated narratives in many children's picture books is easy to take for granted, to consider a given. What is actually a given, however, is the assumption that the readers of picturebooks will have learned to take information from their pools of knowledge in particular ways in order to make sense of texts. In other words, readers/listeners will take the knowledge that they have gained from direct or secondary experiences outside of texts and use this knowledge to make sense within texts.

Learning ways of taking information from experience in order to make sense of texts is fundamental to the process of literary socialization. For Maple Nursery School preschool children, Life-to-Text interactions in group storyreadings were part of an initiation process into particular ways of taking information from experience and bringing it to bear upon texts. These interactions provided a kind of apprenticeship to ways of using such information by offering the children mediated literary experiences wherein an adult storyreader monitored and guided literary sense-making.

The Storyreader as Mediator between Real and Implied Readers

One kind of information that often played a key role in the interpretation of printed materials in off-the-rug nursery-school literacy events was knowledge of and familiarity with the producers or users of the materials. A distinguishing feature of the picture-books used on-the-rug, on the other hand, was that there was anonymity and considerable distance between writers and readers. Since writers could not rely on readers' personal familiarity to contribute to the meaning of print messages, they had to rely, instead, on some generalized view of the knowledge and experience of their audience. In describing kinds and orders of discourse, Moffett (1965, 1968) has stressed this situation. He describes published discourse as "impersonal communication to a large anonymous group extended over space and/or time" and suggests that such discourse necessitates a kind of "one-way transmission" (1968, p. 33) of message.

The notion of one-way transmission of message is similar in many respects to the unilateral sense-making that Scollon and Scollon (1980) suggest is a distinguishing feature of essayist literacy. Several literary theorists, notably Booth (1961) and Iser (1974, 1980), have described the phenomenon of spatial and temporal separation of writers and readers of essayist literacy by developing the literary notion of the "implied" or fictionalized reader. Chambers (1977) and Tabbert (1979) have used the concept to consider several theoretical aspects of the nature of literature intended for children.

The implied reader

The concept of the implied reader can be summarized as follows: Writers of both fictional and nonfictional works for publication (i.e., essayist literacy) are separated from their audiences by greater or lesser distances in both time and space. Because such writers never know their readers, they cannot rely upon the personal experiences or knowledge stores of particular individuals to provide a background against which texts can be read and interpreted. Instead, interpretive information must be contained in the text. Of course, for writers to include in their texts everything that readers need to understand the texts, or to explain everything there is to be explained, is impossible. Instead, readers actively and continuously participate in the creation of meanings by bringing their own life and literary experiences to bear upon texts.

Writers, however, have no way of knowing specifically what their anonymous and distant readers bring to texts. Furthermore, since there is no face-to-face interaction between authors and readers during the actual reading, there is no opportunity for writers to repair misunderstood passages or offer further explanations where needed. As a result, consciously or unconsciously writers create or imply readers within texts themselves. These fictionalized readers are not real persons. Rather, the implied reader is an abstract concept—the "reader *in* the book" (Chambers, 1977). As Chambers has rightly pointed out, the nature of the reader implied by the text is revealed in the language the writer uses, the references he or she makes with and without explanation, the complexity of the sentences, and the attitude assumed toward the reader. Analysis of these aspects of a text allows us to construct a picture of the reader who is implied.

Children's books, of course, are less sophisticated than classic fiction or scholarly articles. They do, however, imply readers by their lexical and syntactic structures, cultural and literary references, and plot and character complexities. Booth (1961) argues that:

> . . . the implied author of each novel is someone with whose beliefs on all subjects I must largely agree if I am to enjoy his work. . . . Regardless of my real beliefs and practices, I must subordinate my mind and heart to the book if I am to enjoy it to the full. The author creates, in short, an image of himself and another image of his reader; *he makes his reader,* as he makes his second self, and *the most successful reading is one in which the created selves, author and reader, can find complete agreement.* (pp. 137–138) [emphasis added]

Booth's description proposes that the real reader of a work must, to some extent, take on or match up with the characteristics of the reader implied in the work in order to read that text "successfully." Although Booth is discussing fiction, his proposition applies to nonfiction essayist literacy as well. To read nonfiction pieces successfully, real readers must take on or match up with the characteristics of the readers who are implied in these works.

The storyreader as mediator and monitor

Nursery-school storyreading sessions were characterized by two features that seem contradictory: (a) storyreadings centered around essayist literacy that necessitates one-way or unilateral sense-making by the writer as he fictionalizes a reader in the work; and (b) storyreadings were social interactions wherein adult reader and child listeners cooperatively negotiated the meanings of written texts. The contradiction is resolved as the nature of storyreading emerges. Primarily through Type II Life-to-Text interaction sequences, the storyreader was transforming the reading of essayist literacy from a unilateral to a joint sense-making process. In order to provide for joint sense-making, the storyreader guided the children in Life-to-Text interactions in which she mediated between child listeners and text. That is, she continuously monitored the match between the reader implied in the text and the real reader/listeners who sat before her listening to the text.

To help them make sense of texts, the storyreader guided the listeners to take on the characteristics of the readers implied in particular books. To shape real reader/listeners into implied readers, or whenever a mismatch between the two seemed to occur, she overrode the textual narrator and became the narrator herself, annotating the text and trying to establish some sort of agreement between real and implied readers. The storyreader mediated by alternating between two roles—spokesperson for the text and secondary narrator or commentator on the text.

In order to mediate, the storyreader had to continuously assess and interpret both the text—its lexical and syntactic structures, the storyline, temporal and spatial sequences, the amount and kind of information carried by the pictures and by words, and the interrelationships of these two kinds of information—*and* the sense that the listeners were making of it all. Listeners' sense-making was monitored by the reader's paying close attention to their responses. Some indications of the children's sense-making were direct—unelicited responses to the text (e.g., a child asked a specific question about the story or made a comment that indicated confusion about the information) or elicited responses to the text (e.g., the reader asked the listeners to identify specific items or answer questions about events in the story). Other indications of making sense of the text were indirectly revealed by listeners' attentiveness, facial expressions, gestures, and postures. The reader also relied on her knowledge of what children of certain ages would generally know and not know and on her intimate knowledge of the common and individual experiences of her particular listeners.

Modifications to the text

Storyreader mediation occurred both in advance of and in response to children's responses. Based on a general sense of what children would and would not understand, the storyreader sometimes altered the text in advance in order to prevent what she expected might become a mismatch between real and implied readers. There were several modification strategies used by the storyreader. Often she simplified the text by significantly altering it.

The beginning of one book, *Florina and the Wild Bird,* by Chronz and Carigiet, for example, reads:

> There was once a mountain child,
> her name Florina,
> and when the summer came and the
> sun beat down from a cloudless sky
> she bade her valley home goodbye.

This text is rather complex: it is written in rhyme, five clauses comprise the first sentence, the vocabulary is sophisticated, and the syntax is unusual. However, the reader's rendition of the text was different:

> Once upon a time there was this little girl.
> Her name Florina.
> And when the summer beat down from the sky, she
>   said goodbye to her little house.

As we can see, the reader took the first complex sentence of the text and broke it into three simpler sentences that were, presumably, easier for the children to follow. In addition to sentence structure, vocabulary was altered: "mountain child" became "this little girl" (with the reader pointing to a picture of the girl to clarify); "bade her valley home goodbye" was changed to "said goodbye to her little house" (which is simpler in both vocabulary and syntax); and "cloudless" was omitted altogether.

Several other modifications were made to the first page of text, which was composed of 12 rhymed sentences similar in construction to the first sentence. Finally, the whole page was followed by the reader's succinct summary, "they're going *up* the mountains." As she said this, she raised the pitch of her voice and tapped a picture of the little girl's family and then a picture of the mountain. In this way, lexical and syntactic information were supported by the prosodic features of the oral reading and by the reader's explicit identification of the mountain setting in the pictures.

In addition to simplifying syntax and word choice, the reader also sometimes altered texts by summarizing, omitting, or failing to call to the children's attention verbal or visual information that she believed to be unimportant or beyond the children's understanding. For example, one picture-book showed a ''pretend'' doctor's office to accompany a textual reference to the story characters' ''playing doctor.'' Although the reader pointed out several of the details of this illustration, she made no reference to a sharply down-turned ''clinic cures'' graph pictured on the wall of the office. This omission is not surprising if considered in terms of the disparity that probably existed between the reader implied in the book and the real reader/listeners who sat on the rug in front of the storyreader. In order to ''get'' the joke in the picture and text, the reader implied in the book understood: the lexical meaning of ''clinic cures''; the relationship in our culture between clinic cures and doctors and their work; the print and configuration conventions of line graphs; that clinic cures should increase in number in order for a doctor to be considered competent; the absurdity of a patient visiting a ''quack'' doctor whose clinic cure record was so bad it had gone off the chart.

It would certainly not be impossible to explain some or all of this information to the listeners. Although we can only speculate, it is also possible that the author included this humor for adult readers. Regardless of what kind of reader is intended, however, it is significant that in a decision that was automatic, rather than deliberate, the reader simply omitted this aspect of the story instead of trying to explain it to the three-to-five-year-old children who were her listening audience. In this way, she mediated between text and children.

Examples of the storyreader's modifications to texts give us a sense of the way the storyreader mediated between implied and real readers as she read to the children. These examples also illumine some of the assumptions that the storyreader had about these preschool children: they understood simple sentence constructions better than complex ones, they had limited lexicons from which to draw, they could handle shorter texts more easily than longer ones, and they could not easily understand certain levels of humor. Many of the textual revisions, omissions, and alterations made by the storyreader were similar to the modifications in language patterns made by adults in white, Western societies when they talk to children.[1] Reading modifications give us some

---

[1] For an insightful description of the assumptions underlying the model of children's language learning in white, Western, primarily middle-class culture and of the ways adults in these groups act on their assumptions, see Ochs and Schieffelin, in press.

insight into how the adults in the nursery-school setting assumed that children learned to make sense of written texts.

The dialogic pattern of storyreading interaction was very effective in providing the storyreader with information about the listeners' sense-making or the extent to which the children, as real reader/listeners, matched with the readers fictionalized in texts. When real readers seemed mismatched with the implied readers, the adult storyreader often led the children in a dialogue that was patterned by reader-questions and listener-answers, or the reader's incomplete phrases and listener-completions. Mediation did not occur only at the end of storyreadings; it was not a process of quizzing the children with after-the-fact comprehension questions. Rather, mediation occurred at any time during a storyreading as the reader shaped the listeners into the image of the implied reader, monitored the match between implied and real readers, or worked to alleviate a mismatch.

The strategy of storyreading mediation used by the teacher in this study was clearly a process of two-dimensional sense-making; the very young reader/listeners were not faced with the task of making sense of an author's unilateral text. Instead, they received a great deal of instruction—confirmation of their correct sensemaking and negation of their incorrect attempts. If they misunderstood or became confused, they were allowed to try again; specific textual passages or pictures that caused confusion were pointed out, and the proper ways to make sense were explained. In one storyreading, for example, the key event in understanding temporal sequence occurred between two pictures, and had to be inferred; but the children had difficulty with the sequence. They did not realize that in-between a picture of a boy headed menacingly toward a snowman and the next picture showing only the base of the snowman, the snowman had been knocked down.

To guide the children closer to the image of the reader implied in the text, the storyreader initiated an interaction sequence in which she recycled pages of text and illustration, emphasizing temporal language and pointing out the ways that the pictured actions were temporally related to one another. In this way, the children received direct, mediated instruction in how to use their knowledge in order to make sense of text. An important part of this instruction was how to "read" or get meaning from both the pictures and words in books and how to integrate these two kinds of information. Part of the children's early literary socialization, therefore, was learning to infer from pictures and words in ways that made logical and narrative sense of a book as a whole rather than as a number of discrete pieces.

Storyreading Segment 9:² Father Christmas (Briggs)

Focal Points	Reader		Listeners	
	Verbal	*Nonverbal*	*Verbal*	*Nonverbal*
	[RP: (the page is divided into a series of 11 small frames like a comic strip) 1) Santa holds coat up to fire; 2) puts on slippers; 3) makes tea; 4) stuffs turkey; 5) carries turkey in a pan to stove; 6) makes pudding; 7) walks by presents inside door; 8) puts bubbles in hot bath; 9) in tub, singing; 10) showers, sings; 11) dries off]			
→	AND HERE'S THE SONG. GEE, THIS MUST BE CHRISTMAS			
→	DAY. I HEAR "Hark the Herald Angels Sing." (sings)	points to picture #4; in background of kitchen is radio with musical notes and words, "Hark" etc. * * *		

²The transcription conventions used in Sharing Segments 1 and 2 and in the Storyreading Segments throughout this monograph are described in detail in Chapter 3, pp. 30–36.

This inferring task is nicely illustrated by Sendak's apt description of the nature of picture-books and picture-book reading as a "juggling act" (in Lanes, 1980). Like circus-juggling, it takes three balls to juggle the sense-making in picture books: (a) making sense of pictures, (b) making sense of text, and (c) relating the two to each other and to the structural or narrative whole of the text. If any of these "balls" is dropped, the act of sense-making will suffer. In the storyreadings I observed over 18 months, the storyreader performed a complicated juggling act of her own in order to help the children keep all three balls in the air by inferring appropriately from texts and pictures.

In the storyreader's mediation of the picture book in Storyreading Segment 9, the intertwining of pictorial and textual information is quite clear. The book that was being shared was a wordless book about Santa Claus; as the segment begins, he had just returned from his annual trip around the world delivering presents. As we will see in this segment, the storyreader worked hard to help the children draw proper inferences from the text and the pictures in relation to the overall narrative.

Many separate inferences underlay the teacher's simple remarks: "And here's the song. Gee, this must be Christmas Day. I hear 'Hark the Herald Angels Sing' right on the radio." These inferences included the following:

1. A zig-zagged speech-balloon connected to the radio in the kitchen-picture indicated that a song was coming over the air waves.

2. The printed words in the balloon were the words to one phrase of a common Christmas carol.

3. The pictured musical notes indicated that the words were being sung rather than spoken.

4. The radio's location in the same comic-strip frame as Santa indicated that he was listening to the song as he worked.

5. A Christmas carol playing on the radio suggested that it might now be Christmas Day itself (instead of Christmas Eve, as it had been when the story began).

Each inference based on the pictures and each inference based on the words had to be integrally related to and built upon the others in order to conclude that it was Christmas morning, and that Santa was preparing his Christmas dinner. All of these inferences also had to be related to the information conveyed by the ten other picture frames on the page and the five utterances made by Santa Claus (e.g., in frame #10, after he had heard it on the radio, Santa showered and sang "Hark the Herald

Angels Sing'' to himself). In turn, all of this information had to be related to previous and later pictures and text so that the total story made logical and narrative sense.

The storyreader's mediation in this example emphasizes that the children were not expected independently to make all of these inferences and relate them to one another. Rather, the storyreader made the inferring process explicit for the children by remarking specifically that there was a song, the song suggested that it was Christmas Day, and Santa was hearing the song. She provided more information by pointing to the zig-zagged speech-balloon attached to the radio as she herself sang the words of the song and then explained that the song was coming over the radio. This example makes it clear that as the storyreader was mediating between children and story, she was conveying to the children a model for drawing inferences from decontextualized, printed texts.

Making Sense of Texts

What I have been describing in this chapter is a process of mediation wherein the storyreader interfaced between the readers implied in children's books and the real reader/listeners of the nursery school. This mediation process was effected primarily through a series of what I have called Type II Life-to-Text interactions that focused on making sense of individual texts. Life-to-Text interactions were characterized by reader-listener exchanges aimed at helping the children use their knowledge in order to make sense of literature. The emphasis in interactions of this sort was on what was happening in the texts themselves, as opposed to either the physical behavior that was to accompany or precede reading (Type I Readiness interactions) or ways in which book information related to or could be used in reader/listeners' lives (Type III Text-to-Life interactions).

One way of looking at Type II Life-to-Text interactions is to consider them in relation to what Prince (1980, 1982) has called ''metanarrative'' signals to readers concerning ways in which particular parts of texts are to be read and interpreted. Prince has suggested that narrative texts include both narrative statements that advance the narrative itself and metanarrative signs or narrative self-references that concentrate on the codes according to which readers make sense of narratives. For example, as Prince has demonstrated, ''Mary was crying'' is a narrative statement; it advances the plot or action of a narrative. In the sentence,

"Mary was crying; this was a mystery," however, the second clause is not a narrative statement but a metanarrative signal to the reader about how to read and interpret the first clause concerning Mary's action or state of mind.

Children's narratives, as well as those for adults, contain metanarrative signals to the reader. In the verbal interactions around printed narratives, the adult storyreader in this study provided a wealth of metanarrative information in addition to the information found in the text itself. The storyreader essentially transformed the usually internalized and automatic reading process of the literate adult readers of this community into an outwardly explicit and gradual sense-building process for its literary apprentices (Cochran-Smith, in press).

The storyreader offered metanarrative information and hence instructed the children in how to make sense of literature by signalling them to use, or using for them, four kinds of knowledge as they read and interpreted texts: knowledge of the world, of literary conventions, of story or narrative, and of how to respond as a member of a reading audience. The storyreader did not directly remind the children to use these four types of knowledge at specific points in stories. Nor did she consciously engage in metanarrative activity. On the contrary, the storyreader's metanarrative commentary occurred because she wanted to share a good (i.e., funny, entertaining, interesting, informative, scary, or timely) story with the children.

The context of storyreading was never to teach the children how to read or understand a story, and the goal was never to offer instruction in how to enjoy a story. Rather, the context of storyreading was shared understanding itself, and the goal was enjoyment itself.

Despite the fact that instruction was neither the goal nor the context of storyreading, implicit in the reader's interactions with the children was a model of how four kinds of knowledge could be used in order to make sense of texts. Each of these is discussed and illustrated with segments of actual storyreadings in the pages that follow.

Using knowledge of the world

In many reader-listener interaction sequences, the reader guided the children to use their world knowledge to recognize the objects, persons, places, and actions that were verbally or pictorially presented. In these sequences, the reader either called the children's attention to certain items, invited them to identify these items, or—when they seemed unable to do so themselves—identified the items for them. These sequences were often introduced by reader language such as, "what's that?" "*is* that a . . . ?" "look at that . . ." or "that's a . . ."

Labeling. One way of taking information from one's general knowledge of the world was to identify and correctly label the items, actions, and characters in books. In the story being shared in Segment 10, for instance, a little boy was building a snowman. Arrow-marked interactions point out how the storyreader guided the children to use general world knowledge in order to label correctly the orange object that was used for the snowman's nose.

As Storyreading Segment 10 shows, the teacher encouraged the children to use their knowledge of the characteristics of various items in order to figure out the identity of the item that became the snowman's nose. Although the meatball suggestion was ignored and the carrot suggestion was rejected with only a circular gesture toward the snowman's round nose, the reader generally tried to get the children to consider the shape and the color of the item pictured in relation to the knowledge they already had about the shapes and colors of the items they suggested. The reader did not explain why the Easter egg idea was not plausible in a winter story, but the suggestion itself was made playfully, and the reader responded in kind by chuckling at the child's joke.

Storyreading Segment 10 The Snowman (Briggs)

	Reader		Listeners	
Focal Points	Verbal	Nonverbal	Verbal	Nonverbal
→	Amy: WHAT'S THAT HE'S GOT, BEN?	points to pictures of boy adding	Anna, Jody: Carrot!	
→	THAT'S NO CARROT!	round, orange object to form snowman's nose; taps round ob-	?: Carrot! Mark: Meatballs! Meatballs! (calling out excitedly)	

(continued)

	Reader		Listeners	
Focal Points	*Verbal*	*Nonverbal*	*Verbal*	*Nonverbal*
		ject in circular motion		
			Bobby: Meatball! Meatball! Meatball!	
			Anna: __ __ Kris: Oranges!	
→	(laughs) YES, KRIS, I THINK YOU . . . THAT'S RIGHT!			
			?: Meatballs, meat-balls, meatballs! Anna: They're oranges! Jody: Oranges! ?: Tangerine?	
→	WELL, IT'S KIND OF OVAL LIKE A TANGERINE.	makes oval shape with hands		
			?: Oranges. Mark: Meatball! ?: Tangeriiiiine! (draws out)	
→	DOES IT LOOK MORE LIKE A TANGERINE? I DON'T KNOW; IT DOESN'T TELL ME.	turns book to herself for a closer look		
			Brad: Hey (excited) know what? Maybe it's a egg! (playful)	
→	(chuckles) BUT IT'S NOT WHITE. (chuckles)			
			Brad: Maybe it's a Easter egg . . .! ?: Orange Brad: that they sav-ed from Easter! (laughs)	
		* * *		

In addition to guiding the children in their naming of pictured items or the characteristics of pictured items, the storyreader frequently helped the children with definitions of words that the children did not seem to know, or that the storyreader assumed they would not know. This defining strategy frequently occurred very quickly as the storyreader repeated sentences from the text with synonyms substituted for troublesome words.

Similarly the storyreader sometimes simply paused in her reading of a text and provided explicit lexical information. When a text mentioned that a boy painted a mural, for example, the reader simply interrupted the text and inserted, "he painted a big picture; a mural is a bi-ig picture," as she tapped the mural in the illustration.

Taking information from one's knowledge of the world was important not only for identifying items but also for pointing out their particular characteristics that helped the reader to make appropriate inferences about characters, time and place settings, and actions. In Storyreading Segment 11, for instance, the book being shared was a loose retelling of "King Midas" featuring a young genie. In the interaction sequences marked with arrows, we can see how the reader guided the children to infer that the genie's mother, who had just appeared on the scene, was a magical creature just like her son.

In this example, the text specifically revealed the identity of the female character who was pictured (she was Oliver's mother), and the reader remarked that she was a magical lady. When the children seemed rather blank about all this, however, the storyreader made explicit the process according to which she herself had inferred this information

Storyreading Segment 11 The Sweet Touch (Balian)

Focal Points	Reader		Listeners	
	Verbal	*Nonverbal*	*Verbal*	*Nonverbal*
	Amy: Then "they were both sound asleep when Oliver's mother flitted (right) into the room. She had been looking for Oliver all that night. 'My, what a mess,' she murmured			

(continued)

Storyreading Segment 11 *Continued*

	Reader		Listeners	
Focal Points	*Verbal*	*Nonverbal*	*Verbal*	*Nonverbal*
	softly. 'What am I gonna (t: going to) do with that boy?'''			
→	SEE HIS MOTHER IS A MAGICAL PERSON, TOO. SHE'S A MAGICAL PERSON.	points to mother		children look over, blankly
→	DOES SHE LOOK LIKE A *REAL* LITTLE LADY?			
			Nat: Mmm hmm. (quietly)	
→	SHE'S KIND OF TINY. AND WHAT DOES SHE HAVE ON HER SHOULDERS LIKE OLIVER? WHAT DOES SHE HAVE UP ON HER SHOULDERS?	points to wings		
			Mark: I don't know . . .	
			Nat: Wings! (exclaiming)	
→	CAN YOU SEE THOSE WINGS? THAT'S RIGHT, NAT KNOWS.		Nat: Wings!	
→	JUST LIKE LITTLE OLIVER HAS WINGS; AND I THINK SHE DOESN'T HAVE ANY COLOR ON HER CLOTHES, DOES SHE?			
			Anna: She has white on her color.	
→	YES, SHE'S ALL WHITE	TP * * *		

about the character. She urged the children to notice certain pictured details—the mother didn't look like a real mother; she was very small; she had wings on her shoulders like her son did; and she was dressed all in white—in order to infer the mother's most important attribute. To reach the conclusion that the mother was a genie like her son, textual information had to be considered in relation to both the children's knowledge of the world (e.g., comparison of the size of Oliver's mother with the size of other adult women) and information already presented in the text (Oliver had wings in this story and *he* was a genie). In this Text-to-Life interaction sequence, initiated in response to the children's confusion about the identity of the mother character, the storyreader clarified the process of making inferences in picture books.

Labeling and the interrelationships of texts. In many interaction sequences, the children were called on to recognize or identify items and objects. Many of these sequences resemble the mother-child picture-book dialogues described by Ninio and Bruner (1978), who suggested that very young children learn the concept of labeling through the adult-dominated conversation that surrounds the activity of looking at the pictured items in books. The initial questioning pattern used by the mother in Ninio and Bruner's study and by the storyreader in this study is particularly similar ("what's that?", "that is a . . .", "is this a . . . ?"). The differences between the two, however, are very important.

Ninio and Bruner's description indicates that via an adult-child dialogue, a 10- to 18-month-old child was learning both the concept of lexical labeling and specific labels for various pictured items. The three-to-five-year-old children in Maple Nursery School, on the other hand, had long since achieved the concept of lexical labeling; furthermore, although they were introduced to some new labels, they were already familiar with the names for most of the items that they were called upon to identify. Hence, nursery-school storyreading interactions built upon both the children's prior achievement of lexical labels and the adult-child dialogue of early storyreadings.

Ninio and Bruner's child was exposed to labels in isolation; the child in their study was called upon to identify or confirm the identity of discrete, specifically pictured objects in picture-books. The nursery-school children, however, were guided to identify or recognize the characteristics of objects, characters, places, and actions in relation to the overall context of the particular story being shared. The reader called the children's attention to relationships among the various parts of pictures and to the relationships implied between the pages. Hence, the nursery-school children were called upon continually to balance their world knowledge with textual information in order to make sense of texts.

That the children were expected to see relationships between items and in relation to overall texts is indicated by the language patterns used in these interaction sequences. Frequently the children were asked to make comparisons (e.g., "well, it's kind of oval *like a tangerine . . .*"; "does it look more *like a tangerine?*"; "does she look *like a real live lady?*"; "and what does she have on her shoulders *like Oliver?*"; ". . . just *like little Oliver* has wings"). These analogic relationships imply a more sophisticated use of world and textual knowledge than simple identification of discrete items. Furthermore, the nursery-school children had to do a great deal of inferring in order to achieve the identification of items. They had to conclude, for example, that a pictured item was an orange and not a carrot, because of their world knowledge that oranges are round and orange-colored and their textual knowledge that the nose of the snowman in the picture was round and not long and skinny.

In interaction sequences of this sort in which children were, in a sense, taught to take information from their knowledge of the world to make sense of printed texts, two very important rules of reading were made explicit. First, *when one reads a book, he or she must integrate all the information given.* Items cannot simply be identified in isolation; rather, the relationships that objects, characters, places, and actions have to one another have to be figured out and accounted for. That is, everything in the text ought to make sense on a holistic level and should also be consistent with one's knowledge of the world. Second, the *reading process requires that the reader make many inferences.* Neither the text nor the pictures explicitly provide all the information needed; instead, the reader/listener uses the information that is provided in conjunction with the information he or she already has of the world. Hence, the reader/listener takes an active role in the process of making sense of texts.

Connotations. Barthes' *S/Z* (1974) is helpful when considering ways in which readers use their knowledge of the world to make sense of text. Barthes describes five narrative codes or groups of norms in terms of which narrative is made legible or readable. His fifth code, the cultural, is used to describe the many codes of knowledge or wisdom to which texts implicitly refer. Barthes suggests that fluent readers continuously, and more or less unconsciously, call up needed information from a broad array of past experiences in order to understand texts. They read and interpret texts in terms, for example, of their concepts of "Italian-ness" or "The Code of Psychology" when these are implicitly referred to in texts. The kind of knowledge Barthes describes is more complicated than knowledge of the labels or physical attributes of objects and places. What Barthes is describing is a way of taking information from a broader kind of knowledge that acts as a framework within which texts can become accessible or readable. Storyreading Segment 12 illustrates how this way of using world knowledge was integral to storyreading. In this example you will see how the storyreader helped the children frame their reading of one part of a pirate adventure in terms of connotations for the phrase, "walk the plank."

We can see in Segment 12 that in order to understand what was happening to the little girl in the picture, it was not enough for the children to label "plank" and the action, "walking." Rather, "walking the plank" needed to be related to all of the things that the phrase commonly connotes—pirate ships and treasure and rescues—or all of what Barthes might call "The Code of Pirateness." The world experience that the nursery-school children had with "pirateness" was their

Storyreading Segment 12: Come Away from the Water Shirley (Burningham)

| Focal Points | Reader | | Listeners | |
	Verbal	Nonverbal	Verbal	Nonverbal
	Amy: WAIT A MINUTE! (excited) WHAT'S HAPPENED TO HER HERE?	points to Shirley on plank	Andrew: Walk the plank!	
→	WALK THE PLANK LIKE IN PETER PAN? LIKE WHEN THEY TRIED TO GET WENDY TO WALK THE PLANK?	* * *		

own dramatization of "Peter Pan." Thus, when a child labeled the story character's action as "walking the plank," the storyreader built on this label by relating it to Wendy's walking the plank in the Peter Pan story. Mention of this literary reference called upon the children to use their previous knowledge of pirateness as a framework for understanding pirates and pirate ships, walking the plank, falling overboard, and using a map to dig for buried treasure (all of which were to be parts of the story).

When the nursery-school listeners did not seem to have the world knowledge that was needed to make all of a particular text accessible, the storyreader tried to supply this knowledge for them or remind them of it. To make sense of the humor of the book in Storyreading Segment 13 for example, the listeners needed to use their knowledge of the habitats and characteristics of various kinds of animals. For most of the text, however, the children did not seem to "get it." Consequently, as arrow-marked sequences point out, the storyreader attempted to fill in for them or prod them toward the needed referential framework.

In this example the teacher was filling in for the children the knowledge they apparently did not have about animal traits and habitats. As she supplied this information, it served as a framework within which the children could interpret the text and pictures to make sense of the text as a "joke," as something that was amusing.

Storyreading Segment 13: Animals Should Definitely Not Wear Clothing (Barrett)

Focal Points	Reader		Listeners	
	Verbal	Nonverbal	Verbal	Nonverbal
	Amy: [LP: sheep in muffler, wool sweater, winter hat—looks very hot] "Because a sheep might find it terribly . . ." HOT TO WEAR ALL THAT CLOTHING! (laughs)		Davey: Hot! (no response from the children)	

Storyreading Segment 13 *Continued*

	Reader		Listeners	
Focal Points	*Verbal*	*Nonverbal*	*Verbal*	*Nonverbal*
	LOOK AT THE POOR THING! (laughs)	points to sheep		
→	(Pretends to pant)	points to all the sheep's clothing		
→	DO YOU KNOW THAT SHEEP HAVE TO PANT VERY MADLY TO GET THE HEAT OUT OF THEIR BODIES? THEY DON'T GET WATER COMING OUT OF THEIR BODIES LIKE PEOPLE. THEY DON'T PERSPIRE. THEY JUST HAVE TO GO HAH-HA-HA-HAHHH (panting) LIKE CANDY (a dog) DOES WHEN SHE'S REALLY HOT.		Melissa: No.	several children pretend to pant, look at Candy
	LOOK AT HIM!	points to picture		
			Melissa: But he should have a drink!	
	HE'LL HAVE TO DRINK AN IMMENSE AMOUNT OF WATER.	* * *		

Like knowledge of labels, connotative knowledge of the world had to be related to the events of each text as a whole. There was consistent encouragement by the storyreader for the listeners to use their prior experiences of the world in order to make sense of texts holistically. For example, the teacher explained about Santa Claus's false teeth in one story by providing the referential framework of one child's grandfather who removed his denture plate to entertain the children when he visited the nursery school. However, the teacher did not suggest the false-teeth reference in isolation; rather, she offered it in relation to what Santa Claus was doing in that particular story.

Relevance in reading. During interaction sequences of the kind I have been describing here, the nursery-school children were exposed to some new knowledge. More important, however, they were being consistently instructed in how to take information from their knowledge of the world (both old and new) in order to make sense of whole texts. They were not simply asked, "what's that?" but rather "what's that *he's got in his hand?*" or "what did this boy *get for his birthday?*" The rule seemed to be this: *when one reads a text, he or she must realize the relevance of various objects and their attributes for the text as a whole, and integrate knowledge of the world with knowledge of the text.*

This rule of relevance in reading was especially clear when the nursery-school children volunteered information or personal incidents. When the information was not relevant to the text, however, the storyreader either tried to make it relevant by linking it to the text in some way, or discouraged the child from sharing the information during the storyreading. In Storyreading Segment 14, two children offered personal incidents as the storyreader was sharing a book about the fossilization process. Notice that the storyreader linked the first child's information to the book. When she was unable to link the information contributed by the second child, however, she discouraged the child from sharing her story.

In Storyreading Segment 14, following the text that explained what happens to animals when they die, Alan volunteered information about a friend's gerbil. The storyreader related this piece of information to the text by asking about the gerbil's burial and whether Alan thought it might become a fossil. Similarly, when Alice mentioned seeing a fish, the storyreader tried to tie it to the text by asking whether Alice's fish was dead like the fish described in the text. When Alice's story turned out to be completely irrelevant to fossils, the storyreader turned back to the text. Despite Alice's continued efforts to tell about her trip to Maryland, the teacher did not allow her to regain the floor with this irrelevant information.

A comparison of the way the teacher responded to these two children makes explicit the rule of relevance in reading: *a reader must take information from his or her knowledge of the world in ways that are related to the information contained in the text at hand.* Hence, even though the text was about the fossilization of a fish, Alice's fish story was not appropriate. Alan's story of a buried gerbil, however, *could be*

Storyreading Segment 14: Fossils Tell of Long Age (Aliki)

	Reader		Listeners	
Focal Points	*Verbal*	*Nonverbal*	*Verbal*	*Nonverbal*
	Amy:		⌈(several children talk- ing—indiscernible)	

	THAT FISH BECAME
	A FOSSIL . . .
		points to
		picture
			⌊Alan: ___ ___ ___ and
			  when his gerbil
			  died, he took it to
			  the garbage.	

→	AND DID HE BURY IT SOMEWHERE?			

			Alan: He ___ ___ ___
			  (several children still
			  talking)	

→	IS IT GONNA TURN INTO A ROCK AND BECOME A FOSSIL, DO YOU THINK? BE MASHED INTO ROCK?			
			Alan: Yeah. (uncertain)	
→	I DOUBT IT. I DOUBT IT.	shakes head TP		

	(CONTINUES READING)
	". . . The minerals in
	the water were left
	behind in the fish
	bones, (and) after a
	very long time the
	minerals changed the
	bones into stone."
	THIS FISH WAS
	CHANGED INTO A
	FOSSIL.
		points to
		series of
		pictures
		showing
		fossiliza-
		tion of
		fish
			Alice: Am-. . .
			
			Alice: Hey Amy,
			  Amy, guess what?
			
			Alice: Down in Mary-
			  land, me and my
			  daddy, we was on
			  the dock and we saw
			  a big, big, big fish.	

	WHAT?			
	OOOH! (interested)			
→	A DEAD ONE?		Alice: No it wasn't	shakes

(*continued*)

Storyreading Segment 14 *Continued*

Focal Points	Reader		Listeners	
	Verbal	*Nonverbal*	*Verbal*	*Nonverbal*
	OH, LUCKILY IT WAS STILL ALIVE, HUH? THAT WAS LUCKY FOR *THAT* FISH.		dead. It swum away.	head
			Alice: Hey, guess what?	
→	YEAH? YOU SEE THE OTHER FISH THAT IT ATE IN- SIDE OF HIM?	points to picture	Nat: Both of them are dead?	
→	YES, BOTH OF THEM ARE DEAD, AND THEY BOTH TURNED INTO STONE.			
			Nat: How come they're *both* dead?	
		turns back to pre- vious page		
→	WELL, THIS ONE WAS INSIDE THIS ONE, AND THE BIG ONE DIED AND ALL THE MEAT ROTTED OFF (*in lower pitch, scowls*).—THE SKIN AND THE MEAT AND ONLY THE BONES WERE LEFT. THAT'S WHY THEY CAN TELL. THE BONES TURNED INTO STONE.			
			Alice: Amy, down in Mar . . .	

Storyreading Segment 14   *Continued*

	Reader		Listeners	
Focal Points	*Verbal*	*Nonverbal*	*Verbal*	*Nonverbal*
→	THAT'S STRANGE ISN'T IT? DID THIS PLANT TURN INTO STONE?	holds up fossil	Alice: Down in Mar . . .	
→	DID IT?		Nat: (nods) Yeah	
→	THAT FERN TURNED INTO STONE, DIDN'T IT?	nods		
			Alice: Hey Amy, Amy, guess what?	
	WHAT (unenthusiastically)?	TP		
			Alice: Down in Mary- land they got . . .	
→	HEY MARK, MARK, SEE THAT FERN IN THE PICTURE? THAT FERN BE- CAME STONE (raises voice over Alice)	points		
		* * *		

made to be relevant to the printed information and therefore was allowed. Through different kinds of teacher responses to their contributions the nursery-school children were learning that they could not take randomly from their knowledge of the world, but only in ways that specifically tied text and experience.

Using knowledge of literary conventions

Literary conventions can be considered "not simply as the implicit knowledge of the reader but also as the implicit knowledge of authors" (Culler, 1975, p. 116). Conventional understandings about literature act as frameworks within which readers are able to make sense of texts; likewise, authors are able to create texts because of shared assumptions about the ways that texts work. The nursery-school storyreader guided the children to make sense of texts in terms of two general sets of literary conventions: bookmaking conventions and genre conventions.

Bookmaking conventions. Several storyreading interactions centered around the conventions of published books, including some of the conventions of printed language. Most frequent were interaction sequences in which the storyreader introduced books according to their titles. The procedure for introducing a book by its title was extremely consistent. To begin a book, the reader called for the children's attention, held up the front cover of the book that she was about to read, told the children how the title functioned (e.g., "now, this *is called . . .*" or "this one *is about . . .*"), and read the title of the book while pointing to the words and showing the cover-picture. These introductory actions served both to reinforce the rug-time framework that separated bookreading from all other nursery-school activities and to indicate that the title of a book offers important information about what is inside. In this way, the children were exposed to the idea that titles give some general idea of what books are about and provide frameworks within which readings occur. A similar closing procedure wherein the reader again held up the front cover of a book and repeated its title signalled the end of the reading framework.

In addition to introducing the children to the convention of book titles and cover illustrations as orienting frames, nursery-school storyreading interactions also exposed them to other book and print conventions. These included: the dedication of a book to a particular person; the use of printed words to represent sounds; the use of print size and paginal arrangement to represent meaning; the use of comic-strip speech-balloons to indicate what characters say; and the idea that books are written by real persons or authors.

It is difficult for us, as fluent readers, to uncover the assumptions we automatically make when we look at simple children's books. And yet, as I have indicated previously, we are not born with instincts about how to relate picture-book texts and illustrations; we learn how to do this. A basic book convention in which the nursery-school children were instructed was that within a single book the printed text and pictures go together.

For example, if the text tells us that a little dog is going down the street, and the pictures show a black Scotty with a red collar and three puppies trailing behind her, we probably can infer that the dog in the text is a black Scotty, as shown in the picture. The nursery-school children did not have much difficulty making this assumption; this was due, in part, to the fact that the storyreader often transformed indefinite pronouns in texts into definite ones and supported the verbal text by pointing at the appropriate pictures. Thus, when the text read, "I saw *an* enormous goldfish coming at me,'' the storyreader read, ''I saw *this* enormous goldfish coming toward me'' and pointed at or tapped the picture of the fish.

Genre conventions. Knowledge of the genre of a particular text provides the reader with an important metanarrative signal about how the text is to be read. In effect, it says to the reader: *read this text in the light of other texts of this same kind; expect this text to be related to others in its generic class.* Tabbert (1979), quoting Jauss (1975), comments on the importance to the reading process of the reader's expectations for a particular genre, or what Jauss calls the reader's ''horizons of expectations'':

> The analysis of the literary experience of the reader . . . describes the response and impact of a work within the definable frame of reference of the reader's expectations; this frame of reference for each work develops in the historical moment of its appearance from a previous understanding of the genre (Jauss in Tabbert, p. 94).

At the nursery school, reader/listeners' expectations for particular kinds of books were limited because their general experience with books was limited. And yet, even for these three-to-five-year-old children, there was—in several Type II Life-to-Text sequences—evidence of the beginnings of generic instruction. That is, the teacher encouraged the children to read and interpret individual books in light of their belonging to particular groups of works. In the arrow-marked sequences in Storyreading Segment 15, for example, the storyreader offered the children information about the genre of the book being shared: ''wordless picture books.'' This information functioned as metanarrative—a signal about how the book was to be read and interpreted.

In Segment 15, the storyreader specifically related one wordless book to the reading of a similar wordless picture-book that the children had read several times during the preceding month. In doing so, the storyreader offered the children metanarrative information about the genre, ''wordless picture-book'' and reminded them that in making sense of a book of this kind, they needed to look carefully at the pictures and construct the narrative that was visually implied. In this example, Tabbert's ''horizon of expectations'' about a particular kind of book is aptly demonstrated. The storyreader's implicit message to the children was something like this: *think of the book, X; think of the way you read the book, X; this new book, Y, is in the same class of books as X; read Y in the same way that you read X.*

Storyreading Segment 15: The Snowman (Briggs)

Focal Points	Reader		Listeners	
	Verbal	*Nonverbal*	*Verbal*	*Nonverbal*
→	NOW REMEMBER THAT BOOK, *FATHER CHRISTMAS*?	holds up "Snowman" book		
			(several children talking)	
→	YOU REMEMBER *FATHER CHRISTMAS*?			
			Susie: "Father Christmas"? No.	
→	YEAH, THE ONE . . .			
		holds up book to first page; taps pictures	Several: Yeah, yes, no.	
→	NOW, YOU HAVE TO *WATCH* THE PICTURES AND SEE WHAT HAPPENS . . .			
		* * *		

A key illustration of learning to use knowledge of the conventions of literary genres was the children's experiences with a riddle book that was a favorite at the nursery school, and consequently was read several times over the 18-month period in which I observed. In Storyreading Segment 16, you will see how the reader worked to frame the children's reading of the book within the conventions of the genre, "riddle."

In trying to help the children make sense of the text in Storyreading Segment 16, the teacher emphasized that the way into the book was via the generic conventions of the riddle. As she introduced the book, she explained the task of the reader/listeners ("okay, see how many we can get") and emphasized immediately that the thing to do with this book was to "get it" by guessing ("nope, guess again . . . guess again"). After reading the question-half of the riddle, the storyreader paused to allow the children to try to come up with the answer-half and encouraged them to guess again and again. Children's responses to some of the

Storyreading Segment 16: Silliest Pop-Up Riddles Ever (Cerf)

	Reader		Listeners	
Focal Points	*Verbal*	*Nonverbal*	*Verbal*	*Nonverbal*
→	Amy: ANDREW, HONEY, BRING THE RID-DLE BOOK OVER. I'LL DO THAT ONE FIRST, AND THEN I'LL BE ABLE TO DO THIS ONE. OKAY, ANDREW?		(children getting settled on rug, some squabbling over seats, etc.)	
→	WOULD YOU LIKE TO HEAR THOSE SILLIEST POP-UP RIDDLES EVER?	holds up book		
			Andrew: Mmmm hmm.	
→	OKAY, SEE HOW MANY WE CAN GET.			
→	OKAY, THESE ARE THE SILLIEST POP-UP RIDDLES. [PIC: man sitting on bed in pajamas] OKAY, NOW, "what do you take off last before getting into bed?"	TP		
			Curt: Your clothes! ?: Your clothes!	
→	NOPE, GUESS AGAIN.			
			Anne: Pajamas! (yelling out)	
	NO, YOU DON'T TAKE OFF YOUR PAJAMAS . . . WHEN YOU GET		?: Your clothes	

(continued)

Storyreading Segment 16 *Continued*

	Reader		Listeners	
Focal Points	*Verbal*	*Nonverbal*	*Verbal*	*Nonverbal*
→	INTO BED GUESS AGAIN			
			?: Your clothes Andrew: We give up.	
	NOPE "Your feet off the floor (in laughing voice)"			
			Joannie: Yeah . . .	
→	(laughs)			
→	HA! HA! HA! THAT'S A RIDDLE!	TP * * *		
	[PIC: raspberry rider on a horse]			
	Okay, "what is red, has bumps, rides a horse and lives in the prairie?"			
→	LOOK AT THE PICTURE.	points to picture of rider		
→	THE PICTURE CAN HELP YOU.			
			Curt: Cowboy!	
→	CAN YOU GUESS, BEN?			
			Ben: I don't know.	
	THE LONE RASPBERRY!			
→	(laughing)		(no response)	
→	THE LONE RASPBERRY! HA! HA! HA!			
			Andrew: How 'bout the lone ra . . ., the lone ranger?	
→	YEAH, IT'S SUPPOSED TO			

Storyreading Segment 16 *Continued*

Focal Points	Reader		Listeners	
	Verbal	*Nonverbal*	*Verbal*	*Nonverbal*
→	SOUND LIKE THE LONE RANGER, BUT IT'S PRETENDING THAT YOU DON'T KNOW HOW TO SAY LONE RANGER. THE LONE RASPBERRY! IT'S A RIDDLE. IT'S A CUCKOO RIDDLE! (laughs)	* * *	(no response)	

riddles indicated that they were beginning to understand both this question-answer form and that there was a more or less standard answer for each riddle question.

In many of the interaction sequences, the storyreader provided further metanarrative information about the riddle: she directly explained that the way to respond to a riddle was to laugh, and she modeled that response by laughing in an exaggerated way herself. The storyreader's comments told the children that riddles were funny: *the appropriate response after the question-half of a riddle was to guess or try to answer, but the appropriate response after the answer-half was to laugh.* Finally the reader also tried to help the children understand the basis of the humor of the riddles in the book, which included encountering the unexpected, playing with double meanings, orthographic rearrangement, and phonological similarity.

As we saw in the "lone raspberry" riddle, the reader tried to help the children see that riddle questions were not supposed to be answered or understood in the same way that everyday questions were answered. "The lone ranger" might be a good response to a question concerning a rider on the prairie, but it was not a good response when the question about the rider was a riddle. So the reader explained, "Yeah it's supposed to *sound like* 'the lone ranger,' but it's pretending that you don't know how to say, 'lone ranger' " and made explicit the process of using one's knowledge of genre to read and make sense of riddles.

That the children were slowly learning to make sense of riddle texts in terms of their expectations for this genre was indicated by their own "reading" of parts of the same riddle book during a storyreading more than a year after the reading in Segment 16. Notice the children's use of some of the conventions of the riddle (see Storyreading Segment 17).

As Storyreading Segment 17 indicates, Nat knew the question-and-answer pattern of riddles, but did not understand that he had to pause and wait for the listeners to guess before he gave the punch line. Also, Nat did not read his riddle in the announcing prosody that the adult storyreader (and Mark) always used for riddles. Mark, on the other hand, had internalized many aspects of reading riddles: he knew the two-part question-and-answer form; he knew the correct combination of announcing prosody and pausing; he reached a crescendo immediately before the punch line and laughed hysterically after he had revealed the answer. As his sleep-without-a-bird riddle shows, however, Mark did not fully understand why it was that riddles were funny, but he had the form, the delivery and the appropriate response for this genre under control.

Storyreading Segment 17: Silliest Pop-Up Riddles Ever (Cerf) (Note: the storyreaders, Nat and Mark, are children.)

Points	Reader		Listeners	
Focal Points	Verbal	Nonverbal	Verbal	Nonverbal
		(a puppet show has just concluded, so Nat goes behind the stage to "read" the riddle book)	Amy (the teacher): Okay, Nat has a couple riddles to do.	
			Amy: Jeffrey? Be really quiet, we can't hear Nat's riddles too well.	
→	Nat: Uh, where do ya get milk from? (in hur-	holds up picture of two-horned		

Storyreading Segment 17 *Continued*

Points	Reader		Listeners	
Focal Points	Verbal	Nonverbal	Verbal	Nonverbal
→	ried, mumbled voice) Nat: A milk truck (doesn't wait for others to answer).	cow/milk truck (in "pop-up" style; one is overlaid)	Mark: A cow! (yelling) (Mark starts to laugh hysterically; several imitate him) Amy: What has one horn and gives milk? (very slowly and distinctly repeats Nat's riddle) Anna: A cow! Mark: Ooooh-ahhh! Aaahhhh! (laughs hysterically) Amy: A cow? It has *one* horn? A cow has *two* horns, doesn't it? Amy: Wait . . . okay, wait, put . . . I can't hear Nat . . .	several children laughing; Jeffrey playing loudly with blocks; Nat starts another riddle— (indiscernible) walks over to Jeffrey and other children several minutes of reorganiza-

(*continued*)

Storyreading Segment 17 *Continued*

	Reader		Listeners	
Focal Points	Verbal	Nonverbal	Verbal	Nonverbal
				tion, getting children set-tled, etc.
		Nat is turning pages	Amy: Okay, do you want to do this one? (to Nat)	points to riddle page Nat has open
			Amy: Okay, go back to this page. Okay, hold it up . . . hold it up . . .	helps Nat find place, helps him to hold book up and out toward children
			Amy: That's it!	
	Nat: What's the best way to get a squirrel? (sort of mumbling)		Davey: I'm so glad it's . . .	
			Amy: Wait, say it louder, I couldn't hear you.	
	Nat: What's the best way to catch a squir-rel, climb up a tree and act like a nut? (very fast, breathless, doesn't pause to allow any of the listeners to answer)			
				several minutes pass while Nat leaves puppet stage; Mark goes behind stage to "read" some riddles

Storyreading Segment 17 *Continued*

Points	Reader		Listeners	
Focal Points	*Verbal*	*Nonverbal*	*Verbal*	*Nonverbal*
	Mark: HOW CAN YOU SLEEP WITH-OUT A BIRD? (no one really hears this)			many children moving around, talking
			Amy: All right, wait . . . Jeff-rey, could you guys come over a minute? We can't hear. We can't hear. Amy: It's too much noise.	moves toward Jeffrey's group
	Mark: I DON'T NEED THE BOOK.	hands riddle book to Amy		
			Amy: Oh, no, no, but . . .	
	Mark: AMY, I DON'T NEED THE BOOK. (insisting)			
			Amy: Okay	
→	Mark: HOW CAN YOU SLEEP . . . (dramatic pause) WITH-OUT A BIRD? (very clear, in perfect rid-dle intonation; (then pauses to allow listeners to supply answer)			
→			Amy: How can you sleep without a bird? (repeating the riddle question for Mark)	
→	Mark: BE-			

(*continued*)

Storyreading Segment 17 *Continued*

Points	Reader		Listeners	
Focal Points	*Verbal*	*Nonverbal*	*Verbal*	*Nonverbal*
	CAUSE . . . YOUR BED CAN'T FLY! (loud, delivering 'punch line', very pleased with himself)	starts to laugh hysterically		several other children join in the laughter
			Amy: Okay, do you know any others?	
	Mark: YEAH.		Amy: All right, you know any other riddles?	
→	Mark: WHAT HAS, WHAT IS, A KEY THAT CAN KICK VERY HARD?			
			Nat: A kangaroo!	
→	Mark: NO . . . (pauses, ready for the 'punch line') . . .			
→	A DONK . . . (long pause) KEY-KEY. (quieter, slightly uncertain)			adults applaud several children start to laugh with adults
			Amy: Oh, that's funny! A *don*-KEY!	
→	Mark: WHAT KEY LIVES IN THE ZOO?		Amy: What key lives in the	

Storyreading Segment 17   *Continued*

Points	Reader		Listeners	
Focal Points	Verbal	Nonverbal	Verbal	Nonverbal
			zoo? (repeating for Mark) Nat: Donkey! Linda: Elephant zoo key! (referring to plastic animal-shaped keys purchased at the zoo)	
→	Mark: NO-OOOOH! (voice mounting, excited) . . .			
→	A MON-KEY! (excited, all ready to laugh)			
			Amy: Yes, that's very funny!	several children start to laugh, applaud

Using knowledge of narrative

Many analyses of narratives have been suggested.[3] Despite differences among these analyses, they all agree that a narrative centers around the actions of a protagonist who is trying to reach a goal of some sort. Many Life-to-Text interaction sequences in nursery-school storyreadings aimed to help the children make sense of texts by understanding these basics of narrative: characters and actions.[4]

---

[3]The work of Propp (1958) and Bartlett (1932) were seminal in this area. See also, for example, Mandler and Johnson, 1977; Maranda and Maranda, 1971; Rumelhart, 1975; Stein and Glenn, 1978; and Thorndyke, 1977.

[4]Much of the nonfiction intended for young children is written in narrative form; hence reader-listener interaction sequences around characters and actions were found in readings of both fiction and nonfiction selections.

The nursery-school storyreader worked hard in many interaction sequences to help the children use information from their developing knowledge of narrative structure in order to make sense of texts. There was a great deal of emphasis on story characters with questions like these: who is this character? how does he or she feel? why? what does the character's action tell you about how he or she feels? how will this person feel if a certain thing happens? what is the relationship between the feelings and actions of characters in this story? how have these feelings changed during the story? what do these characters want or need? why do they want or need this particular thing? All these questions had to do with the general topic of characterization in literature. They focused on understanding kinds of character traits and personalities, character developments and changes, and characters' motivations for actions.

There was also heavy emphasis during interaction sequences on the actions occurring in texts. Interaction sequences of this kind essentially tied characters and actions together and focused on helping the children find answers to such questions as: what is happening here? what happened before this? how are what is happening now and what happened before related to one another? what might happen later in the story? how did this happen? why did this happen? is what is happening real or imaginary? what is the relationship between what is happening and specific characters in the story? how will this action affect specific characters? All these questions were related to plot in literature. They focused on understanding sequences of actions, temporal and spatial relationships among various actions, cause and effect, the status of each action, and relationships between characters and actions. The relationship between character (feelings and needs) and action (what the character does about these feelings or needs) was the crux of many of the stories to which the nursery-school children were exposed.

It is obvious from the foregoing questions that there is a great deal of overlap between knowledge of actions (what is happening?) and knowledge of characters (to whom is it happening?). This overlapping relationship between character and action is perhaps the key to narrative; it is also one of the features of nursery-school storyreading that made it different from previously reported situations in which children were encouraged to acknowledge, provide, or repeat the lexical labels for discrete items or single actions.

As I have suggested earlier, through interaction sequences that helped the children use information from various kinds of knowledge, the storyreader made explicit the process of reading and making sense of texts. In sequences that helped them use knowledge of narrative, the storyreader, in effect, showed the children how to use the information in both pictures and verbal texts in order to make inferences about characters, actions, and the relationships between the two. Knowledge of characters and actions was to be integrated not only with one another but also with world knowledge, knowledge of literary conventions, and knowing how to respond as a member of the reading audience.

Using knowledge of character in narratives. One of the most important aspects of narratives used in making sense of texts was knowledge of characters, that is, understanding how characters felt in stories, the traits of particular characters, and ways in which characters responded or might respond to situations. Storyreading interactions essentially told the children that: (a) *it was important to make inferences about characters by integrating the information in pictures and texts;* and (b) *this information played an important role in what happened in a story.*

In Storyreading Segment 18, for example, notice how the storyreading emphasized the reciprocal relationship between how a character felt and what she did.

Storyreading Segment 18: Flicks (dePaola)

| Focal Points | Reader | | Listeners | |
	Verbal	Nonverbal	Verbal	Nonverbal
	Amy: [PIC: series of frames—1) title; 2) girl with birthday cake; 3) tries to blow candles; 4) tries harder; 5) looks disgusted; 6) throws pail of water on cake; 7) cake is melting, but girl looks pleased] HAPPY BIRTH-			

(*continued*)

Storyreading Segment 18 *Continued*

	Reader		Listeners	
Focal Points	*Verbal*	*Nonverbal*	*Verbal*	*Nonverbal*
	DAY TO YOU (singing) . . . AND SHE TRIES, BUT . . .	points to 3, points to 4		
	WHAT HAPPENED?			
→	LOOK AT HER FACE.	points to 5	Anne: She can't . . .	
	HOW DOES SHE FEEL?			
→	ANGRY?		Several: Angry, sad . . .	
→	SO LOOK WHAT SHE DID (laughs)	points to 6		
→	SHE WENT AND GOT A . . .	points to 6		
			Nat: Threw water on her cake.	
→	YEAH, A BIG PAIL OF WATER TO POUR ON.			
→	IS SHE HAPPY NOW?	points to 7		
			?: Yeah.	
→	BUT LOOK AT HER CAKE, LOOK AT THE FROSTING! (laughs)	points to 7		
			(no response)	
→	SHE'S HAPPY THE CAN-DLES ARE OUT, BUT LOOK AT			

Storyreading Segment 18 *Continued*

	Reader			Listeners	
Focal Points	*Verbal*	*Nonverbal*		*Verbal*	*Nonverbal*
	HER NICE CAKE, ALICE. A WRECK-Y CAKE (laughs)			(no response)	(Alice hits picture of spoiled cake)
		* * *			

The sequence in Segment 18 and others like it allow us to uncover some of the bookreading rules about using knowledge of characters that were implicit in reader-listener dialogue:

1. Pay attention to the actions of characters.
2. Pay attention to the facial expressions of pictured characters for information concerning how the characters feel.
3. Notice how the feelings of a character are sometimes the result of his or her actions.
4. Notice how the actions of a character are sometimes the result of his or her feelings.

These bookreading rules emphasized the importance of textual integration. It was not enough for the listeners to look at a picture or hear a text and simply realize how a character felt. They had to understand how a character felt in relation to both the actions that caused the character to have that feeling or that might result from that feeling and in relation to the structure of the narrative as a whole. The reader also helped the children infer character traits on the basis of actions and utterances. The message underlying this sort of inference was that characters could be judged according to the ways they behaved in texts.

Using knowledge of action in narrative. It was very difficult to separate reader-listener interaction sequences that focused on character from interaction sequences that focused on action. This difficulty arose from the fact that the reader so consistently integrated the two in her conversations with the children. Nevertheless, it is possible to point out some of the features of reader-listener sequences that focused on action in narratives. The focus of these sequences was, loosely, what we call "plot" in narrative, that is, what was "going on" in a story. Storyreadings of wordless books provide key examples of the storyreader's emphasis on the action of a story. In Storyreading Segment 19, you will see how the storyreader centered the dialogue around the action or plot of the story.

Storyreading Segment 19: Flicks (dePaolo)

	Reader		Listeners	
Focal Points	Verbal	Nonverbal	Verbal	Nonverbal
	Amy: This is called "Rhonda Rolls Along" [PIC: series of frames—1) title; 2) girl gets skates; 3) puts skates on; 4) starts to skate; 5) falls on behind; 6) ties pillow on behind; 7) skates; 8) starts to fall; 9) falls on chest; 10) puts pillow on front; 11) skates and slips; 12) falls on side; 13) crawls toward worktable; 14) "do not disturb" sign on door; 15) peeks out; 16) skates happily inside rolling "walker"]	holds up title		
→		* * * points to 3, 4, 5		
	SO RHONDA PUTS 'EM ON, SKATES ALONG. UH OH, WHAT HAPPENED?			
			Curt: Fell!	
→	FELL ON HER BUTT! (laughs)			

	Reader		Listeners	
Focal Points	*Verbal*	*Nonverbal*	*Verbal*	*Nonverbal*
→	AND NOW WHAT'S SHE DOING?	points to 6		
			Melissa: Tying his suit . . .	
→	NOW WHAT'S SHE DO TO FIX HERSELF UP? SO THAT SHE DOESN'T HURT HER BUTT ANYMORE?	points to 6		
		points to 6		
			?: Got up . . .	
→	SHE GOT UP AND SHE TIED HER . . .	points to pillow		
			Anne: Tied her teddy bear!	
→	SHE TIED A BIG . . . PILLOW RIGHT ONTO HER BUTT, SO THAT WHEN SHE FALLS DOWN NEXT TIME SHE WON'T GET HURT.			
		* * *		
	(laughs)		(several children laugh)	
→	SO LOOK, OFF SHE GOES SKATING, NOW LOOK WHAT HAPPENS!	points to 7, 8		
→	SHE SKATES ALONG, SKATES ALONG AND SHE FELL RIGHT ON HER . . . DID SHE FALL RIGHT ON HER BUTT?	points to 8, 9		
			Nat: Chin . . .	
→	YEAH, SO NOW WHAT'S SHE GOTTA DO?	points to 10		
		* * *		

In Segment 19, the storyreader repeatedly questioned the children about the little girl's actions of roller skating, falling, protecting herself with pillows, and building a walker. This interaction sequence suggests that there are specific aspects of action in narrative that can be identified as foci of the storyreader's commentary. Especially important among these are interactions that emphasized: (a) temporal sequence of actions (e.g., "So look, off she goes skating. *Now look* what happens!"); (b) the relationship between the causes and effects of actions (e.g., "Now what did she tie onto, what did she do *to fix herself up? so that she doesn't hurt* her butt anymore?")(c) relationships between what had happened and what would happen (e.g., "Yeah, so *now what's she gonna do?*"); and (d) the status of items, actions, or events as real or imaginary (e.g., "what was he doing *really?*").

Not all of these occurred in every storyreading; their occurrences in individual storyreadings depended to some extent on the nature of the particular book being shared and, of course, on the responses of the listeners. Nevertheless, interaction sequences that revolved around these four aspects of narrative action repeatedly occurred in storyreadings. Each aspect is described and illustrated below.

Storyreading Segment 20: Come Away from the Water Shirley (Burningham)

Focal Points	Reader		Listeners	
	Verbal	*Nonverbal*	*Verbal*	*Nonverbal*
→			Alice: Where are the pirates?	
			Alice: Where are the pirates?	
→	REMEMBER WHAT HAPPENED? DID YOU SEE WHAT			
→	HAPPENED?	TP back to sword-fight picture		
→	*THERE* WERE THE PIRATES, SHE WAS PLAYING WITH HER SWORD, AND . . .	points to fight picture		

Storyreading Segment 20 *Continued*

	Reader		Listeners	
Focal Points	*Verbal*	*Nonverbal*	*Verbal*	*Nonverbal*
	THAT'S THE SIDE OF THE BIG SHIP, SEE?	points to diving overboard picture points to ship in background	Susie: I can't see!	
→	SO OFF SHE GOES DOWN INTO THE WATER. WHERE ARE THE PIRATES? DOES ANYBODY SEE THEM?			
			?: No.	
→	YOU KNOW WHERE THEY WENT?	turns page to rowboat scene		
			Andrew: Up, up!	
→	THEY'RE STILL LEFT *UP* ON THE SHIP, HUH?			
		* * *		

Temporal sequence of actions. In her questions and comments to the children, the storyreader underlined the proper temporal sequence in which story actions occurred. The storyreader's comments were often linguistically marked by words that denoted temporality (e.g., after, now, then, before, a long time ago), and by voice stress on morphemes that indicated verb tenses. Storyreading Segment 20 provides an illustration of interaction around the temporal sequence of narrative action. Here you will see how the teacher emphasized the relationships in time of the various actions in the story.

In Segment 20, a child was confused about the sequence of actions in the story; she did not realize that *first,* Shirley was fighting with the pirates on the ship, *then,* she jumped overboard leaving the pirates on the ship, *then,* she got into a rowboat. The storyreader's response to the child's confusion reemphasizes the storyreader's role as a teacher of inference. That is, just like the key to making sense of a text in general, the key to making sense of temporal sequence in a text was based to a great extent on knowing how to draw inferences from the information in texts and pictures. The storyreader made explicit this process of knowing-how by pointing to appropriate pictures and commenting: (a) Shirley was fighting with the pirates; (b) Shirley jumped overboard; (c) Shirley dived down past the side of the ship into the water; (d) Shirley is now in a rowboat; therefore, (e) the pirates must still be up on the ship where Shirley left them.

Storyreading Segment 21: Barbapapa's New House (Tison and Taylor)

Focal Points	Reader		Listeners	
	Verbal	*Nonverbal*	*Verbal*	*Nonverbal*
	[RP: Barbapapa looks at his small house]			
	"Barbapapa was wondering if their house (is big) (t: was large) enough. He and Barbamama have seven children now."			
→	I THINK THEY'RE GONNA NEED A NEW HOUSE, DON'T YOU THINK SO?	TP		
			Several: Yeah.	
	[LP: All Barbapapas (B) crowd into house]			
	[RP: house bursts apart]			
→	DO YOU THINK THAT HOUSE IS BIG ENOUGH	points to house		
			Several: No.	
			?: Yeah! (being silly)	
	NOPE			
→	THE HOUSE IS TOO			

Storyreading Segment 21 *Continued*

	Reader		Listeners	
Focal Points	*Verbal*	*Nonverbal*	*Verbal*	*Nonverbal*
	SMALL. (sad voice) LOOK AT THAT, IT EVEN BREAKS A LITTLE BIT WHEN THEY ALL GET IN-SIDE. (sad voice) "Frank told them of an old abandoned house nearby." (hushed tone on 'abandoned')	points to picture		
	So "Barbabelle was cry-ing 'cause she had broken her beads." (sad, crying voice)	points to beads mimes crying		
→	SEE BARBABELLE? HER WHOLE NECK-LACE BROKE. [LP: B's in front of old house] [RP: cut-away view of house with B in each room]	TP		
	"The house was beauti-ful although it needed a lot of work."	* * *		
→	SEE, IT'S KIND OF A WRECK-Y OLD PLACE, ANDY? "It was fun for the whole family to work together. They quickly did the repairs and Barbabeau painted a (picture) (t: a mural) on the wall."	points to picture		

(continued)

Storyreading Segment 21 *Continued*

	Reader		Listeners	
Focal Points	*Verbal*	*Nonverbal*	*Verbal*	*Nonverbal*
→	SEE HOW THEY'RE PAINTING A PIC-TURE UP ON THAT WALL 'CAUSE THIS HOUSE IS TOO WRECK-Y. (says ''wreck-y'' in low, disgusted voice)	points to picture * * *		

Causes and effects of actions.   Intertwined with storyreader commentary that stressed the temporal sequence of narrative actions was commentary that stressed cause and effect. Interaction sequences of this kind centered around both the causes of various actions and their effects; these were often considered in relation to characters' feelings or states of mind. Storyreading Segment 21 includes several Life-to-Text sequences that underlined actions caused and affected by other actions and by characters' mental states.

In Segment 21, the storyreader repeatedly pointed out to the children the cause and effect relationships of various actions: the Barbapapas' house broke a little (effect), because it was too small (cause); the Barbapapas needed a new house (effect), because theirs was breaking apart (cause); Barbabelle cried (effect), because her necklace broke (cause); the new house needed work (effect), because it was ''wreck-y'' (cause); and they painted a mural on the wall (effect), because the house needed work (cause). The metaphorical overlay of the Barbapapa story (a vague ecological message about urban destruction and pollution) was not important in this storyreading. Rather, the reading revolved around sorting out the basic actions and why they occurred.

• *Relationships between prior and forthcoming actions.*   Part of making sense of the action in narrative is understanding actions or events that *have* occurred in relation to actions or events that *will* occur. This process of making predictions about actions was explicit in many storyreading interactions. In Storyreading Segment 22 some of the in-

Storyreading Segment 22: Snow White (Werner)

Focal Points	Reader		Listeners	
	Verbal	*Nonverbal*	*Verbal*	*Nonverbal*
		* * *		
→	WHERE'S SHE GOING, DEARIE, IN HER BOAT?	taps picture of wicked witch on her way to see Snow White		
→	WHERE IS SHE OFF TO, SUSIE?		Susie: To the woods. Several: the woods . . .	
	"She felt certain that her plan would succeed, for the magic spell of the Sleeping Death could be broken only by . . ."			
	(makes kissing sound) love's first kiss."	mimes kissing		
→	[RP: Snow White waves to seven dwarves, off to work]		Alice: I'm scared. Susie: She's gonna have a bite of the apple and she's gonna be dead. (announcing)	
→ →	"and certain that no lover would find Snow White, asleep in that (part) (t: in the forest) (so off she went). ". . . 'Be careful!' said the seven little men. 'Watch out for the Queen.' And		Nat: Not for real! Susie: I know. Now she'll be sleepin'; she's gonna be sleepin'.	

(continued)

Storyreading Segment 22 *Continued*

	Reader		Listeners	
Focal Points	*Verbal*	*Nonverbal*	*Verbal*	*Nonverbal*
	Snow White promised that she would.''			
→	IS SHE GONNA WATCH OUT FOR THE QUEEN?		?: No.	
→	SHE WILL WATCH OUT FOR THE QUEEN.	nods head; points to Snow White		
	DO YOU THINK *THAT* LOOKS LIKE THE QUEEN?	points to witch in boat (back a page)	Several: No.	
	SHE WAS DIS- GUISED (in hushed voice) IN RAGGED CLOTHES, HUH?	points to witch	Alice: Yeah, wicked . . .	
→	DO YOU THINK SNOW WHITE'S GONNA KNOW THAT THAT'S THE QUEEN?		?: No-oh Nat: Wicked witch.	
→			Davey: She's gonna know it's a witch! (excited) Alice: Wicked Witch!	
→	YEAH, SHE'S GON- NA THINK, "OH YEAH," THAT'S A WITCH!	* * *		

teractions initiated by both storyreader and listeners centered on predicting narrative action and outcome.

In Segment 22, questions like "Is *she gonna* watch out for the queen?" and "Do you think *she's gonna* know that's the queen?" not only gave the children opportunities to predict Snow White's actions, but also alerted them to the fact that she *would* act. That is, the storyreader's comments indicated to the listeners that there would be a significant development in the narrative, and in this way provided metanarrative information about how a particular part of the text was to be read. The metanarrative function of the storyreader's commentary about prior and forthcoming events was especially clear when the storyreader prefaced her questions with exclamations (e.g., "*Uh oh!* What are they gonna do with his loose tooth?") that signalled to the listening group both that a particular kind of event would occur and that the listening audience ought to respond to that event in a particular way.

To a certain extent, the nursery-school children had internalized the strategy of predicting narrative action. Their own predictions and comments on others' predictions of forthcoming actions indicated a growing sense of the structure of narrative and the way narrative action works. In Segment 23, you will see one little boy refute a peer's prediction, make his own prediction about narrative action, and then confirm the correctness of his own prediction.

One way of thinking about interaction sequences that centered on the relationships between prior and forthcoming actions and on cause and effect relations is to consider them in the context of two reading codes described by Barthes (1974). He suggests that fluent readers continuously frame their understanding of narratives in terms of various codes of knowledge. One of these codes (Barthes's "hermeneutic code") alerts readers to the questions or enigmas in narratives and then leads to their solutions. In other words, one way that readers make sense of texts is to form questions about events and then read to find the answers to these questions. In Type II Life-to-Text interactions, part of what the storyreader was doing was helping the children frame their understanding of parts of texts in terms of questions and answers about narrative action. For example, in the "Snow White" reading (Segment 22), we saw the storyreader help the children to raise questions (e.g., "Is she gonna watch out for the queen?") and then emphasize the answers to these questions (e.g., "She *will* watch out for the queen").

Barthes also describes a narrative code that helps readers frame their reading of narratives in terms of their understanding of the logic of

Storyreading Segment 23: Fish Is Fish (Lionni)

	Reader		Listeners	
Focal Points	*Verbal*	*Nonverbal*	*Verbal*	*Nonverbal*
		* * *		
	IT'S NO GOOD FOR HIM OUT THERE, IS IT?	taps picture of a fish out of water		
→			Davey: No-ooo!	
→			Ben: He'll die	
			Davey: Huh-uh! (insisting)	
→			He'll . . . the . . . the frog is gonna put him back in	
		TP	the water. (breathless).	
→	[PIC: frog helps fish into water]		See!	points to picture
	"Luckily, the frog who had been hunting butterflies nearby, saw him. And with all his strength, he pushed him back into the pond."			
→			Davey: See! I told you! (to Ben)	points to picture—nodding head
		* * *		

cause and effect relationships (Barthes's "proairetic code"). In Type II Life-to-Text interactions, the storyreader frequently urged the children to predict the logical effects of various actions. As we saw in the "Fish Is Fish" storyreading (Segment 23), some of the children themselves had internalized this strategy and framed their understanding of the narrative by predicting logical effects (e.g., "He'll die"; "Huh-uh . . . he'll . . . the frog's gonna put him back in the water").

Status of actions. Many Type II Life-to-Text interaction sequences focused on the status of various narrative events and actions. In Life-to-Text interactions of this kind, the major emphasis of conversa-

Storyreading Segment 24: And To Think That I Saw It on Mulberry Street (Geisel)

	Reader		Listeners	
Focal Points	Verbal	Nonverbal	Verbal	Nonverbal
→	WHAT DID HE REAL- LY SEE ON HIS STREET? WHAT DID HE SEE, JEFFREY? WHAT DID HE SEE?	holds up book to last page with original cart and horse.		
			Jeffrey: All that . . . junk!	gestures gener- ally toward pictures
→	DID HE SEE *ALL* OF THESE THINGS?	turns pages back slowly to pictures	Jeffrey: Yeah.	
→	DID HE?	of imaginary		
→	MARK, MARK DID HE *REALLY* SEE ALL OF THESE?	scenes	Nat: Junk! All that junk!	
			Nat: This, this is junk, junk!	points to pictures
			Jeffrey: Junk!	
	IT'S JUNK? YOU MEAN IT'S WRECK-Y?			
→	BUT DID HE *SEE* THIS?			
		points to dif- ferent pic- tures of boy's imaginings	Mark: Yes.	
→	BUT DID HE *SEE* THAT?	points to sleigh	Nat: But that's not the only thing, but that's what he said.	
→	HE *SAYS* . . .	nods head emphatically		
→	HE'S JUST *SAYING* THAT HE SEES LOTS OF DIFFER- ENT THINGS? HUH?			
	NAT?		Nat: Nup.	
→	DID HE SEE A ZEBRA?	points to picture		
			Mark: Yes! (impatient)	
→	DO YOU THINK HE COULD?			
			Mark: Yes.	
→	I DON'T KNOW. (doubtfully)	shakes head	Nat: Yup, yup, yup.	
→	DO YOU THINK			

(*continued*)

Storyreading Segment 24   *Continued*

Focal Points	Reader		Listeners	
	Verbal	*Nonverbal*	*Verbal*	*Nonverbal*
	ZEBRAS LIVE IN HIS TOWN? DO ZEBRAS PULL CARTS? DO THEY, JEFFREY?			
→	IS HE *TRICKING* HIS DAD?			
			Jeffrey: Mmm hmm	
→	IS HE? IS HE TELL-ING HIM ALL THOSE THINGS HE COULD SEE WITH A CHAR-IOT? LOOK AT THAT FAST CHARIOT!	points to picture	Jeffrey: No.	
			Jeffrey: That's neat.	
→	HOW 'BOUT THAT? BUT YOU KNOW, HE DOESN'T . . . A REINDEER DOESN'T PULL A CART WITH WHEELS . . . WHAT DOES IT NEED?			
			Jeffrey: A sled!	
→	AND HOW 'BOUT THAT?	points to elephant		
→	THAT LOOKS KIND OF CRAZY BE-CAUSE THAT ELE-PHANT . . . THAT'S AN INDI-AN ELEPHANT. HE COMES FROM INDIA. AND INDI-ANS, ELEPHANTS DON'T GO IN COLD PLACES . . .			
	DO THEY?			
		* * *		

tion was on sorting out real and imaginary fictive actions, events, and situations. This distinction was not synonymous with the differences between fiction and nonfiction, nor with differences between fantasy and realism. Rather, the distinction was based on the status of action as it was embedded within the world created in the text. For example, a fantasy story could have some actions that were real and some that were imaginary within the fantasy world itself.

In Storyreading Segment 24, a young boy imagined a whole parade of outrageous creatures and people as he walked home from school (all of these were pictured in the book); but when he reached home, he simply told his father he had seen a cart and a horse. In this example you will see how the storyreader emphasized the difference in status between the actions of the boy walking home from school and talking to his father and the action of all the creatures in the boy's imagined parade.

In Segment 24, the storyreader worked hard to help the children realize that the parade of creatures had been completely in the boy's imagination. She seized on Nat's suggestion that the boy was *just saying* that he saw those things, then repeatedly asked whether the boy *really saw* each item. She raised questions about the real qualities of reindeers, elephants and zebras and about the likelihood of having zebras in one's own hometown. In this way she emphasized to the listeners that they had to use their knowledge of the world in order to clarify the status of the action in the narrative. Interaction sequences in which the teacher strived to convey the real-imaginary distinction were common in storyreadings.

Responding as a reading audience

In her analysis of the development of communicative competence in the Kaluli children of Papua New Guinea, Schieffelin (in preparation) suggests that part of what these children had to learn in order to "be Kaluli" was how to feel about various actions, events, and situations. Schieffelin argues that Kaluli children learned how to feel primarily through verbal interactions with adults who consistently molded the children's assumptions and expectations for particular situations. Schieffelin's arguments shed light on the fourth kind of knowledge that the nursery-school storyreader encouraged her listeners to use in order to make sense of texts: knowledge of how to respond to texts as members of a reading audience.

The storyreader shaped the children's responses to story events by both modeling their feelings (i.e., the storyreader herself appropriately responded as an audience member) and suggesting feelings that the children ought to have or exploring feelings that they might have about various textual events. For example, audience members were encouraged to respond with sadness to a story character's loss of a pet or with laughter to a story figure's silly actions. In this way the nursery-school children were exposed to a process of making sense of texts that included responding or feeling appropriately about the events, actions, characters, and situations that occurred in books.

Modeling response.　Often the teacher instructed the children in how to respond to stories or parts of stories by responding appropriately herself. In Storyreading Segment 25, notice how the teacher modeled response by exaggerating her own laughter at the humor in the book.

Storyreading Segment 25: Animals Should Definitely Not Wear Clothing (Barrett)

Focal Points	Reader		Listeners	
	Verbal	*Nonverbal*	*Verbal*	*Nonverbal*
	"Animals should definitely . . . not wear clothing because it would be disastrous for a porcupine!"		(no response)	
		holds up picture of porcupine with quills		
	WHAT WOULD HAPPEN TO THE PORCUPINE'S CLOTHES? (laughing very hard)	sticking out of clothes		
→		hand up to mouth		
			Davey: Picking out, it would picking out.	
	THEY WOULD GET PICKING?			
			?: Holes.	
→	WHAT WOULD HAPPEN?			
→	(laughs)	points to porcupine		
			?: Holes, holes, holes.	

Storyreading Segment 25 *Continued*

Focal Points	Reader		Listeners	
	Verbal	*Nonverbal*	*Verbal*	*Nonverbal*
→	THEY WOULD PRI-CK ALL THEIR CLOTHING AND MAKE HOLES?			
→	(laughs hard)	hand to mouth, shakes shoulders		
	PRICK IT?		Curt: That's funny.	
			Melissa: Yeah, that's funny.	
			(several children sort of laugh)	
		* * *		

In Segment 25, the message that the storyreader was giving the children was essentially this: *This is funny; appropriate audience response is laughter.* Some of the children seemed to "get" the message and commented explicitly: "That's funny; Yeah, that's funny." As the reading continued, the storyreader repeatedly signaled to the audience that they should laugh. She put her hand to her mouth, mimed laughter with shoulders shaking and head bobbing, and laughed out loud, exaggerating her response. This kind of behavior is a particularly clear example of the storyreader offering metanarrative information to the children; that is, the storyreader's actions can be understood as metanarrative signals to the audience on how to read parts of texts—as funny, sad, surprising, dismaying.

Instructing response. In some interaction sequences, the reader did not model audience behavior; instead, she talked about appropriate audience response. That is, she asked the children to discuss how they felt about particular story characters or events, or she suggested ways that they might be feeling. In Segment 26, the storyreader first suggested the response that listeners ought to feel, then described and

Storyreading Segment 26: Alexander and the Terrible, Horrible, No Good, Very Bad Day (Viorst)

Focal Points	Reader		Listeners	
	Verbal	*Nonverbal*	*Verbal*	*Nonverbal*
	YOU KNOW THAT KID REALLY HAD A TERRIBLE TIME, DON'T YOU THINK?	pats book		
			Nat: Yeah. (not very interested)	
→	DON'T YOU FEEL SORRY FOR HIM?			
			Nat: Mmm Hmm . . .	
→	EVERYTHING? I FELT BAD WHEN HE BIT HIS TONGUE. THAT REALLY HURT.			
			Nat: I felt bad when he got his foot stuck in the elevator.	
		* * *		

explored her own response. Notice how one child picked up on the storyreader's example and offered a similar response of his own.

Especially important in helping the children learn how to feel about parts of texts were the prosodic features of the storyreader's readings of and conversations around the texts. Prosody was also important in conveying information about the three other kinds of knowledge that the children needed to use in order to make sense of texts. These are discussed below.

Contextualization Cues and Making Sense of Texts

Gumperz (1977) has pointed out that what he calls "contextualization cues" carry a major part of the interpretive load in conversation. These cues are primarily the prosodic and paralinguistic features of language, such as intonation and stress, pitch, register, rhythm and loudness, but can also refer to "any aspect of the surface form of utterances which, when mapped onto message content, can be shown to be functional in the signalling of interpretive frames" (p. 199).

Cook-Gumperz and Gumperz (1982) further suggest that adults usually communicate in several modalities at once so that verbal, kinesic, and contextualization cues together signal interpretive frames. For young children, on the other hand, contextualization cues, particularly prosodic ones, are foregrounded; that is, they are essential rather than supplementary interpretive signals. For children to make the transition from oral to written culture, Cook-Gumperz and Gumperz argue that children need to learn a "new system of solely syntactic and lexicalized cue-ing" (p. 18).

The ideas of Gumperz and Cook-Gumperz are helpful in pointing out an important feature of Type II Life-to-Text storyreading interactions. In the preceding pages I have been discussing primarily *what kind of* verbal information the storyreader supplied for listeners or encouraged listeners to use in order to make sense of texts. The notion of "contextualization cues" as interpretive signals for conversational inference provides insight into *how* the storyreader provided some of this information.

Storyreading Segment 27: My Mama Says There Aren't Any Zombies, Ghosts, Vampires, Creatures, Demons, Monsters, Fiends, Goblins, or Things (Viorst)

Focal Points	Reader		Listeners	
	Verbal	Nonverbal	Verbal	Nonverbal
	[LP&RP: across bottom of pages, boy carrying groceries in sequence of four pictures—having difficulty] "But when we went shopping at the supermarket (on) Friday, my (mom) (t:mama) told me to carry the bag with the eggs. And I said			

(continued)

Storyreading Segment 27 *Continued*

	Reader		Listeners	
Focal Points	Verbal	Nonverbal	Verbal	Nonverbal
	it was too heavy for me.			
→	(complaining)			
→	And she said, you can do it, you can do it.	nods head		
→	(conversational, encouraging)			
	It's heavy, I said. Too heavy for me.			
→	(complaining)			
	Oh, you can do it, she told			
→	me. (encouraging, impatient)			
→	I can't, I said.	shakes head		
→	(whining)			
	You can too, she told me.	points to each in		
→	(insisting)	series of pictures TP		
	[LP: boy drops bag in air on top of angry lady]			
→	"And that's how we got scrambled eggs all over our shoes. (explaining)	nods head points to picture		

A great deal of the interpretive information the storyreader provided to the children was tied up with the prosodic and paralinguistic accompaniments of her reading and conversations around texts. The nursery-school storyreader was a literate adult reader who, unlike the children to whom she read, already knew how to get meaning from the syntactic and lexical features of written language. Hence, when reading aloud, she was able to mediate between listeners and written texts by inserting into texts prosodic features that signaled familiar interpretive frames to the audience.

Storyreading Segment 27 offers an example of the way in which contextualization cues provided interpretive information. Notice how the storyreader provided extra information by varying the volume and intonation of her voice and by accompanying the reading with head movements and changes in facial expression. In this way, the repetitive text ("I can't . . . You can . . .") was transformed into a text that varied significantly as the mother-son dialogue progressed.

In Segment 27, the storyreader stayed close to the words of the text. What was essential, however, were the prosodic features of the reading and the paralinguistic accompaniments to the reading. By changing from complaining to encouraging to whining to insisting tones of voice, by pointing at the pictures in correct sequence, and by alternately shaking and nodding her head, the storyreader provided a great deal of information in addition to that conveyed by the lexical and syntactic features of the written text. In this and other storyreadings, the storyreader signaled adverbs of manner in dialogue by reading the dialogue in the appropriate manner herself. In this way, she provided the listeners

Storyreading Segment 28: Barbapapa's New House (Tison and Taylor)

| Focal Points | Reader | | Listeners | |
	Verbal	Nonverbal	Verbal	Nonverbal
	[LP: wrecking machinery starts to tear houses down on their street] "Now they had lived there happily for some time when it was decided that all the old houses in the street had to be destroyed."			
→	WRECKED DOWN! (whispering, anxious voice)	on "down" makes sudden downward motion * * *		

with information about both *who* was talking in stories and the *manner* in which they were talking.

Information concerning dialogue between characters was not the only kind of information conveyed by contextualization cues. Frequently, lexical information was conveyed this way as well. Lexical referents, sentence construction, and contextualization cues jointly conveyed meaning. Notice in Storyreading Segment 28, for example, how lexical information about the word, "destroyed," was supplied by the reader's verbal explanation, as well as by the pitch, volume, stress, and intonation of her voice.

Contextualization cues also provided information about how characters felt and how their feelings were affected by the events and actions of the story. The prosodic cues conveyed by the reader supported the verbal information in the text and the visual information in the pictures. Information about how to respond as an audience member was also conveyed via prosodic features of the reading. Often the storyreader not only specifically verbalized to the listeners the way that they should evaluate parts of a narrative, but also emotionally responded herself through appropriate verbal intonation, pitch, and volume. In instances of this kind, the storyreader essentially told the children: *read this particular part of a story as sad or happy or suspenseful.* She also showed by the tone of her voice that she, as one audience member, was responding in these ways.

Summary

As many examples have shown, what emerged from this study was a picture of storyreading events in which the storyreader demonstrated a process of using knowledge of the world, literary convention, narrative, and audience membership in order to make sense of texts. Information in all four of these categories was jointly conveyed by verbal annotations on texts and pictures and by contextualization cues. Together these made the language strategies needed for group storyreading transitional between those used to interpret conversation and those used to interpret essayist literacy.

As Maple Nursery School preschoolers mature and become literate readers, they will have to learn to interpret decontextualized written language without the support of verbal annotation and contextualization cues and, eventually, without the support of illustration. At these beginning stages of literary apprenticeship, however, all these features of storyreading helped the children to use their knowledge to make sense of texts.

As reported in this chapter, the nursery-school children were exposed to a process of literary sense-making wherein four kinds of knowledge had to be used together in order to understand a text. For example, both world knowledge and knowledge of narrative might be needed to help a reader infer the cause and effect of a particular action. This general sense-making process, implicit in scores of nursery-school storyreadings, had an endless number of specific configurations. In other words, for different books and different audiences, the four kinds of knowledge were combined in different ways in order to allow reader/listeners to find sense in the texts. This characteristic of nursery-school storyreading was underlaid by two important rules of the reading process: (a) one must *come to different kinds of books in different ways and read differentially, depending on reading audience, genre, reading purpose, and setting;* and (b) *readers themselves contribute actively to the reading process by bringing their individual knowledge to bear upon texts* (hence one book can have many realizations).

In addition to making sense of the information within texts, storyreading interactions also guided the nursery-school children in making sense of texts in relation to the world. Ways to use texts in the world are described in Chapter 10.

Just Like They Did in the Book:
Text-to-Life Interactions

I have been describing the literary socialization of the preschool children who attended Maple Nursery School. As I have shown, both ways of preparing for and behaving during storyreading (Type I Readiness interactions) and ways of using one's experiences in order to make sense of texts (Type II Life-to-Text interactions) were guided by the storyreader within adult-child social interactions. These interactions were not one-sided or adult-controlled; rather, they were jointly negotiated sessions where children's sense-making was highly respected and accounted for. As I have suggested, Type II Life-to-Text interaction sequences were aimed at helping children make sense of individual texts. The direction of these interactions was outside-in; that is, they centered around the extra-textual information needed in order to make sense within texts. In this way Life-to-Text sequences transformed the act of bringing one's knowledge to bear upon texts from an automatic, internalized process to a deliberate, explicit one.

In the pages that follow, Type III Text-to-Life interaction sequences are described. Unlike Life-to-Text sequences that were outside-in, Type III Text-to-Life interaction sequences were inside-out. They were aimed at helping the children compare, extend, or relate textual information to matters outside texts. In other words, Text-to-Life interactions focused on helping the children apply a book's information, meaning, message, topic, problem, or theme to their lives. Life-to-Text sequences focused on the text itself: what is happening here? what is this object? what kind of person is this character? Text-to-Life sequences, on the other hand, invited listeners to consider the relevance of the texts to their own situations: what does this book tell you? how does the information relate to your current experience? what would you decide to do if you were in this situation?

These Type III Text-to-Life interactions sometimes occurred outside of the text-reading frame, often after storyreadings had concluded. During a storyreading of a book about guinea pigs, for example, the storyreader pointed out to the children that in the book a group of children sat in a circle to form a pen for their guinea pig (a Type II Life-to-Text interaction). The storyreader then underlined the relevance of this book event for the nursery-school children's own lives: "Shall *we* try to make a big circle like that so the guinea won't get out? . . . We could try it out when we go outside" (a Type III Text-to-Life interaction). Later, after both this storyreading and the larger rug-time episode were completed and the children were playing outdoors, the teacher brought the guinea pig outdoors and helped the children sit in a circle to form a ring around their pet. As they did so, the storyreader reminded the children of the guinea-pig story and commented that their own actions were "just like they did in the book" (another Type III Text-to-Life interaction).

Although the outdoor interaction did not occur until after the rug-time storyreading event, it still gives us insight into the nursery-school children's use and application of book knowledge in the world. Type III Text-to-Life interactions that occurred after storyreadings and referred back or related to prior storyreadings conveyed an important message about book knowledge and information: *the contents of books can be both directly and indirectly applied to real-life situations.* This idea was a powerful part of the nursery-school children's orientation to book-reading.

Ways of Using Books

Primarily through Text-to-Life interactions with the storyreader, the nursery-school children were exposed to several different ways of coming to books or using books in the world. In some cases, whole books were used in one general way (e.g., the guinea pig book was generally used to acquire information about the nursery-school pet guinea pig); in other cases, individual parts of books were used in various ways. Four major kinds of Text-to-Life interactions emerged from the data. These interactions centered on using books for: (a) counseling or problem-solving, (b) ways of knowing or gaining access to various kinds of information, (c) stimulating the imagination, and (d) entertaining oneself or others. These four ways of coming to books were supported by the ways that reading and writing were used in off-the-rug literacy events at the nursery school. They were also supported by and highly consistent with the ways that the nursery-school adult community used books in their homes. Many of these uses have been discussed in Chapter 4.

Using books for counseling

The nursery-school storyreader frequently selected books to read aloud to the children because she believed that the books contained topics or issues that were important in the children's lives. Like the parents in Chapter 4 who selected books for their children's "problem-solving," the nursery-school storyreader did not believe that books offered direct answers to children's problems, or that bookreading itself actually solved problems. With the parents, the nursery school story-reader did believe, however, that bookreading served as a kind of counseling vehicle that could be "therapeutic for everyone" by opening up topics for discussion or by acknowledging the legitimacy of children's feelings. In Type III Text-to-Life sequences that focused on counseling, the storyreader encouraged discussion of the children's own experiences in relation to the experiences of story characters or in relation to the general topics of books. Discussion of this sort was not aimed at exploring the motivations or responses of story characters (Life-to-Text interactions), but rather at exploring the emotions of nursery-school children themselves.

Storyreading Segment 29 is a key example of a counseling interaction sequence. The verbal interaction in this excerpt was prompted by the introduction of a book with which all the nursery-school children were familiar; this segment underlines the nursery school relationship between storyreading and helping children work through psychological dilemmas. In this segment, you will see the storyreader accept and encourage the children's discussion of their fears about nighttime and darkness.

In Segment 29, the storyreader listened to and legitimated the children's expressions of fear and anxiety concerning nighttime, darkness, and being alone. This counseling discussion was evoked and fostered by

Storyreading Segment 29:[1] There's A Nightmare in My Closet (Mayer)

	Reader		Listeners	
Focal Points	*Verbal*	*Nonverbal*	*Verbal*	*Nonverbal*
	"There's a nightmare in my closet!" (loudly— over children)	holds up book, points to words of title page	[several: Nightmares! Nightmares!	many children finding places to sit, talking
→	HEY! "There's a nightmare in my closet!"	holds up book to first page	Andrew: I always hear a strange noise when I go to bed.	many children talking, running around rug
→	YOU DO?	puts book down in lap	Curt: Yikes! A nightmare's comin'! (shouting)	
→			Andrew: Bangin' on the window.	
	IS . . . SOMEONE'S BANGING ON YOUR WINDOW AT NIGHT, TOO?			
			Andrew: Ye-ah, and I can't see it.	children suddenly quieter
			?: Nightmare!	
→	IS IT WHEN YOUR ROOM IS VERY DARK THAT THAT HAPPENS? (seriously)			
→			Andrew: Yes . . . (quietly)	
			Curt: Andrew, guess who's knocking at your	

(continued)

[1]The transcription conventions used in Sharing Segments 1 and 2 and in the Storyreading Segments throughout this monograph are described in detail in Chapter 3, pp. 30–36.

Storyreading Segment 29 *Continued*

Focal Points	Reader		Listeners	
	Verbal	*Nonverbal*	*Verbal*	*Nonverbal*
			window? (yelling and still not settled on rug) Sandman! (yelling/ singing) (laughs)	
→	THE SANDMAN IS DROPPING LITTLE GRAINS OF SAND IN YOUR EYES SO THAT YOU'LL GO TO SLEEP?		Curt: I know . . . (yelling)	
→	IS THAT WHAT'S HAPPENING?			
			Andrew: No. (quietly) Curt: A robber! (shouting)	
→			Andrew: Yeah, it must be a robber. (tense)	
→	WHAT WOULD HE WANT TO TAKE OUT OF YOUR ROOM, ANDREW?			
→			Andrew: I think my teddy . . .	
	YOUR TEDDY BEAR? WOULD HE TAKE YOUR TOYS, TOO?			
				Andrew nods
→	YOU THINK SOME- ONE WANTS TO TAKE STUFF OUT OF YOUR ROOM?			
			⌐Several children start to talk all at once (excited)	
→			└Ben: Me too . . . wa . . . my bas- ketball! and my stickball!	several chil- dren talking

Storyreading Segment 29   *Continued*

	Reader		Listeners	
Focal Points	*Verbal*	*Nonverbal*	*Verbal*	*Nonverbal*
→			Davey: A . . . a robber took my, uh, paper watch away! (breathless)	gets up on knees, leans toward reader
→	DID HE? AND BEN, WHAT CAME INTO YOUR ROOM THAT YOU WERE TELL- ING US ABOUT A SECOND AGO?			
			Ben: I don't know . . .	Mark begins playing with and pounding on a block fort nearby
			Ben: I don't know . . .	
→	WHAT WAS IT?			
→	IS IT WHEN YOUR ROOM WAS COM- PLETELY DARK THAT SOMETHING COMES?			
		* * *	Ben: Uh huh.	

both the reader's selection of this particular book and by the responses and encouragement given by the reader to the children. As is apparent in this example, the storyreader did not prompt discussion of the nighttime fears of the storybook boy, but rather encouraged exploration of the fears of the listeners. In many storyreadings, the teacher made it clear that there was a tie between the text and the counseling discussion by bringing the children's comments back to the book, or by asking them to compare their experiences with those in the book.

It is difficult to know the role that counseling-oriented Text-to-Life interaction sequences actually played in helping the nursery-school chil- dren deal with their fears and anxieties. That the children themselves repeatedly requested and animatedly responded to books that contained particular topics (monsters, nightmares, fears, anger), however, offers a hint of the power of these topics in the children's lives. Further, the children themselves sometimes framed their concerns in terms of storybook characters or events, and sometimes recycled bits of storybook texts into their own conversations on related topics.

Text-to-Life counseling interaction sequences did not occur *only* around such topics as nightmares, demons, ghosts, and monsters. They also occurred often within readings of books about children's feelings. The storyreader used these bookreading situations as vehicles for initiating counseling interactions that explored children's feelings of anger, pride, likes and dislikes. She guided the children in discussions in which understanding of book events and understanding of real-life events reciprocally enriched one another. The major focus was on creating a framework within which the children's feelings could be sorted out.

Some Text-to-Life counseling interactions were initiated by the children, and some were initiated by the teacher; some were more or less anticipated by the teacher, and books were deliberately chosen with counseling or "therapy" in mind. For example, when one child's grandmother died, the teacher pre-selected a book that dealt with a fictional child's loss of a pet and specifically stated that the book was for the little girl. Counseling interactions were not heavy-handed, didactic sermons by the adult storyreader. That is, the storyreader did not explicitly state the "moral" or "lesson" in books, and then stipulate how these morals ought to be practiced in the children's everyday lives. Rather, as both nursery-school parents and nursery-school teacher claimed, the books were used as vehicles for opening communication between children and adults.

What is most significant about Text-to-Life counseling interaction sequences is the use of bookreading as a way of dealing with children's feelings. This use of bookreading is related to the self-expression purpose of writing described in Chapter 6. Like writing for self-expression, counseling interactions during and after bookreadings conveyed the message that children's feelings were both acknowledged and accepted by adults. Just as important, however, counseling interaction sequences were underlaid by the message that book topics, incidents, and issues were related to the vital issues and dilemmas of real life and could pave the way for discussing and dealing with such issues. Hence, discussion of book topics and themes could promote understanding of the children's own lives.

Using books as a way of knowing

Both in their homes and in off-the-rug nursery-school literacy events, Maple Nursery School preschoolers were exposed to the use of printed materials as a way of knowing or acquiring information in many different areas. Bookreadings were used at the nursery school to introduce forthcoming experiences, to follow up on prior experiences, to relate experiences to one another, to verify information, to acquire information in new areas, and to frame current experiences.

A key example of this use of bookreading was the framing of the nursery-school experience itself. On the third day of the new school year in September, the teacher shared with the children a book about going to nursery school. During this storyreading, the teacher consistently guided the listeners in Text-to-Life interaction sequences that framed their own new experience of coming to nursery school in relation to the fictional description of the nursery-school experience. Although this use of bookreading is related to the counseling interactions described before, the focus is on structuring actual experience rather than exploring feelings and emotions. This nursery-school approach to framing new life experiences in relation to reading experiences is very much in keeping with the remarks of one nursery-school parent, quoted earlier: "If something's happening, the first thing I do is to go and read about it."

The nursery-school group frequently went on outings to local museums, stores, and other points of interest. For most of these trips, the children were introduced to the topic of interest prior to going on the trip by hearing a book on the subject. For example, the children heard *A First Look At Fish* (Selsam & Hunt) before traveling to a large tropical aquarium to see and buy fish for the school's fish tank and *Eskimos* (Bringle) before traveling to an Eskimo art shop for a brief talk and view of native Eskimo art objects. During these bookreadings, the children were invited to acquire information which could subsequently be used to frame the new experiences and knowledge they would gain on the outings. During and after trips of this sort, the storyreader referred back to the readings and pointed out relationships between real and book experiences. In this way, book knowledge became a basis for grounding knowledge gained through primary life experiences. Such use of book knowledge underlines a way of knowing that was characteristic of the Maple Nursery School community: knowledge was frequently grounded in print (either as an introduction or follow-up to life experiences) and then supplemented, clarified, elaborated upon, or complemented by primary experience.

In addition to providing knowledge that framed actual experience, bookreadings were also used at the nursery school to provide knowledge or information that could be directly and immediately applied to current situations. Printed information was favored as a way of finding out how to do things in the world—how to dye fabrics, how to care for a pet. The nursery-school children were also encouraged to use books as references when they needed information about various topics. When, for example, a child wanted to identify a stone or a bird's nest, he or she was helped to find the information in a text rather than told the information orally.

This is not to suggest that every nursery-school activity had a book or print base. However, a significant characteristic of the nursery-school use of books was the range of situations and topics for which bookreading functioned as a primary way of knowing. Books were used as sources of knowledge not only as reference guides or nonfiction works, but also to structure personal experiences—to provide frameworks within which experiences could make sense and be assimilated with other experiences. This use of bookreading as a primary way of knowing about "just about everything" was the result of learning and experience with the patterns of bookreading implicit in the activities of the community. At both the school and at home, literacy was meaningful in many contexts, and its use as a source of knowledge across contexts was quite consistent.

Using books to stimulate the imagination

Many parents commented during interviews that bookreading was highly preferable to watching television. Unlike television, which promoted passive spectatorship, bookreading actively stimulated their children's imaginative and mental growth. The nursery-school teacher indicated her strong agreement with this parental sentiment and frequently selected for storyreading books that would widen the children's horizons by presenting new ideas, situations, and events. In this way, bookreading was used as a vehicle for broadening the intellect or stimulating the imagination.

In addition to this general orientation to bookreading as imagination-stretching, many Text-to-Life interaction sequences during storyreadings made explicit this way of using or coming to books. In Text-to-Life sequences of this kind, listeners were encouraged to imagine themselves in the places of story characters, to ponder their own feelings if they were in circumstances similar to those in books, to use story events or circumstances to recall or imagine their own experiences, and to increase their awareness of some of the sensory stimuli around them.

Storeading Segment 30 illustrates how the storyreader used story-readings to invite the children to stretch their imaginations. Notice how she continuously tied the children's imaginings to the details of the setting in the book and, reciprocally, used the book details to elaborate on the children's imaginings.

Storyreading Segment 30: Barbapapa's New House (Tison and Taylor)

	Reader		Listeners	
Focal Points	Verbal	Nonverbal	Verbal	Nonverbal
		(has just pointed to each room of story charac-ters' new house)		
→	WHICH ROOM WOULD YOU LIKE TO LIVE IN, DAN?	holds book out to Dan		
			Dan: Na-ah (scanning page), this room!	points
→	OH, THE PRETTY ROOM WITH THE PICTURES?	taps picture		
→	HOW 'BOUT YOU CLAY?	holds book out to Clay		
			Clay: I'd like to live in, uh . . . (long pause)	points to gym
→	THAT'S WHERE THE ATHLETE . . . THAT'S LIKE A GYM.	nods points to picture	Clay: I'd, uh, I	

(continued)

Storyreading Segment 30 *Continued*

	Reader		Listeners	
Focal Points	Verbal	Nonverbal	Verbal	Nonverbal
			would like in . . . there.	points to science room
→	OH! YES, WITH ALL THE INSECTS AND THE MUSHROOM PICTURES.	nods		
		pointing to details of picture	Dori: I like it, I'd like this one.	
		nods to Dori	Mark: I like . . . this one.	gets up and points to picture
			Davey: Amy, I li--	points
→	OH, THE ONE WITH THE TELESCOPE SO YOU CAN LOOK AT THE STARS! (to Mark)			
		* * *		

Text-to-Life interactions like those in Segment 30 invited story listeners to use books as vehicles for stretching their imaginations, increase their sensory awareness of things around them, and participate actively and creatively in discussions concerning these things.

Using bookreading to entertain

The adults in the nursery-school community stressed that at-home bookreading was used mainly as a way of entertaining their children. Although at the nursery school bookreading was also used to entertain, entertainment was not its major purpose. As the storyreader's reminders during storyreading sessions have pointed out, rug-time bookreading was often characterized for the children as "a time for learning new things," but never characterized as "a time for having fun." Fun and entertainment, were, however, features of many bookreadings; adults and children laughed together and seemed to delight in sharing many of the stories with one another. That the children enjoyed bookreading was evidenced by both their frequent requests for bookreadings and the willingness of most of the children to sit and listen to three or more bookreadings in succession. That the storyreader acknowledged entertainment as one of the legitimate uses of bookreading was evidenced by both her willingness to honor children's storyreading requests (even when she personally or professionally disliked certain books) and her selection of books on the basis of their appeal and popularity with previous groups of children.

Further testimony to the children's conception of bookreading as a pleasant and entertaining way to spend time was their election to sit quietly and look at books during periods of free play. Many children regularly chose bookreading from among the various activities (e.g., game-playing, dramatic enactments, role playing, art projects) that filled the first part of mornings at the nursery. During self-selected bookreading activities, individual children or pairs of children sat on the rug and paged through individually-chosen books, often studying each picture carefully. Although individuals within pairs pointed out items of interest to one another, bookreading of this kind was a largely silent activity. If adults were nearby, however, children requested that they read aloud to them.

Storyreading Segment 31: Would You Rather (Burningham)

Focal Points	Reader		Listeners	
	Verbal	*Nonverbal*	*Verbal*	*Nonverbal*
	[LP: above—elephant drinking bath; below—eagle stealing dinner]			
→	"(or) would you rather . . . an elephant drank your bath water?" (playful)	points to top		
			Chorus: No-ooooooo! (rising and falling shout)	

(*continued*)

Storyreading Segment 31 *Continued*

Reader			Listeners	
Focal Points	Verbal	Nonverbal	Verbal	Nonverbal
→	Or "an eagle stole your dinner?"	points to picture	Chorus: No-ooooooooo! (very loud)	many children standing, laughing, hopping
	[RP: above—pig wearing overalls; below—hippo sleeping in boy's bed]			
→	"(or how 'bout let) a pig (try) (t: tried) on your clothes?"	points		
			Chorus: No-ooooooo!	hopping, squealing, jumping
→	"Or a hippo (let him sleep) (t: slept) in your bed?"	points		
			Chorus: No-oooooo!	
→	WOULDN'T THAT BE NICE? (playful)			
			Chorus: No-oooooo!	
→	THEN YOU MIGHT HAVE TO SLEEP ON THE FLOOR (laughing)!	TP	⌐?: No-ooooooo! └ ?: No-oooooo ?: No-oooooo!	
		* * *		

Entertainment as a way of coming to books was implicit in some of the Text-to-Life interaction sequences within storyreadings themselves. In sequences of this sort, "having fun" or being entertained by the text was primary; that is, texts were used almost as toys, as things to be played with. Storyreading Segment 31 is a clear illustration of this use of books. In it you will see how the storyreading interaction became a game—with the reader suggesting absurdity after absurdity and the listeners responding with louder and louder squeals of "no-oooh!" As Segment 31 indicates, some Test-to-Life interaction sequences featured a way of coming to books for fun and entertainment; in these sequences, books prompted light-hearted interaction between reader and listeners.

Bookreading as Part of Shared Knowledge

The preceding description of four ways that books were used at the nursery school centers on the uses of individual books before, during, and following storyreadings. In addition to these particular instances, the characters, themes, and plots of storybooks also played a general role at the nursery school as they became parts of shared knowledge and experience. Bits and pieces of storybook elements were used by and for the children as points of reference to describe current experiences or as analogic bases according to which new experiences could be structured. Although on a simpler level, shared literary knowledge was assumed at the nursery school in much the same way that understanding of phrases like "Cinderella story" to describe a baseball team's victory, or "Romeo and Juliet" to characterize young lovers is assumed in certain adult communities. Use of such descriptions assumes that perceivers understand the current situation (a baseball team's victory), the literary reference (the fairy tale, "Cinderella"), and the appropriate connection between the two (like Cinderella's, the status of a baseball team changed, rather magically, from defeat to triumph).

Understanding of the literary references made at the nursery school required the same three layers of understanding as did these analogies. For example, as a group of children played a card game with the teacher, a boy remarked that the character on his card "looked just like Corduroy." The teacher and children looked at the playing card, smiled and agreed. This simple comparison required that perceivers understand the appropriate parts of the current situation (the manner of dress of the male figure pictured on the playing card), the literary reference ("Corduroy," a stuffed-bear storybook character who was the center of a series of children's picture-books often shared at the nursery school), and the appropriate connection between the two (like Corduroy, who always wore overalls, the playing-card figure was dressed in overalls).

The teacher made a similar kind of comparison when one child, decked out in a white headpiece and carrying a flower, wanted to have a bridal procession. Because several other costumed children insisted on participating, the bride proceeded down the "aisle" in the company of a soldier, a sailor, a fireman, and a Mexican peasant complete with sombrero and shawl. The teacher's remark that the procession was "just like Babar's wedding," alluded to the similarity between the strange bridal party and the unlikely bridal procession in one of the stories of Babar, an elephant character in a popular storybook series.

As these examples point out, literary themes, characters, and events became part of the shared background knowledge and experience assumed by nursery-school participants. References of this kind were not made constantly; each nursery-school event or item was not compared to some other known event and certainly was not compared to some literary event. Rather, literary knowledge was simply a part of the larger repertoire of shared experiences that were referred to on various occasions.

Drawing from their repertoire of experiences, the children also included story characters, plots, and themes in their creative expressions. Spontaneously, they included in their drawings "Cinderella" or "Snow White" and various other literary characters. With adult direction, they made cut-out figures of "Paddington Bear," "the good bird," and other story figures. Some of the stories that the children had heard at the nursery school were also enacted dramatically with an adult narrator telling the story and the children assuming the various parts of "Peter Pan," "Paddington Bear" or "The Little Fireman." Occasionally the children also drew from literary knowledge for their unprompted and unsupervised dramatic games of "Three Billy Goats Gruff" or "Cinderella." In these instances, children more or less spontaneously took on the roles of story characters, and other children responded with the appropriate supplementary characters and actions.

Summary

The most prominent aspect of the ways books were used at Maple Nursery School was the range of situations for which book knowledge was relevant. The children were exposed to a literary orientation in which bookreading played key roles in cognitive, social, and imaginative growth and development. Paramount to this orientation was the perception that books could provide not only access to information concerning what we might call nonfiction topics or areas of interest, but also knowledge that helped to structure personal experiences and elucidate various aspects of individual psychological and social development. This made bookreading a way of knowing about an extremely broad array of life experiences. Book knowledge was not the only way of knowing in this community, but book knowledge was one of the primary avenues of access to knowledge, as well as one of the major ways of supplementing, verifying, complementing, and making sense of other avenues of knowledge.

This chapter, along with Chapters 4, 5 and 6 of this monograph, points out the striking consistency between home and nursery-school ways of using books. Although parents emphasized bookreading for entertainment and nursery-school storyreadings stressed bookreading as a way of knowing or acquiring information, books were used in both settings in each of these two ways, as well as for counseling about personal situations and for imaginative growth. For this reason, the children were confronted with little disparity between pre-nursery-school and nursery-school orientations to books and printed materials. Rather, nursery-school experiences functioned to extend, enrich, and complement the home literary experiences of this group of preschoolers.

CHAPTER 11

Conclusions

In *The Making of a Reader*, both *what* young children in one nursery school knew about print and *how* they came to know it have been described. We saw that in this preschool community, despite the fact that they did not know how to read or write in the conventional sense, three-to-five-year-old children knew (or were coming to know) a great deal about print.

1. They knew that reading and writing were integral and meaningful parts of their everyday world.

2. They knew that reading and writing were effective ways to accomplish many of their own purposes and meet many of their own needs.

3. They knew that they could be and probably would be readers and writers throughout their lifetimes.

4. They knew how to organize and use contextualized print for their own social purposes.

5. They knew how to interpret contextualized print in relation to many of the environments and situations in which it occurred.

6. They knew how to relate contextualized print to the oral language that often surrounded it.

7. They knew that decontextualized print was different from contextualized print and required different interpretive strategies.

8. They knew how to prepare for and attend to the decontextualized print of storybooks.

9. They knew how to use their knowledge of the world in order to make sense of storybook texts and pictures.

10. They knew how to use information gained from texts and apply it in many ways to their own lives.

11. They knew that reading and writing were used consistently in the major home, school, and community contexts that comprised their lives.

12. They knew that reading and writing were used regularly in these contexts to structure and explain their life experiences.

The preschoolers in this setting were coming to know so many things about print because of their continual participation with adults in literacy events organized in order to meet a wide variety of social, transactional, and informational needs in their lives. These literacy events involved joint adult-child participation. In these events, adults acted as intermediaries between children and contextualized print by taking on whatever parts of the events that the children could not perform themselves. Gradually, children took on more and more of the roles in literacy events, with uses of print preceding skills.

The children were coming to know that special language strategies were needed to interpret storybooks because of the unique physical and psychological framework that signaled preparation for storyreading events. This framework set apart the reading of decontextualized print from all other nursery-school activities and from all other reading and writing events. The children were learning how to make sense of decontextualized print, because they were daily involved in mediated storyreading sessions. In these sessions, the storyreader essentially instructed them in how to use their knowledge to make appropriate inferences, evaluations, and responses to texts and how to take the knowledge they found in books and apply, use, or relate it to their lives.

In short, this monograph has documented the process wherein children were becoming readers in one setting. This documentation provides an important addition to a growing body of research in early literacy. The major contribution of this monograph, however, is neither to prescribe for educators and parents a particular model of literacy nor to generalize about early literacy on a global scale. Rather, the major contribution of *The Making of a Reader* is to offer a way of looking at, thinking about, and talking about early literacy that can help others see more clearly some of the issues involved in studying and making decisions about this process. In other words, it is my hope that this monograph will not stipulate to others *what* to think about children's early experiences with print, but rather that it will raise questions for them about *how* to think about it.

The way of looking at early literacy that underlies this work is ethnographic in its perspective. That is, it is based on the belief that the meaning of all human behavior, including print-related behaviors and habits, is embedded within social and cultural contexts. This perspective allows us to identify the literacy events and contexts that are significant to particular social groups and helps us to understand the meaning that these events have for participants. This perspective also helps us to uncover some of the assumptions about early literacy that are implicit within the print practices of a community. These include:

1. Whether or not literacy for children is assumed by adults.
2. Where literacy is primarily located by the adults of a community (in the school, the church, the home).
3. What role (if any) a community assumes bookreading and book knowledge will play in children's lives.
4. What value and importance (if any) are placed on books, bookreading, and other print-related materials and activities.
5. The range and breadth of situations (if any) within which literacy is culturally and socially relevant and meaningful for members of the community or social group.

It will be useful to examine more closely *The Making of a Reader* as a way of seeing, thinking about, and talking about children's early literacy experiences. The way of looking that underlies this study is founded on careful observations over considerable time in one setting. It is important to emphasize that these observations were not random or unguided. Rather they were systematic observations aimed at teasing out and pulling apart patterns of behavior that explained, from a participant's perspective, the meaning of literacy in one setting. Observations were guided by awareness of literacy patterns that had been identified in research in other cultures and in other social groups, and by an overall perspective that views literacy as a cultural and social phenomenon.

Looking at Literacy from an Ethnographic Perspective

What can we learn by looking at early literacy from an ethnographic perspective? Essentially we can learn what children and adults in particular settings are actually doing with print and how they are doing it. We can get at the real nature of what is going on in one classroom, one preschool, or one home setting. What can be gained from studies of this sort is in striking contrast to the results of reading research wherein the object of attention and, to a certain extent, the nature of the findings are predetermined according to what we have been told—by teaching manuals or cognitive models—that literacy is all about.

This is not to argue that these sources are invalid or incorrect. Rather, it is to suggest that we do not yet know enough about how children become readers to limit our attention to children's performances of particular skills or competencies. Instead, we need a way of looking at early literacy based on the systematic search for patterns of literacy behavior in particular cultures or social groups. Such an approach allows us to see literacy as a social and cultural phenomenon that can organize events for children and adults and can be organized by children and adults for their own purposes (Schieffelin and Cochran-Smith, in press).

The Making of a Reader offers one example of the value of this way of looking. It peels away some of the layers of meaning of early literacy in one particular group which has been considered effective and successful in preparing its children for school literacy. It is important to remember that much of what has been written over the years about children's early reading and writing experiences has been based on studies where researchers, readers, and subjects shared a common cultural background. For this reason, many assumptions were made by both writers and readers of the research about the nature and significance of particular literacy experiences. The cultural factors in these experiences were not made clear.

An ethnographic perspective on early literacy offers a way of looking more critically. With a close look at a single case, *The Making of a Reader* begins to pull apart an often taken-for-granted picture of literacy. It makes explicit many of the implicit aspects of early literacy in one community; hence, its explanation of how children become readers is a cultural explanation. Close studies of other preschool populations may yield different descriptions of early literacy patterns embedded within different layers of context. Applying the framework suggested here may also yield many questions not considered in this study. *The Making of a Reader* questions whether any single description is sufficient and useful for describing patterns of literacy and suggests, instead, that there may be many ways of becoming literate. This work also provides terminology that may suggest useful variables for studying early literacy.

The underlying perspective of *The Making of a Reader* allows us to see several important aspects of early literacy in one community. Of special importance is the realization that there were many layers of context that surrounded storyreading and that were interrelated to one another:

1. The organization of time and space at the nursery school was very important, especially in the way that it supported the distinction between the children's experiences with contextualized print and decontextualized print.

2. Rug-time clearly marked the need for a particular set of interpretive and interactional strategies.

3. The material culture of both the nursery school and nursery-school homes supported early uses of reading and writing and pointed to some of the community's assumptions about their children's eventual literacy.

The idea of multiple layers of context helps to build a way of looking at early literacy and makes it clear that, for this community, reading and writing were not isolated groups of skills used only in a school setting. Rather, the ways that adults in this community helped children come to reading and writing and use reading and writing were parts of a consistent, continual, and overlapping preparation for a kind of literacy that was embedded within both a larger educational context and an almost limitless number of social contexts.

An ethnographic perspective for looking at early literacy helps us to see both children and adults as active, significant participants in the making of readers. Because detailed and systematic observations of literacy events were made for this study, it was possible to see that literacy events were jointly undertaken through social interactions. From other perspectives we can sometimes only see those aspects of literacy that are officially "taught" to children, or that children are able to accomplish independently in testing or interview situations. With an ethnographic view, we can document children *in the process* of becoming literate; we can see their emerging and developing literacy as it occurs in everyday situations. Rather than seeing literacy as an endpoint based on a theory of what children need to know in order to become literate, we can see what children actually do know about print, and we can gain many insights about how they come to know it.

For example, observation and analysis of literacy events in Maple Nursery School allowed us to see children actively learning literacy. We were able to observe and analyze how the children organized literacy events for their own social purposes and, in the process, sorted out rules for using and interpreting print in various ways. We saw children learning how to develop written language strategies through the mode of oral language. We also saw that adults figured prominently in the literacy-learning process by playing important intermediary roles.

Reading: A Broad Definition

The single case upon which *The Making of a Reader* is based suggests that reading and writing were much more than decoding and encoding, and that early literacy was much more than preparation for breaking the code. Rather, early literacy involved knowing how to do the following.

1. Effectively organize and use print for one's own purposes.
2. Use the appropriate strategies for interpreting contextualized print in a wide variety of situations.
3. Use oral language to interpret and organize written language.
4. Prepare mentally and physically for reading the decontextualized print of storybooks.
5. Make sense of storybook texts by:
   a. Consistently balancing and relating world information and textual information.
   b. Bringing relevant world knowledge to bear upon a text.
   c. Interpreting textual language in terms of common connotations.
   d. Relating pictures and texts on a holistic level.
   e. Understanding literary conventions.
   f. Appropriately inferring from pictures and texts.

6. Use storybook texts in one's own life by:
   a. Knowing the kinds of information contained in books.
   b. Seeing relationships between book events and real life situations and experiences.
   c. Coming to books for entertainment and relaxation.
   d. Using books as avenues of access to knowledge and information on a wide array of topics.

None of these aspects of early literacy is directly related to the processes of encoding or decoding print. The perspective I have been describing here allows us to see these aspects as a foundation for literacy to which the important mechanical skills of encoding and decoding can later be added. Close study of this single case makes it clear that encoding and decoding were preceded and supported by a great deal of knowledge about how to use print. Without knowledge of how to use print, the abilities to encode and decode print are meaningless.

Terms and Dimensions for Looking at Early Literacy

An ethnographic perspective helped us to see what adults and children in one setting were actually doing with print and how they were doing it. *The Making of a Reader* began with careful systematic notetaking on nursery-school literacy events, supplemented by audio-recording of storyreadings. The recording/transcribing system described earlier offered a way to capture on paper the nature of storyreading events. Detailed transcription allowed us to see some of the subtleties of storyreadings: (a) the kinds of talk that surrounded it; (b) the interrelationships between texts, pictures, oral commentary on texts, and the prosodic and paralinguistic accompaniments to the oral presentation of texts; and (c) the interplay between storyreading participants. This recording/transcription system allowed us to see that storyreading events were social interactions that centered on the cooperative negotiation of textual meaning.

The terminology used in this analysis pinpoints several features of early literacy that may be helpful in guiding other investigations. As I have made clear throughout this monograph, it is not suggested that these features of early literacy are universal. Rather, these are suggested as some of the dimensions according to which early literacy varies, and they are proposed as a way to compare and contrast early literacy in various social settings.

Literacy event. The notion of a literacy event is very important. It can help us see the contexts within which people use print, the ways they organize print for various purposes, the kinds of talk that accompany uses of print, and the nature and extent of social participation and interaction. Participants' comments on and references to literacy events can also help us to tease out the meanings that these events have for participants themselves, and can help us to identify the relevant contexts within which literacy events occur in given social groups.

Contextualized print-decontextualized print. The contextualized print-decontextualized print distinction is a salient conceptual tool for looking at children's early print experiences. In the case studied here, the distinction was highly consistent with the location of literacy events, the norms for interaction during literacy events, and the types of strategies used for interpreting print. We need to know whether this distinction operates in other social groups and, if so, how it organizes literacy events for people.

Adult as intermediary, child as active learner. To describe the nature of participation in literacy events, I have used the terms, "adult as intermediary" and "child as active learner." These terms emphasize the active roles played by both adults and children in the literacy-learning process and stress the social, interactive nature of literacy events. These terms may not be appropriate descriptors for adults and children in other social groups, but the terms can provide researchers with an initial way of looking and can provide a basis for comparison.

The Making of a Reader identifies several dimensions according to which storyreadings to young children may vary. These dimensions and the terminology we can use to talk about them provide a way of comparing storyreading events, both in situations where storyreadings are very different from those described here and where they appear, on the surface, to be the same. For example, in the community studied for this monograph, nursery-school storyreading and library storyreading to the same group of children looked very much alike and even featured the same storybooks. As my analysis points out, however, nursery-school storyreading was characterized by interaction and mutual negotiation of the sense of texts. In library storyreadings, on the other hand, the adult storyreader performed a unilateral text. The dimension of interactive negotiation, along with several other dimensions described later, help to point out some of the subtle and obvious differences between storyreadings, and provide a way to compare the storyreadings that occur in various settings within social groups.

Storyreader as mediator-monitor. This monograph describes the adult storyreader as one who monitored the match between the readers implied or fictionalized in texts and the real readers to whom she read, and then mediated any discrepancies between the two by supplying or guiding the listeners toward the information needed in order to make sense of texts.

Storyreading as interactive negotiation. Storyreading is described in this monograph as interactive negotiation between storyreader and story listeners. The variable, interactive negotiation, is actually comprised of two characteristics of storyreading that occur together in the group studied here: social interaction and cooperative negotiation.

Social interaction. Social interaction is a term that is used to describe a storyreading event as one in which both reader and listener participants are actively, verbally involved during the storyreading process. That is, during individual storyreadings, both reader and listeners deviate from the text and ask questions, make comments, offer explanations, and relate personal experiences.

Cooperative negotiation. Cooperative negotiation is a term indicating that the meanings of texts are jointly worked out by reader and listeners; the verbal actions of each are mutually dependent, and the sense that listeners are making of individual texts is highly respected by the storyreader who acts as both spokesperson for the text and, more often, secondary narrator and commentator on the text.

Readiness interaction sequences. *The Making of a Reader* identifies three kinds of interaction sequences that occur during and, in the case of readiness sequences, before storyreading events. Readiness sequences prepare children to attend to and understand decontextualized print. They alert children to the fact that unique interpretive and interactional language strategies are to be used for the decontextualized print of storybooks. Readiness sequences focus on the physical behaviors that are expected to accompany or precede the reading of storybooks and on the attending behaviors that are to continue throughout individual storyreading events.

Life-to-text interaction sequences. Life-to-Text is the terminology used to describe interaction sequences where a storyreader guides children in their interpretations of individual texts. These sequences center on the kinds of knowledge that readers need to bring to bear upon texts. These areas of knowledge function as frames within which various parts of texts become accessible.

Text-to-life interaction sequences. Text-to-Life is the phrase used to describe interaction sequences where a storyreader guides children in their application and use of individual texts. These sequences center on the ways book knowledge can function in the world.

Implications for Teachers, Parents, and Researchers

The framework for looking at early literacy suggested by *The Making of a Reader* can have important implications for three groups of people who are vitally interested in how children become readers: educators, parents, and researchers.

Implications for teachers

Educators, both curriculum developers and individual classroom teachers, can use this sort of approach for looking in their own classrooms to uncover the patterns that exist there. If teachers adopt this kind of classroom approach, they might address several important issues:

1. What kinds of print experiences are the children in my classroom having?
2. Is there a variety of print experiences?
3. Are the children having experiences with contextualized print? with decontextualized print?
4. Do the children in my classroom use print for their own social purposes? If so, how do they organize print for these purposes? For what purposes do they use print?
5. What is the role in literacy events of teachers or other adults in my classroom? Do children and adults jointly participate in literacy events?
6. Do participants in reading and writing events interact with one another? If so, how?
7. For what purposes do the adults in my classroom use reading and writing?
8. Do children participate in the literacy events organized by adults? If so, how?
9. What kinds of talk are related to reading and writing? What kinds of talk are encouraged or discouraged?
10. What messages about print underlie the way print is used and the talk that surrounds it?
11. In what classroom contexts are reading and writing relevant and meaningful?
12. How do the children in my classroom see reading and writing? Do they equate it with decoding and encoding? If not, what else do reading and writing encompass?

13. Do storyreading events occur in my classroom? If so, what are the events like?

14. Are storyreadings socially interactive? Are they cooperatively negotiated?

15. What messages about bookreading are implicit in the nature of storyreadings?

16. What kinds of talk precede, occur together with, or follow storyreading?

17. What messages about the language strategies needed for the interpretation of decontextualized print underlie this talk?

There are no preferred answers to these questions. There is no ideal model of literacy implicit in them. To read such a model into these questions would be to misunderstand the fundamental purpose of this monograph. As I have stated before, the purpose of these questions is not to suggest to others what to think or do about early literacy, but to suggest how to think about it. Regardless of the nature or extent of the literacy events that occur (or do not occur) in a given classroom, there are important messages about reading and writing implicit in these events or in their absence, and there are important assumptions about literacy that underlie these events. By adopting the way of looking described here, educators can begin to peel away the layers of context surrounding particular configurations of literacy and discover how their own classroom environments organize literacy experiences for young children. With this kind of information, teachers and curriculum developers can then begin to make decisions about the appropriateness of the literacy experiences for their particular communities and about the balance of the literacy experiences offered to children.

Implications for parents

Parents are also vitally interested in how children become readers. They too can use the way of looking at early literacy described here in order to observe in classrooms and preschool situations that serve their children, or will be serving them. Parents can raise many of the same questions that educators ask of their own classrooms. Parents might be most interested in considering:

1. What kinds of literacy events occur in this classroom?

2. Do the children in this classroom have experiences with contextualized print? with decontextualized print?

3. Who uses print here?
4. Do children use print for their own social purposes?
5. What is the role in literacy events of teachers and other adult helpers in this classroom?
6. Do the children and adults jointly participate in literacy events?
7. Do the children participate in storyreading events? If so, what kind of an event is storyreading?
8. Who can talk during storyreading and for what purpose?
9. If storyreadings include interactions, what kinds of interaction sequences occur?
10. What is the role of the adult storyreader during storyreading events? What is the role of the child?

Again, there are no preferred answers to these questions and no ideal model of literacy implied. Parents will be able to make their own judgments and decisions about the kinds of literacy experiences that are most appropriate for their children. By adopting the way of looking described here, however, parents will have a great deal of information upon which to base their decisions.

Implications for theory and research

The Making of a Reader also has important implications for theory and research in children's learning, particularly in their learning of language and literacy. The study reported in this monograph identifies a number of key dimensions of the making of readers in one middle-class, school-oriented community. Future research can address the question of whether or not, and to what extent, the dimensions of literary and literacy socialization identified here are characteristic of other middle-class nursery-school, day-care, or home environments across the country. Along similar lines, *The Making of a Reader* provides a basis for comparison of children's early reading and writing in this community with those of other communities.

The results of current research in early literacy (Anderson, Teale, and Estrada, 1980; Heath, 1982b; Miller, Nemiouanu and DeJong, in press; Schieffelin and Cochran-Smith, in press) together with the results of the study reported here emphasize that there are both similarities and differences among children's early reading and writing experiences cross-culturally and cross-nationally. It is important to identify the specific points of similarity and difference by comparative analysis of case studies. Eventually, comparisons of this sort will build an "ethnography of early literacy" that will provide important information to researchers and practitioners in a number of fields.

One feature of children's learning that has been emphasized recently is the notion that early learning can be scaffolded or supported by adult-child dialogue. As I have discussed earlier, Ninio and Bruner (1978) describe a mother-child storybook dialogue in which a mother elicited labels for discrete items pictured in the book. Ninio and Bruner suggest that in this "scaffolding" dialogue the adult provided specific language structures and slots upon which her child's learning of lexical labels was built. Similarly, Snow and Goldfield (1980) have pointed out the potency of the bookreading situation for language learning. Like these analyses of picture-book dialogue and like Cazden's (1980) analysis of peek-a-boo games, the storyreading interaction analyzed in this monograph can be seen as scaffolding dialogue wherein the specific questions, comments, and incomplete phrases of the adult storyreader provided a foundation which child listeners could use to sort out and integrate various aspects of stories and show that they were able to do so.

The Making of a Reader also provides some insight into the nature of child development. Vygotsky (1978) suggests that children develop through social interaction, particularly in social relationships with other people. Vygotsky argues that children learn how to complete certain tasks on their own by first performing those tasks with the help of others. The storyreading events analyzed in this monograph provide one example of Vygotsky's "zone of proximal development," or children's potential level of learning. Story listeners were able to make sense of printed texts with the help of an adult mediator-monitor who instructed them in how to use their knowledge of the world in order to understand texts. These mediated storyreadings served as a transition to new language strategies and might well have contributed significantly to the children's later abilities to make sense of texts on their own.

The patterns of literary socialization described in this monograph are closely related to patterns found in the acquisition and development of children's language. Much of child-language theory and research is built on white, Western, middle-class communities; this research reveals a dialogic model for the development and acquisition of children's early language. The interactive storyreadings detailed in *The Making of a Reader* suggest a continuation of this dialogic model. As pointed out earlier, even the texts of children's storybooks are designed to invite conversations between adult readers and child listeners. The texts, therefore, feed into and encourage a conversational storyreading pattern, which in turn builds upon the dialogic model of language learning established in early adult-child interactions. In this way, storyreading study provides further insight into culturally organized patterns of adult-child interactions. In a larger sense, this monograph also contributes to our understanding of some of the assumptions about the nature of language, learning, and children that underlie particular cultural orientations to literacy.

Finally, this study contributes to the beginning outlines of a developmental framework for one type of literary socialization. Most of the previous investigations of adult-child book-related interactions related to this type of literary socialization have focused on children under three years of age (Magee and Sutton-Smith, in press; Miller, Nemoiuanu and DeJong, in press; Ninio and Bruner, 1978; Snow and Goldfield, 1980). All of these revealed dialogic patterns of interaction that featured labeling or responding routines within specific language structures and slots. A recent British study (Cuff and Hustler, 1981) describes storyreading to six- and seven-year-old children in a school setting. Storyreadings in this study were more or less verbatim readings of the texts followed by interaction sequences wherein children were invited to tell stories of their own to indicate their grasp of the story's relevance for their own lives.

The Making of a Reader, which focuses on children between the ages of three and five years, fills in part of the gap between the two age groups above: children under three years and children over six years of age. Taken together, all of these studies allow us to generate a developmental framework for a particular kind of literary socialization. This framework is founded on social interaction. It begins with a dialogic labeling routine for the discrete items and actions shown in picture-books. Building on both the labeling routine and the dialogic pattern, which in turn builds on early language-learning patterns, mediated sense-making of storybook texts develops. At this level of development, an adult mediator-monitor helps the child to accomplish the task of making sense of a written text by guiding him or her—*as the story-reading proceeds*—to use particular kinds of knowledge as frameworks for making sense of texts. Cuff and Hustler's work suggests that so-cially-interactive storyreading may then become non-mediated reading of texts accompanied by mediated application of texts; that is, the adult storyreader helps the children make sense of the text, after they have heard it, by helping them apply the text and relate it to their lives.

Eventually, children who are becoming literate in the formal sense must learn to make sense of written texts without the support of the social, oral, dialogic kind of storyreading described in all of these studies. They must learn to read unilateral, decontextualized texts in largely solitary and silent fashion. All of the earlier phases of storyreading mentioned here, however, may proceed and contribute significantly to an endpoint—"the literate adult reader"—as defined by a particular community. As the research in early literacy continues to grow, and as gaps in this research are filled with case studies in various social groups, we will begin to be able to investigate the existence and usefulness of a developmental framework for understanding storyreading experiences.